ALTERNATIVE OKLAHOMA

Alternative Oklahoma

CONTRARIAN VIEWS OF THE SOONER STATE

Edited by

DAVIS D. JOYCE

Foreword by

FRED R. HARRIS

UNIVERSITY OF OKLAHOMA PRESS : NORMAN

ALSO BY DAVIS D. JOYCE

Edward Channing and the Great Work (The Hague, 1974)

History and Historians: Some Essays (Washington, D.C., 1983)

(with Michael Kraus) *The Writing of American History,* rev. ed. (Norman, 1985); paperback ed. (Norman, 1990)

(ed. and abr.) *A History of the United States* by Edward Channing (Lanham, Md., 1993)

(ed.) *"An Oklahoma I Had Never Seen Before": Alternative Views of Oklahoma History* (Norman, 1994)

(with Tibor Glant) *United States History: A Brief Introduction for Hungarian Students* (Debrecen, 1996)

(with Palmer H. Boeger) *East Central University, 1969–1989: The Wagner Years* (Ada, Okla., 2001)

Howard Zinn: A Radical American Vision (Amherst, N. Y., 2003)

Library of Congress Cataloging-in-Publication Data

Alternative Oklahoma : contrarian views of the Sooner State / edited by Davis D. Joyce ; foreword by Fred R. Harris.

   p. cm.

Includes bibliographical references and index.

ISBN: 978-0-8061-3819-0

1. Oklahoma—History. 2. Oklahoma—Social conditions. 3. Minorities—Oklahoma—History. 4. Oklahoma—Biography. I. Joyce, Davis D., 1940–

   F694.5.A73 2007

   976.6—dc22   2006026753

The paper in this book meets the guidelines for permanence and durability of the Committee on Production Guidelines for Book Longevity of the Council on Library Resources, Inc. ∞

2   3   4   5   6   7   8   9   10

To the memory and spirit of Woody Guthrie

Contents

Foreword

Fred R. Harris

Born and raised in Oklahoma and twice elected to the United States Senate from the Sooner State, I've always agreed with the words that Thomas P. Gore, one of Oklahoma's first two senators, used in closing his farewell address to the Senate. He said on that occasion: "I love Oklahoma. I love every blade of her grass. I love every grain of her sand. I am proud of her past. I am confident of her future."

I've always been an admirer of Senator Gore's, too—but not because I think he was always right. To my mind, he was wrong, for example, in opposing Woodrow Wilson's League of Nations—opposition that helped cause him to lose his Senate seat the first time. To my mind, Senator Gore was also wrong, once he was back in the Senate, to eventually turn against Franklin D. Roosevelt and oppose the New Deal, thereby costing him his seat a second and final time.

What I like most about Senator Gore was that he was not afraid to stand up for what he believed in. When I myself was first elected to the U.S. Senate in 1964, the late Senator Richard Russell of Georgia was still an active and powerful member of that body, although he had served with Senator Gore so many years before. Senator Russell told me a story about Gore. He said that one time, long before the Senate had microphones, Senator Gore was involved in a heated debate with another member of the Senate, when at one point the other senator turned to Senator Gore and said under his breath, so that it couldn't be heard in the galleries,"If you weren't blind, I'd thrash you within an inch of your life!" Senator Russell said that Gore wheeled around toward the other senator and said, "Blindfold the son of a bitch and point him in my direction!"

That he was a fighter is one good reason I'm an admirer of Senator Gore's. But I admire him warts and all. And that's the way I am about Oklahoma, too.

I love my home state. And I love it warts and all. We don't do ourselves or anybody else any favors by writing and teaching a kind of sugar-coated, everything-was-always-hunky-dory kind of Oklahoma history.

And that brings us to the reason for *Alternative Oklahoma: Contrarian Views of the Sooner State*. With this collection of engaging essays about Oklahoma and its past, Davis D. Joyce has put together an informative and worthwhile volume that says to the reader, in the well-known words of Oklahoman Paul Harvey, "And now for the rest of the story."

There were a lot of hard times, as well as good times, in Oklahoma's history. But surely you could say the same thing about every state. I recently went back and reread John Steinbeck's *The Grapes of Wrath*, set in our state's Depression and Dust Bowl days of the 1930s. My annotated study edition of the book quoted an Oklahoma congressman as angrily charging, when *The Grapes of Wrath* first came out, that it was a pack of lies. I don't think so. When the late Dewey Bartlett was governor of Oklahoma, he tried to popularize—with pins and other promotions—the term "Okie," the same way that 1960s African American leaders sought to adopt the then-pejorative word "black" as a term of self-pride. But Governor Bartlett failed in his own effort. Too many Oklahomans were ashamed to be called Okies. And a lot of them said to me at the time something like, "Old John Steinbeck tried to make us look bad." I didn't agree then, and I don't now. *The Grapes of Wrath* is about good, hardworking, sturdy people trying their best to keep body and soul together in hardscrabble times and conditions over which they had very little control.

There is a lot of conflict, of all kinds, in Oklahoma's history—some of it admirable, some of it shameful. But in what state isn't that true? I received a first-rate education at the University of Oklahoma. But although I minored in history in undergraduate school there, I don't believe that I ever heard of the Green Corn Rebellion, the populist multiracial, multiethnic World War I–era draft-resistance movement in eastern Oklahoma. Nor do I remember ever hearing back then about the horrible 1921 white riot in Tulsa, which led to the brutal murders of so many innocent and upstanding African Americans then living in Greenwood, Tulsa's Black Wall Street, and which irrevocably pillaged and burned that solid and prosperous city section. It was only after President Lyndon Johnson appointed me to the President's National Advisory Commission on Civil Disorders (Kerner Commission) in 1967 that I finally began to get a more complete history of black-white relations in America—and Oklahoma.

It is correctly said that history is written by the winners. And too often, history is also written from the standpoint of the elites. But if we're really going to understand who we are as Oklahomans and how far we've come, we need to learn, and teach, history as it was lived by the losers, too—and those who had to fight hard to keep from losing. And just as we need to be aware, as it has been quaintly put, of "English as she is spoke," we need to know Oklahoma history "as she was lived"—and not just by those on top, but by all the rest, too.

That's where this book comes in. And not a moment too soon.

Editor's Introduction

In stock market jargon, a *contrarian* is an investor who buys shares of stocks when most people are selling—or vice versa. More broadly, a contrarian is a person who takes a contrary position or attitude. This is a collection of contrarian views of Oklahoma history. Notice that "contrarian" here has no negative implication; it does not mean "disagreeable," but rather "different" or "more than meets the eye."

If ever there was a contrarian state, Oklahoma is it. One of the great historians of the state, Arrell M. Gibson, insisted that "anomaly" was a central theme in Oklahoma history, meaning that it differed more from the pattern of state evolution than any other state—think of settlement patterns, the oil boom, or the Dust Bowl, for example. This is not unrelated to the approach to Oklahoma history presented in this volume. Much of the material presented here proudly runs "contrary" to the traditional view of the state's past, cutting against the grain.

Oklahoma celebrates one hundred years of statehood in 2007. Centennials are traditionally a time for celebration. That is the case here as well—although the aspects of Oklahoma's past and present being celebrated here may not be the same as those that are celebrated officially. Here we celebrate women, minorities, common people, radicals, and other groups and topics that traditionally did not make it into the history textbooks.

Textbooks have improved in this regard, of course, since the 1960s—and in part as a response to the movements that dominated that decade, such as the civil rights movement, the anti–Vietnam War movement, the women's movement, and the environmental movement. Before the sixties, one could read most U.S. history textbooks and come away thinking, "Okay, I get it; history is about dead white men—and it never says anything critical of American political leadership or of the role of the United States in the world." But virtually all U.S. history textbooks today are more inclusive, as well as more willing to be critical. Hopefully, Oklahoma history textbooks have made progress in these areas as well; hopefully, this collection of essays on Oklahoma history (and its predecessor, *"An Oklahoma I Had Never Seen Before": Alternative Views of*

Oklahoma History) can contribute to this change.[1] The basic goal is to make the reader see Oklahoma history in a new way: Oklahoma history outside the mainstream, alternative views of Oklahoma history. Sometimes the topic is new or unfamiliar; sometimes an old topic is looked at in a new way.

The historian Howard Zinn had a profound impact on this approach to Oklahoma history with his approach to U.S. history, especially in his million-selling work *A People's History of the United States*. Perhaps the key paragraph in Zinn's book is the following:

> In that inevitable taking of sides which comes from selection and emphasis in history, I prefer to try to tell the story of the discovery of America from the viewpoint of the Arawaks, of the Constitution from the standpoint of the slaves, of Andrew Jackson as seen by the Cherokees, of the Civil War as seen by the New York Irish, of the Mexican war as seen by the deserting soldiers of Scott's army, of the rise of industrialism as seen by the young women in the Lowell textile mills, of the Spanish-American war as seen by the Cubans, the conquest of the Philippines as seen by black soldiers on Luzon, the Gilded Age as seen by southern farmers, the First World War as seen by socialists, the Second World War as seen by pacifists, the New Deal as seen by blacks in Harlem, the postwar American empire as seen by peons in Latin America. And so on, to the limited extent that any one person, however he or she strains, can "see" history from the standpoint of others.[2]

And perhaps the most effective and direct way to make the point here is to write a parallel paragraph for Oklahoma history:

In that inevitable taking of sides which comes from selection and emphasis in Oklahoma history, I prefer to try to tell the story of Oklahoma's prehistory from the point of view of the Spiro Mound people; of Indian removal from the viewpoint of the Cherokees; of the Civil War from the standpoint of the Seminole slaves; of the Run of '89 as seen by the Indians already here; of the coming of statehood as seen by the Sequoyah Convention; the First World War as seen by those who participated in the Green Corn Rebellion; the state's petroleum industry as seen by the workers in the fields; the coalmining industry as seen by the radical Italian labor organizer; the Ku Klux Klan as seen by the victims of the Tulsa Race Riot of 1921; the 1930s exodus as seen by the "Okies" themselves; the state's "macho" image as seen by the victim of domestic violence or the gay individual; the state's failure to ratify the Equal Rights Amendment as seen by women; the University of Oklahoma's much-vaunted football success as seen by the bright students who feel compelled to leave the state for high-quality education and jobs, or by the athlete who never gets a degree; and so on, to the limited extent that any one person, however he or she strains, can "see" history from the standpoint of others.[3]

I like to tell the story of having Danney Goble's book *Progressive Oklahoma* lying on my desk, and having a colleague from outside history see it and remark, "That's kind of an oxymoron, isn't it?" I appreciated the humor, but I also thought, "How sad." Parts of Oklahoma's past, including its progressive, even radical, parts, go largely ignored, forgotten. As David R. Morgan wrote recently in the pages of *The Oklahoma Observer*, "We sometimes forget how radical Oklahoma's political past has been."[4] We forget because the generally conservative political, social, and cultural climate of Oklahoma today does not match up very well with that progressive past. But we must not forget! Some of us find those progressive/radical traditions the most exciting aspects of our past, in part because of their potential relevance for the present and the future.

Jim Roth is a member of the Oklahoma County Commission. When he was elected in 2002, he apparently became the first openly gay candidate to be voted into office in Oklahoma, "which may not be the state many think of when it comes to electing gays and lesbians," the *Tulsa World* suggested. Roth, however, says, "I actually think, and my race demonstrates it, there is really an innate goodness about Oklahoma. There is an individualism. There is a libertarian streak, a progressive streak."[5]

There is indeed a "progressive streak" in Oklahoma. There has long been. That is part of the point of these volumes.

Jacqueline Van Fleet moved to Oklahoma in 1965. She works at a bookstore in Tulsa. "Somehow," she writes, "I have managed to encapsulate myself in a life of 'liberal' thinkers, Unitarians, Democrats, those associated with the University of Tulsa, etc., and keep wondering why everyone thinks Oklahoma is conservative." She knows, of course, that it is. She also knows "perfectly well that state politics are murky from state to state, but I will mention to you that I grew up in Missouri, went to school in Kansas, where I was a Beatnik for a few years, have traveled all over this country and part of the world, but *never* have I seen anything so fascinating as Oklahoma politics." Van Fleet tells of working for passage of the Equal Rights Amendment in Oklahoma. She was on the steps of the state capitol in Oklahoma City after the second defeat in the legislature, and remembers seeing fellow Tulsan Sally Bell, of Bell's Amusement Park in Tulsa, handing out miniature loaves of home-baked bread to everyone who had voted against the ERA. Offended, Van Fleet began to boycott Bell's, insisting that her children not go there, and when they were old enough to understand, explaining to them why. Let her continue the story: "As my children left home for Oklahoma State University and the University of Iowa, I began to receive letters instructing me not to buy pizza from Domino's, and by the way, do you know that Coca Cola. . . .well, I suppose my efforts were not completely wasted!"[6]

Part of what our history teaches us is that our efforts are never completely wasted. Sometimes we succeed, as with Vietnam Veterans Against the War and the Sunbelt Alliance (against nuclear power), both written about in this volume. Sometimes we do not, but we feel we are doing the right thing, and at the very least, consciousness is raised. That is the role that radicals have always played historically. They are always out there—outside the mainstream, re-defining the mainstream—raising the hard questions, pulling the rest of society along, sometimes kicking and screaming. Even those who do not define themselves as radical—by very definition the majority of any given group of people—can usually be brought to acknowledge the important role that radicals play, the changes they help bring about from which all people eventually benefit.

Howard Zinn praised James W. Loewen's book *Lies My Teacher Told Me: Everything Your American History Textbook Got Wrong.* "Every teacher, every student of history, every citizen should read this book," said Zinn. Why? Perhaps quoting the bulk of the final paragraph will explain it:

> Thomas Jefferson surely had it right when he urged the teaching of political history so that Americans might learn "how to judge for them-selves what will secure or endanger their freedom." Citizens who are their own historians, willing to identify lies and distortions and able to use sources to determine what really went on in the past, become a formidable force for democracy. Hugh Trevor-Roper, the dean of Brit-ish historians, has written, "A nation that has lost sight of its history, or is discouraged from the study of it by the desiccating professionalism [or unprofessionalism!] of its historians, is intellectually and perhaps politically amputated. But that history must be true history in the full-est sense.[7]

Just so with Oklahoma history—it must be "true [Oklahoma] history in the fullest sense." Part of the agenda here is to contribute to bringing that about. I even considered as a title *Lies My Oklahoma History Teacher Told Me: Everything Your Oklahoma History Textbook Got Wrong.* But it was too bulky, and obviously too derivative. Besides, this volume is not that comprehensive. A "people's history," said Howard Zinn, "promises more than any one person can fulfill." Similarly, a "people's history of Oklahoma" promises more than any one person can deliver, at least at this time. Not "everything" your Oklahoma history textbook got wrong is included herein; and some of what is included is essentially material considered unworthy of inclusion in the textbooks—or too controversial. By no means does this volume cover all of the topics about taking sides that are listed in the paragraph above. And not all of the ones that are included fit with the ideological approach that might seem to be suggested here. Joseph Bruner, for example, was essentially a right-wing alternative in the area of Indian rights.

The topics here are diverse, ranging from pioneer women social historians to an autobiographical account by a person who grew up both Okie and radical, from an interpretive essay on the African American experience in Oklahoma to an essay based on interviews with diverse Oklahoma women, from the legacy of Woody Guthrie in Oklahoma's "Red Dirt" music scene to gay rights, from the struggle against nuclear power to the struggle against the Vietnam War. Finally, as in *"An Oklahoma I Had Never Seen Before,"* several essays here deal with religion—but not in a traditional manner. Instead, writers such as Alvin O. Turner and Brian Bentel explore the complex interrelationships between religion, freedom, and prosperity (or poverty) in Oklahoma, while Samuel P. Riccobene writes of the sometimes difficult role of a liberal religionist in the Bible Belt, and Marlin Lavanhar attempts to explain why the "liberal religion" of Unitarian Universalism has done so well in Tulsa. The style of the essays is diverse as well, from the traditional scholarly essay to what I like to call the personal/historical essay—historical in the sense of involving change over time, personal in the sense that the author was a participant in the events described.

What ties this diversity together is that it represents an effort to show an Oklahoma that many people have never seen before—a people's history of Oklahoma, Oklahoma history from the bottom up (or the outside in), contrarian views of Oklahoma history. Although much of it has not traditionally been included in the standard treatments of the state's history, such material is clearly interesting, important, and relevant.

NOTES

1. Davis D. Joyce, ed., *"An Oklahoma I Had Never Seen Before": Alternative Views of Oklahoma History* (Norman: University of Oklahoma Press, 1994).

2. Howard Zinn, *A People's History of the United States* (New York: Harper and Row, 1980), 10.

3. Joyce, *"An Oklahoma I Had Never Seen Before,"* x. Essentially, I am quoting myself here.

4. David R. Morgan, "What's the Matter with Oklahoma?" *Oklahoma Observer*, October 24, 2004, 9. The *Oklahoma Observer* plays an important role in the state. It bills itself as "An Independent Journal of Commentary." Surely it is not too much to suggest that it provides an *alternative* to the generally conservative mainstream media.

5. Jim Myers, "Delegate Says Truth His Appeal," *Tulsa World*, July 31, 2004, A-8.

6. Jacqueline Van Fleet, personal communication by e-mail, September 16 and 18, 2004.

7. James W. Loewen, *Lies My Teacher Told Me: Everything Your American History Textbook Got Wrong* (New York: The New Press, 1995), 312. The bracketed insertion in the Trevor-Roper quote is Loewen's. The Zinn quote appears on the cover of the paperback edition.

Acknowledgments

First, sincere thanks to all the contributors, both to this volume and to its predecessor (*"An Oklahoma I Had Never Seen Before": Alternative Views of Oklahoma History*). Anyone who has ever edited such a volume knows two things:

1. There's a lot more work involved in editing a book than in writing one.
2. You couldn't do it at all without your contributors.

Perhaps special thanks should be given to the three repeat contributors: Carole Jane Joyce, Jimmie L. Franklin, and Elizabeth D. Barlow.

Thanks to Howard Zinn and his approach to U.S. history for a major part of the inspiration to take this approach to Oklahoma history.

The first political campaign I ever actively supported was that of Fred R. Harris for the U.S. Senate in 1964—a position not without controversy for a graduate student at the University of Oklahoma when former football coach Bud Wilkinson provided the opposition. My personalized Oklahoma license plate in 1972 read "FRED-72" to show my support for Harris's bid for the Democratic presidential nomination. Clearly, it is a great honor for me to have him on board with a foreword here. It is my belief that he matches up with the approach I take to Oklahoma history better than any other Oklahoma politician, past or present.

On the cover of the predecessor volume was a picture of the water towers at Okemah, one of which reads "Home of Woody Guthrie." The dedication of this volume to Guthrie is a continuing recognition that his life and his music are an inspiration for this approach.

I have retired from full-time teaching, but East Central University continues to play an important role in my life, both professionally and personally. Six of the essays herein are by people with East Central connections: four members of the faculty (Linda W. Reese, Christine Pappas, Alvin O. Turner, and Brian Bentel) and two former students (Amanda Strunk Frady and Marci Barnes Gracey). I would be remiss if I did not also acknowledge the continuing friendship and support of Scott Barton and Bob Vavricka. I also found important support from new colleagues in my position as an adjunct at

Rogers State University in the past few years, including Abe Marrero, Frank Elwell, Paul B. Hatley, David Tait, and Phil Sample.

David Tait is among the teachers of Oklahoma history around the state who have adopted my previous volume for use in their courses. A sincere thank you to all those people—and to the students who have suffered through it, and sometimes even been kind enough to contact me and say thank you.

Finally, I acknowledge the contribution, support, editorial assistance, and patience of my wife, Carole. She has been with me through more than thirty years, and for all of my books but one. Thus, more than once she has had to tolerate my rage at publishers, contributors, deadlines, and especially the computer, which I frequently threaten to throw into the middle of the road (along with our cell phone, but that's a different subject) so that I can drive the car back and forth over it until it is ground to dust. Thank you, Carole; I truly couldn't make it without you.

Alternative Oklahoma

CHAPTER 1

"Petticoat" Historians

THE FOUNDATION OF OKLAHOMA SOCIAL HISTORY

Linda W. Reese

Linda W. Reese holds the Ph.D. from the University of Oklahoma, where she has also taught. She is currently Assistant Professor of History at East Central University in Ada. Reese considers race and gender in the American West to be her major areas of research and writing, and is likely to be best known to readers of this volume as author of the excellent book *Women of Oklahoma, 1890–1920*.

Hers seems a good choice for the lead essay in this collection. It begins with reference to the work of Howard Zinn, which has had a considerable influence on this volume and its predecessor. Furthermore, it chronicles and pays tribute to four Oklahoma women social historians, women who prepared the way for the very kind of history "from the bottom up" that has become so prominent in American historical writing since the 1960s. As Reese shows, these Oklahoma women were pioneers, writing that kind of history long before it became fashionable.

In 1999, Howard Zinn, often described as a "public intellectual," and author of the influential *A People's History of the United States*, agreed to an interview with David Barresi for *Digress Magazine*. Barresi immediately questioned Zinn about the state of the contemporary history profession. One of the distinct changes Zinn described was that a "whole generation" of women historians were now allowed into university faculties and active in historical associations. "These women historians have worked not just in the field of women's history, but all throughout the range of history, bringing new insights and angles," he said. Indeed, most national historians credit the women's movement of the 1960s, as Zinn did, with bringing about this phenomenon.

For the state of Oklahoma, however, a generation of women historians were active a half-century before, capturing the primary sources, marking significant places, perfecting their craft, and contributing a broad perspective to the history of this twentieth-century state. Four names—Anna Lewis, Carolyn Thomas Foreman, Muriel Wright, and Angie Debo—are particularly representative of this group because of their excellence. Two are virtually forgotten now, and all four were frequently undervalued during most of their lives, but these women were responsible for providing the foundation of Oklahoma social history that has developed so richly in recent publications.[1]

A brief biographical profile of the four women reveals much about the nature of the development of Oklahoma and the ways that gender understandings influenced opportunities for professional women. A cluster of attitudes about early-twentieth-century women's roles, appropriate behavior, access to higher education, and possibilities and limitations in the historical profession affected their careers.

All four women were born well before the beginning of the twentieth century—Carolyn Foreman, the oldest, in 1872—and all remained active until their mid-seventies. Angie Debo, who died at the age of ninety-eight, lived long enough to see her life's work celebrated in the state. Both Lewis and Wright were born in Indian Territory, descendants of distinguished Choctaw families. Foreman and Debo were born in Illinois and Kansas, respectively, but Debo arrived in Oklahoma as a child and experienced firsthand the Oklahoma Territory homesteading experience. All came from comfortable, although not wealthy, families who greatly prized education for their children as a necessity for both success and good citizenship. Lewis, Wright, and Debo completed university baccalaureate degrees, and Lewis and Debo earned doctorates in history from the University of Oklahoma. All three of them supported themselves with their historical work and held a variety of positions, but Lewis alone enjoyed the security of a lifetime college teaching position and the virtues of its intellectual context.

Carolyn Foreman was the only one of the four who married, and none of the women raised children. Many women of their generation believed that in order to pursue an active career, they would have to forgo marriage and a family. Angie Debo made a conscious choice not to marry, because, as she told interviewers much later, she felt that a writing schedule such as the one she kept could not accommodate a husband and children. These women observed that professional prominence, especially in fields dominated by men, required sacrifice and single-minded dedication of energies. Lewis later commented, "You can't change a man-shaped culture overnight. . . . Professional women have long recognized that to compete with their men colleagues they must not be just as good, but better."[2]

This network of women historians knew well the questions that their own lives posed, and they knew the cost of their decisions. Each one contributed a different strength to the profession that complemented the others. As they wrote history in Oklahoma, they expanded the range of subjects by including people outside political and social power structures, incorporating primary source material from those involved, and challenging elite interpretations of events.[3]

ANNA LEWIS

In 2003, the Oklahoma Higher Education Hall of Fame recognized the career of Dr. Anna Lewis, in large part because of the efforts of the administration of the University of Science and Arts of Oklahoma. Few knew the history of this fine teacher, except for some of the remaining former schoolgirls who had attended the institution in the days when it was still known as the Oklahoma College for Women. For thirty-nine years, Lewis directed the history department at OCW, introducing each new class of young women to rigorous study and historical investigation. She published two major books, numerous articles, syllabi of lectures, and workbooks. She began an impressive collection of historical artifacts and books for the OCW library, and she served as president of the Oklahoma Association of College History Professors (now the Oklahoma Association of Professional Historians). Between 1917 and her retirement in 1956, she built a career that was unique among the women historians of Oklahoma and impressive by any standards.[4]

Anna Lezola Lewis was born in 1885 in the Choctaw Nation, Indian Territory, to William A. Lewis, a cattleman and banker, and his Choctaw wife, Elizabeth Ann Moore. One of ten children, Anna graduated in 1903 from the Tushkahoma Female Institute, the finest school for girls in the Choctaw Nation. Her mother's death, however, required her to assume responsibility for the home and the care of her younger siblings. She managed to acquire a teaching certificate and taught at Bokchito and Durant city schools, hoping for the chance to attend college and earn a degree. This may have been why, in spite of frequent social activities, Lewis did not entertain enduring male relationships. In a reminiscence, Lewis's niece, Winnidell Gravitt Wilson, wrote that "somehow the time or person was never right to get married."

When her father remarried, Lewis seized the opportunity to leave home. Against the wishes of her family, she sold her Choctaw land allotment and enrolled at the University of California at Berkeley. The intellectual and cultural climate of the San Francisco area seemed so inspiring that her sister Winnie followed her two years later, and the two took advantage of every activity the school offered. Lewis excelled in her studies and quickly formed a mentor relationship with Herbert E. Bolton, California's premier historian of the Southwest. She completed an undergraduate degree in 1915, and after finishing her thesis, "History of the Cattle Industry in Oklahoma, 1866–1893," she earned an M.A. in 1918. George W. Austin, president of the Oklahoma College for Women in Chickasha, recognized Lewis's potential and hired her in 1917 to take charge of the history department and simultaneously create a professional registrar's office at OCW. He once teased her, "I just told Mrs.—— that I had the best history teacher in the state of Oklahoma. I believe it. If I did not, I'd fire you and hire the best." Lewis remained as chairperson of the history department until 1956.[5]

In spite of the demands of the dual job, Lewis pursued graduate work at the University of Oklahoma. In 1930, at age forty-five, she became the first woman to earn a Ph.D. in history at OU, only the second woman in the history of the school to be awarded the terminal degree. She quickly revised her dissertation into her first book, *Along the Arkansas,* an examination of the region drained by the Arkansas, Verdigris, and Canadian rivers. The highly positive reviews of the book applauded her use of original sources and "modern scientific methods," as well as the "humanly appealing factors in the story." Lewis's work documented attempts by the French, Spanish, and English to gain political control of the region, but it also bore the characteristics of good social history. She included the "ways and manners of the frontier," as well as "groups and individuals that came and went, or stayed and worked and maneuvered to keep and develop the region where they had put down stakes."[6]

Lewis published a number of articles in the *Chronicles of Oklahoma.* Her relationship with Muriel Wright, editor of the journal, was a respectful one of long duration. Both Choctaws, they shared an interest in preserving and publishing Native American history. They also worked together on Oklahoma Historical Society field trips and in researching and marking the location of significant historic places. Lewis and Wright directed tours along the route of Coronado's expedition and along the Chisholm Trail, making good use of Lewis's early research expertise. Lewis wrote about a trading post on the Chisholm Trail and was instrumental in locating and placing a monument at Camp Napoleon, a meeting place of post–Civil War Indian unity. She bought the property of the dilapidated Tushkahoma Female Institute and built a home for herself from the original stone. Lewis's later articles discussed people and places significant to Indian Territory, such as Choctaw leader Jane McCurtain and Sue McBeth, missionary to the Choctaws.[7]

Lewis's primary responsibility was to her many students at OCW. She maintained rigorous standards, and she was especially demanding of the history majors. She sent her best students on to Professor E. E. Dale, her graduate school mentor at OU. Dale wrote to her in 1935, "As you know, we have awarded more fellowships and scholarships here to your students than we have to our own and we have, as yet, never had any regrets about any of them." Her favorite course assignments involved sending her students out to track down primary source materials—letters, diaries, interviews, or artifacts of historic importance in Oklahoma—or to tramp over the countryside and locate significant places of the past long overgrown or lost to memory. She once wrote, "History should and does deal with facts; but history is more than facts. . . . Nothing in all the world is more interesting than people. History is the true story of how men and women have built the world." On class field trips she collected artifacts of those human lives—pottery from the Spiro Mounds, a Comanche war bonnet, a spinning wheel belonging to the Cherokee Ross family—and these became the genesis of the OCW museum collection.[8]

Lewis emphasized two themes in all of her teaching, public speaking, and publishing: America's Native American roots and the importance of equal rights for women in the world. She was among the first generation of American academic historians to incorporate race and gender into historical analysis. She lectured extensively on the history of women, their responsibilities and roles: "Many deep-seated customs and attitudes discourage women from entering a chosen profession, or, more frequently restrict their advance," she said, but the future demanded a change in thinking: "Men need to consider women as colleagues, women to emerge from dependence."

In a lecture on teaching history, Lewis maintained that previous historians had focused only on events of long ago. "They wanted a grand theme to write about, and in most cases queens, kings, and knights were on parade," she stated. "Today, historians take into account economic, racial, and cultural sides of life as well as political and military."

Lewis's final book, *Chief Pushmataha: American Patriot,* completed shortly before her death, incorporated all of these themes, and documented the injustice dealt the Five Civilized Tribes at the hands of the federal government. Her own Choctaw heritage and her struggle to achieve her educational and career goals shaped her multidimensional understanding of American history.[9]

CAROLYN FOREMAN

Carolyn Thomas Foreman has undoubtedly been the most consistently underrated historian of the four under consideration, and her work demands a reappraisal from a modern perspective. Even though her contemporaries recognized her as a cultured, gracious woman, her publications drew criticism rarely applied to anyone else at this time. In a posthumous tribute, Angie Debo bluntly wrote, "Carolyn Thomas Foreman became a historian of note mainly because she was above all a devoted wife." Several factors need to be considered in order to understand this slight.

First, Foreman was not born in Oklahoma; she arrived in the area as an adult. Second, she enjoyed a proper seminary education and an extended tour of Europe typical for a young woman of comfortable means. She never had to work to support herself. She did not produce substantially sized narrative books, with the exception of *Oklahoma Imprints, 1835–1907,* her study of the early territorial newspapers. And finally, in 1905 she married Grant Foreman, a successful attorney and well-known Oklahoma historian. Her economic class, her refinement, and her marital status may well have had more influence than her work itself on how she was evaluated as a historian. Her impact on the preservation of the raw materials of Oklahoma history, however, is immeasurable.[10]

Foreman was born in 1872 in Metropolis, Illinois, to John R. Thomas, an attorney, and Lottie Culver Thomas. She was the first of their three children, and the expectations for her were great, especially after the death of one sibling in childhood. Her position in the family was even more influenced by her mother's death when Carolyn was only eight years old. She became her father's confidante and social hostess, a close relationship that would endure for the rest of their lives. Foreman attended private schools in Washington,

D.C., while her father represented Illinois in the House of Representatives, 1879–89, and she completed her education at Monticello Seminary in Illinois. Following graduation, she spent a year in Europe, studying with private tutors. At age twenty-five, Carolyn accompanied her father to Muskogee, Indian Territory, to his new appointment as a federal court judge. They lived in a boarding house until a spacious new home could be built. She would live in that home for the rest of her life; it now serves as an Oklahoma Historical Society museum.

Adjustment to conditions in a small western town of a few thousand people must have been hard for a young woman of Carolyn's advantages, but Muskogee was the center of Indian Territory activity in these years. The federal government, through the Dawes Commission, carried on its termination of tribal control of Indian lands, and pushed for the creation of a new state. Every significant government official and Native American leader found hospitality at the Thomas home. Grant Foreman, a young attorney, worked for the Dawes Commission for a time, and later joined in law practice with Judge Thomas. Grant and Carolyn became an intellectual union as well; they jointly researched, wrote, and promoted historical preservation in Oklahoma for the remainder of their lives.[11]

Although she had written some newspaper stories, Carolyn Foreman's first historical article appeared in the *Chronicles of Oklahoma* in 1927. Before her death, she would contribute eighty-three more articles to this journal, and three additional pieces would be published posthumously, based on her notes. She wrote six books—the most celebrated being *Oklahoma Imprints, 1835–1907* and *Indians Abroad*—and coauthored one. She also contributed articles to other state journals.

In nearly every reference to her work, two points are noted. First, readers were reminded of her marriage to Grant Foreman, and reviewers consistently linked the body of work produced by the two as inseparable and indistinguishable. "Their threads of interest on matters historical were so interwoven, so tightly knit, that it is impossible to separate one from the other," one writer observed. It is true that they spent much of their long marriage traveling around the United States and to Europe, India, and Mexico to conduct research in archives, libraries, and museums. Grant Foreman frequently acknowledged in his own publications the partnership of his wife in their research, and he especially respected her ability to translate French and Spanish documents to be used in his books. His work always received acclaim, however, and hers was found wanting. Somehow her contribution lost value.

For example, in 1931, Foreman wrote to E. E. Dale that he and Carolyn were going out for a "day of historical foraging." Foreman wanted to interview "an old Cherokee woman," and to visit in another Cherokee home. Given current understanding of Native American culture and the appreciation of the position of women in the resilient matrilineal clan structures of the Five (Civilized) Tribes, one wonders how accessible the Cherokee home and how receptive the "old Cherokee woman" might have been to Foreman without the presence of Carolyn.

Grant Foreman preceded his wife in death by fourteen years. She continued to publish until the close of her life.[12]

Indeed, it is in the area of Native American women's history and family history that Carolyn Foreman had a significant impact. Many of her articles for the *Chronicles* consisted of interviews, reminiscences, and biographical sketches of elderly Indian women, including "Aunt Eliza of Tahlequah," "Augusta Robertson Moore," "Aunt Sue Rogers, a Creek Pioneer," "The Bean Family," and "The Jumper Family of the Seminole Nation." Foreman was able to complete these articles because she cultivated a network of women, both Indian and non-Indian, who facilitated the recovery of this history. For example, in her 1931 article on "Aunt Eliza," Foreman wrote that she was "ably assisted by the devoted relatives and warm friends of Aunt Eliza among whom thanks are due." In addition, Foreman documented valuable detailed information about educational opportunities for nineteenth-century women, such as Sophia Sawyer's School for Girls, and the creation of the Cherokee Female Seminary, which became a part of her book entitled *Park Hill*. Foreman's 1954 book, *Indian Women Chiefs*, challenged the misunderstanding that Native American women had no position in tribal affairs, and that they often existed as slaves within their societies. She traced examples of powerful Indian women leaders from the sixteenth century to the twentieth. One reviewer wrote, "This book is a monument to all Indian women. Through its insight future historians and writers have a wealth of new material, and the general reader has a true concept of the American Indian woman."[13]

Still, good reviews of her work were few and far between in Oklahoma, for the second most frequent assessment was that Foreman was not a writer but a researcher, compiler, and collector. Even for one of her most important books, *Indians Abroad*, a study of the experiences of American Indians in foreign lands, Muriel Wright wrote, "There has been no attempt at fine writing by Mrs. Foreman." During World War II, however, the Office of War Information ordered 80,000 copies of *Indians Abroad* to be placed in overseas libraries for servicemen. Other reviewers characterized her style as "prolix and uneven in presentation of the subject matter—even repetitious at times." Angie Debo summed up Foreman's work this way: "She carried on prodigious research on topics never before explored, and produced heavily documented articles, piling facts on facts, with little attempt at organization or interpretation."

Reviewers did acknowledge the extent and value of Foreman's research. Of *Oklahoma Imprints,* a work that involved seven years of effort, a reviewer noted, "There can be no doubt of the great value of the book." Academically trained historians draw on Foreman's exceptional research today to produce accurate descriptions of Oklahoma social history. Foreman's *North Fork Town,* with its genealogy, interviews, cemetery records, and geographic description, provides a fitting historical complement to the fictional setting of Edwin Lanham's Depression-era novel *The Stricklands.*[14]

Given the nature of her work style, her connections to a wide range of Oklahoma citizens outside her own class, and her interest in Native American, women, family, and environmental place topics, it is reasonable to see how she came to suggest an idea that would have major significance for future historians. Foreman valued the small, intimate, personal history recorded in the pre-statehood newspapers that she had researched so long for *Oklahoma Imprints.* In the early years of the Depression, she urged her husband to propose a joint Works Progress Administration and Oklahoma Historical Society project to hire unemployed white-collar workers to index the large newspaper collection owned by OHS. The extensive index has been enormously beneficial to researchers. That completed, Foreman next suggested that before the pioneering generation of Oklahomans was lost, a similar statewide effort should be made to record their memories. Such a collection would create a lasting historical endowment. Her husband directed the joint University of Oklahoma, WPA, and OHS project that resulted in 112 volumes known now as the *Indian-Pioneer Papers.* Angie Debo described this collection as "a storehouse of living history." Because of Carolyn Thomas Foreman's resolute scholarship and perseverance, the raw materials of nineteenth- and twentieth-century Oklahoma social history survived.[15]

The remaining two Oklahoma women historians, Muriel Wright and Angie Debo, produced a greater volume of published work and are far better-known. In a sense they represent the identity of Oklahoma: one from Indian Territory, one from Oklahoma Territory; one the child of a distinguished Choctaw family, one the child of homesteaders; both excellent scholars, and both fiercely proprietary about the history of Oklahoma. Most often they have been analyzed on the basis of a large body of work devoted to Native American history, but Wright and Debo had an expansive vision of the state that allowed them to incorporate many voices into the history they wrote.

MURIEL WRIGHT

Muriel Hazel Wright was born in 1889, at the very moment of transition when the first sections of Indian lands held separately since 1830 were opened for non-Indian settlement. Her grandfather, the Reverend Allen Wright, principal chief of the Choctaw Nation from 1866 to 1870, had proposed the new name for this territory, "Oklahoma." Muriel was one of two daughters born at Lehigh, Choctaw Nation, Indian Territory, to Eliphalet Nott Wright, a doctor, and Ida Belle Richards Wright, a Presbyterian missionary teacher. She was home-schooled by her mother and sent to Presbyterian elementary schools when they were available. Her father held several influential positions as a Choctaw delegate to the U.S. government during the allotment and disposition of Indian lands and the abolition of tribal governments prior to Oklahoma statehood. The family spent extended time in Washington, D.C., where Muriel studied privately after a two-year enrollment at Wheaton College. Upon her return to Oklahoma, she entered East Central State College in Ada, where she pursued a teaching degree, graduating in 1912.[16]

Wright began her career in the rural schools of southeastern Oklahoma. She encountered every challenge present in public education in this new state: one-room facilities in which the upper and lower grades were separated only by a curtain; students of varying ages and races, many of whom could not afford basic school supplies; and positions that required her to teach, coach basketball, direct plays, and serve as both principal and janitor. These conditions and the ignorance that most of her students had of their own past called on her academic training and love of history to create classroom materials.

Throughout Wright's career, she wrote Oklahoma history textbooks. In 1929 she published the first, *The Story of Oklahoma*. *Our Oklahoma* followed in 1939, and *The Oklahoma History* in 1951. Supplemental workbooks accompanied the first two. In addition, along with Joseph Thoburn, she wrote a four-volume adult history entitled *Oklahoma: A History of the State and Its People.*[17]

When Wright published *Our Oklahoma*, she expressed concern in the preface that such a brief volume might not maintain a proper balance and might not "give due consideration to many diverse elements" that made the story of Oklahoma so remarkable. Joseph Thoburn reassured her on that count in his review: "By heredity and environment she might easily have manifested a measure of prejudiced feeling in some instances," he wrote, but "her statements concerning controversial issues are noticeably fair-minded and free from any hint of personal bias."

She had adopted a positive Oklahoma voice as early as the publication of *The Story of Oklahoma*. "Life here is teeming with great possibilities," she wrote in its introduction, "achievements only to be equaled in time to come with the vivid history of its past, which will remain as a spectacular panorama of the 'last frontier.'"

Historian Patricia Loughlin's thoughtful analysis of Wright as a historian describes her as a "confident bicultural woman" who identified her own Choctaw past with progress and positive accomplishment. She transferred that identity to Oklahoma itself and protected it in the history she wrote. Loughlin suggests that this may be one of the reasons why Wright had little patience with Angie Debo's criticism of the role of acculturated Indians such as the Wrights in Indian dispossession.[18]

This does not mean that Wright attempted objectivity in her writing. Had she lived long enough to be familiar with Howard Zinn, she might have agreed with his assessment that objectivity is both impossible and undesirable. "If you think history should serve society in some way; should serve the progress of the human race; should serve justice in some way," Zinn has stated, "then it requires you to make your selection [of information] on the basis of what you think will advance causes of humanity." Zinn insists that this be honestly acknowledged.[19]

Anna Lewis would have challenged Zinn on this position. She received her academic training at a time of momentous changes in the history profession, when moralizing and nationalistic biases were being rejected in favor of meticulous research and analysis. She wrote that in order to teach or write about the past, the historian must "free himself of the burdens, of all his prejudices, and even his principles," like the Pilgrim in *The Pilgrim's Progress*. The problem arises for Zinn's viewpoint when there is a legitimate disagreement over the interpretation of evidence, as Loughlin asserts there was between Wright and Debo—one assuming a positive posture, one assuming a critical point of view. Debo contended, "My research is objective, but when I find all the truth on one side, as has sometimes happened in my study of Indian history, I have the same obligation to become involved as any other citizen." The two wrangled on numerous occasions over different sides of an issue.[20]

Between 1929 and 1974, Muriel Wright wrote or coauthored twelve books on Oklahoma and Indian history. Throughout her life, she traveled across Oklahoma, researching, mapping, and marking historic sites. She identified, wrote descriptions of, and published information about more than six hundred locations significant to Oklahoma history.

She published her most significant book, *A Guide to the Indian Tribes of Oklahoma,* in 1951, and it continued to be a valuable reference source for many years. In the 1986 reprint, Arrell Gibson, premier western historian at the University of Oklahoma, explained the appropriateness of Wright's authorship. He grounded the credibility of the book in Wright's Indian heritage, in her exposure to experienced mentors—Joseph Thoburn, Grant Foreman, and E. E. Dale—and in a lifetime of productive research. Once again, Gibson wrote, Wright discussed the suffering of each of the sixty-seven tribes because of their exile and Trail of Tears to Oklahoma, but "each sketch evolves on a positive note" and includes "revelations of substantive cultural, economic, and social changes made by Indians adapting to the 'new order.'" To the history and government of each tribe, Wright added sections on contemporary life and culture, and public ceremonials and dances.[21]

Wright accomplished her most profound work, however, as editor of the *Chronicles of Oklahoma,* the journal of scholarly studies published by the Oklahoma Historical Society. From 1943 to 1973, she directed the quarterly publication, insisting on high standards of scholarship, critical evaluation of issues, a diversity of articles from all periods of Oklahoma history, and an emphasis on primary sources. In the early days, she often had to supplement the scholarship and rewrite the articles herself in order to bring them up to her publication standards. An analysis of the articles published during Wright's tenure reveals that in terms of subject matter, they were almost evenly split between Indian and non-Indian history. Toward the latter part of Wright's career, the articles became more scholarly, more professional, and driven more by "fact" than by "attitude." She made the "Notes and Documents" section an ongoing source of exciting primary materials inviting further investigation, and she captured biographical and oral history sources that would otherwise have been lost to historians. During her tenure, she wrote or edited ninety-five articles for the journal and reviewed twenty-nine books. Many of these, like the articles of Carolyn Foreman, retrieved the lives of women and dealt with issues of female education and family life.

Patricia Loughlin maintains that Muriel Wright used the *Chronicles of Oklahoma* as the forum for projecting her views. "From this position of power, she influenced and gave shape to the historical interpretation coming out of the Oklahoma Historical Society."[22]

ANGIE DEBO

Angie Debo, who lived to the age of ninety-eight, experienced the respect, honor, and affection for her long career as a historian that none of the other women in this study enjoyed. She wrote thirteen books and published more than one hundred articles on Oklahoma history and Indian history. In addition, she established a political action network that pressured federal government officials to create legislation to fulfill its obligations and to protect the rights of Native Americans. In this area she became what her biographer called her, a "warrior-scholar." Her portrait was hung in the Oklahoma state capitol rotunda, public schools were named for her, and days were set aside in her honor by political leaders, and at the time of her death, she knew that a PBS video of her life and work being prepared for national broadcast had neared completion. Historians Richard White and Shirley Leckie acknowledge her as the scholar who pioneered the "new" Indian history. She wrote from a Native American perspective, and her research moved beyond traditional government documents to include court records, travel accounts, census records, newspapers, oral histories, and ethnology. Much of her acclaim resulted from her lifelong goal, "to discover truth and to publish it." This she did especially well in her major book, *And Still the Waters Run,* a candid description of the criminal activities of national, state, and local figures to extinguish the sovereignty of the Five Nations and to dispossess them of their land and natural resources. There was another reference point for Angie Debo, however, one that has been less-considered: she also wrote about the non-Indian population of Oklahoma and the spirit and character of these people. In this work, she wrote about herself.[23]

Born on a farm near Beattie, Kansas, in 1890, Debo retained vivid memories all her life of the sunshine and green wheat fields that greeted her family on the day in 1899 that they arrived in Marshall, Oklahoma. Her parents, Edward and Lina Debo, sent their daughter to rural elementary schools until she was twelve. There was no high school in the area for Angie to go on to, so she was forced to wait until one was built. She graduated when she was twenty-three years old. At the age of sixteen, she obtained a certificate and started teaching in the rural schools of Logan and Garfield counties. In 1915 she entered the University of Oklahoma, where she encountered Edward

Everett Dale, premier historian of the American West, who introduced her to
the challenge of historical research and writing. Theirs would be an enduring
relationship that shaped her career. She completed a master's degree at the
prestigious University of Chicago in 1924 and began the frustrating and disappointing search for a university appointment. Regardless of the quality and
success of her publications, she would never secure a tenured academic position. She joined the faculty at West Texas State Teachers College (now West
Texas State University) and pursued a doctorate in history at OU under Dale's
mentorship. She earned the Ph.D. in 1933, and her dissertation, *The Rise and
Fall of the Choctaw Republic,* was published the following year. It won the John
H. Dunning Prize of the American Historical Association. Unable to find
suitable employment, she returned to Marshall, where she would remain for
the rest of her life, supporting herself through temporary positions, grants,
and her publications.[24]

In a 2001 article, historian Patricia Nelson Limerick defines a paradox that
she finds in Angie Debo's work. There is the body of literature that Debo
produced, which openly placed before the reading public the corruption,
chicanery, and scandal of the strategies employed by white power brokers
against the original Native American landholders of Oklahoma. The language
she used throughout was blunt and forceful. But there are also her books on
Oklahoma history, such as *Prairie City* and *Oklahoma: Foot-Loose and Fancy-
Free,* that are virtually silent on the Indian past and celebrate the white pioneering spirit and accomplishments. Limerick called this "boilerplate 'frontier and pioneer' writing," in which the reader feels "trapped in a Norman
Rockwell painting." As Limerick tried to unravel the paradox, she came to the
conclusion that the two could not be reconciled, and that the history of
Oklahoma was both—*And Still the Waters Run* side by side with *Prairie City.*
Angie Debo could be generous about the humble, hard-working pioneers
who built a life and a community on land that had been unjustly taken. She
knew both of those truths.[25]

When Debo's works on Oklahoma history are considered rather than her
works on Indian history, their publication dates may be significant. The chro-
nological time frame of U.S. history and the passages of Debo's own life may
have influenced her choice of subject matter. All of them were published in the
1940s, during World War II and the Cold War confrontation with the Soviet
Union. Historians live within and are affected by the culture that surrounds
them. As Debo went about her writing in Marshall, she was confronted by the
wartime sacrifices of death and privation. For a time during the war, she served

as a Methodist minister, and when she buried the dead, she reminded the mourners of their loved one's attachment to the land by repeating, "With this loved soil of Oklahoma which you tilled for so many years I bury you." Perhaps this love of the land that she had experienced through her parents and her own sense of place, as well as the unity and patriotism inspired by the times, made her more inclined to write books that commemorated the best of human values rather than the worst. These were also times of postwar intolerance and fear of subversion. Debo knew firsthand through the rejection of *And Still the Waters Run* the cost of writing a book that "named names" and embarrassed important people. In 1941, her history chapter in *The WPA Guide to 1930s Oklahoma* was mysteriously deleted, and another one was substituted in its place. At least one commentator believed that Anna Lewis's biography of the Choctaw chief Pushmataha had failed to find an established press because of public sentiment against any material that criticized the U.S. government. Debo was in her fifties, and her livelihood depended on her publications. She had already made an established name for herself in the historiography of the American Indian; this was a time to write about the people she had come from and lived among.[26]

Before the publication of *And Still the Waters Run,* Debo took charge of forty employees of the Federal Writers Project in Oklahoma to research and write the WPA guide for the state. Besides planning, supervising and editing, she wrote the chapter on Oklahoma history and submitted the manuscript in 1941. She was horrified to find that the published guide had omitted her essay and replaced it with one full of errors. When the guide was republished in 1986, Anne Hodges Morgan insisted that Debo's chapter be placed in its rightful position. Morgan wrote that the guide was "remarkably well-written" and provided an "excellent key to understanding the cultural heritage and attitudes of Oklahomans." It had become a source of "primary materials about the nation's social history prior to World War II," she continued. Armed with information coming out of the WPA project, Debo wrote *Tulsa: From Creek Town to Oil Capital,* describing it as the "quintessence of Americanism." The book sold out as fast as the bookstores received it.[27]

Debo next received a grant from the publisher Alfred A. Knopf and embarked on her only work of fiction, *Prairie City.* The thinly disguised rural community setting of the novel was actually a love letter to the people of Marshall, Oklahoma. "The whole epic sweep of American history is compressed into the lifetime of these pioneers," she wrote, a theme that she repeated in all of her works about white settlement in Oklahoma.

Prairie City is a composite sketch of small Oklahoma communities from settlement to decline after World War II, and the people who labored to build homes, churches, schools, farms, and businesses on the frontier. It is a story of work, courage, and determination against great adversity. Debo makes it clear in the preface, however, that besides her own personal experience, she "carried on exacting research" in all kinds of records and interviews to be sure that her story was authentic."I hope the people of my community, the finest people I have ever known, will not be disappointed in this book they have helped me write," she concluded. The citizens of Marshall were proud of *Prairie City,* and proud of their favorite daughter.[28]

Oklahoma: Foot-Loose and Fancy-Free appeared in 1949. Debo had placed some of the text from the deleted history chapter of the *WPA Guide* into the opening chapters of this book and began her preface with the statement, "Any state of the American Union deserves to be known and understood." She claimed that she had not really written a history, but had provided the historical background, the context, the "physical setting," so that the state might be recognized as the symbol of the American experience she believed it to be. In this book, Debo at different times applauded pioneer accomplishments and derided the ruthless exploitation of Native Americans. While the tone and content were not as positive overall as in *Prairie City,* Debo was still intentional about linking the Oklahoma character to the solid values of the past.

Her concern for contemporary society was reflected in this statement: "Nobody knows better than they [Oklahomans] that mankind is traveling a perilous road, with annihilation perhaps as the not far distant end," she wrote, "And if they should be building on the edge of a precipice, why building is much pleasanter and even more constructive than looking down into the void. . . . This confidence of course flows out of the experiences of the past, and one generation has felt them all." Angie Debo's intellectual integrity, her superior scholarship, and her unwavering commitment to writing Oklahoma history made her for a time the conscience and voice of Oklahoma.[29]

• • •

In the early part of the twentieth century, Oklahoma had a network of professional female historians who engaged in scholarship that prepared the way for modern social historians. They combed archives, they took down oral histories, they documented historic sites, they created programs for the enhancement of historical preservation, they collected print sources, they prepared educational materials, and they wrote and published new history. Their scholarship broadened the scope of Oklahoma history by retrieving the stories of the non-elite and by exploring topics considered by most professionals as unimportant, "pots and pans" history. They also challenged traditional interpretations of the past, especially with regard to Native American history and gender. At a time when professional positions were nearly nonexistent for women, these historians developed strategies to pursue their research and find auxiliary employment in order to support themselves. They were often overlooked and underrated, they were certainly underpaid, and they frequently faced discrimination in hiring and advancement. The state of Oklahoma owes them a great debt. The historical profession would be much poorer today but for this company of "petticoat" historians.

NOTES

1. Howard Zinn, interview with David Barresi for *Digress Magazine,* March 1999, http://digressmagazine.com/zinn/zinn3.html, accessed July 10, 2004. For a biography of Zinn and his significance, see Davis D. Joyce, *Howard Zinn: A Radical American Vision* (Amherst, N.Y.: Prometheus Books, 2003). For women in the history profession, see Gerda Lerner, "A View from the Women's Side," *Journal of American History* 76 (September 1989): 446–56, and Susan Armitage, "Here's to the Women: Western Women Speak Up," *Journal of American History* 83 (September 1996): 551–59.

2. Winnidell Gravitt Wilson, "Anna Lezola Lewis, Ph.D., 1885–1961," typescript, Anna Lewis Collection, Nash Library, University of Science and Arts of Oklahoma, Chickasha, Oklahoma (hereafter cited as ALC-USAO), 1, 4; Angie Debo, quoted in Patricia E. Loughlin, "Assuming Indian Voices: Western Women Writers, Alice Marriott, Muriel Wright, and Angie Debo" (Ph.D. diss., Oklahoma State University 2000), 161–62; Anna Lewis, "The Rights of Women," ALC-USAO. For an examination of Oklahoma women and gender understanding in this time period, see Linda W. Reese, *Women of Oklahoma, 1890–1920* (Norman: University of Oklahoma Press, 1997).

3. Carolyn Foreman (1872–1967): J. Stanley Clark, "Carolyn Thomas Foreman," *Chronicles of Oklahoma* (hereafter cited as *Chronicles*) 45 (Winter 1967–68): 368–75. Anna Lewis (1885–1961): Winnie Lewis Gravitt, "Anna Lewis: A Great Woman of Oklahoma," *Chronicles* 40 (Winter 1962–63): 326–29. Muriel Wright (1889–1975): LeRoy H. Fischer, "Muriel H. Wright, Historian of Oklahoma," *Chronicles* 52 (Spring 1974): 3–29. Angie Debo (1890–1988): Shirley A. Leckie, *Angie Debo: Pioneering Historian* (Norman: University of Oklahoma Press, 2000); Peter N. Stearns, "The Old Social History and The New," in Mary Kupiec Cayton, Elliott J. Gorn, and Peter W. Williams, eds., *Encyclopedia of American Social History,* (New York: Scribner, 1993), 1: 237–50.

4. "Inductees Named to Higher Education Hall of Fame," http://arapaho.nsuok .edu/~tne/Past%20Issues/09162003/News/Inductees.html, accessed August 29, 2004; USAO grant writers were Dr. Dan Hobbs, Kelly Brown, and Julie Bohanon; Gravitt, "Anna Lewis," 326–29; Dan Hobbs, "Dr. Anna Lewis," typescript, ALC-USAO;

Linda W. Reese, "Dr. Anna Lewis, Historian at the Oklahoma College for Women," *Chronicles*, forthcoming.

5. Wilson, "Anna Lezola Lewis," 1–2; Gravitt, "Anna Lewis," 328; Anna Lewis, handwritten memoir, ALC-USAO. The name of the woman Austin was talking with was left blank in Lewis's memoir. For histories of OCW, see Rex Harlow, *George W. Austin: His Life and Work* (Oklahoma City: Rex Harlow, 1927); Dixie Belcher, "A Democratic School for Democratic Women," *Chronicles* 61 (Winter 1983–84): 414–21; Cynthia Savage, "Oklahoma College for Women: Oklahoma's Only State-Supported College for Women," *Chronicles* 80 (Summer 2002): 176–203.

6. David W. Levy to Linda Reese, May 23, 2003. The University of Oklahoma History Department awarded tenure to the first female faculty member, Judith Schneid Lewis (no relation to Anna Lewis), in 1987; Jacqueline Goggin reported that between 1893 and 1935, 334 women received the Ph.D. in history in the United States. Although they were trained at coeducational institutions, few were hired by such schools. Most women with advanced degrees were employed by high schools, libraries and archives, and women's colleges. See Jacqueline Goggin, "Challenging Sexual Discrimination in the Historical Profession: Women Historians and the American Historical Association, 1890–1940," *American Historical Review* 97 (June 1992): 771. *New York Times*, January 15, 1933; *Books*, February 12, 1933; Martin Heflin, "Books," clipping, *The Bandwagon*, January 1933, 23, ALC-USAO.

7. Bob L. Blackburn, "Oklahoma Historians Hall of Fame—Anna Lewis," *Chronicles* 73 (Fall 1995): 358–60; R.G.M., "The Smoking Room," clipping, June 14, 1953, ALC-USAO; Elmer L. Fraker, "1956 Historical Society Tour over the Old Chisholm Trail," *Chronicles* 34 (Summer 1956): 240–45; Winnidell Wilson, "Notes," ALC-USAO; Anna Lewis, "Camp Napoleon," *Chronicles* 9 (December 1931): 359–64.

8. E. E. Dale to Anna Lewis, March 22,1935, E. E. Dale Collection, Box 39, Folder 19, Western History Collections, University of Oklahoma, Norman, Oklahoma (hereafter cited as WHC-OU); Anna Lewis and Howard Taylor, *Problems in Oklahoma History* (Oklahoma City: The Economy Co., 1931), Preface; "Indian Relics and Early Pictures Contained in the College Museum," clipping, n.d., ALC-USAO.

9. Anna Lewis, "The Rights of Women," ALC-USAO; Anna Lewis, "The Teaching of History," ALC-USAO; clipping, D. L. Birchfield, "Anna Lewis, Choctaw Historian," review of *Pushmataha, American Patriot* by Anna Lewis, *Spirit Talk* 2 (1994): 21–23, ALC-USAO; William F. Semple, review of *Pushmataha, American Patriot*, by Anna Lewis, *Chronicles* 37 (Summer 1959): 255–56.

10. Angie Debo, "A Dedication to the Memory of Carolyn Thomas Foreman, 1872–1967," *Arizona and the West* 16 (Autumn 1974): 215.

11. Ibid., 215–18; Clark, "Carolyn Thomas Foreman," 368–75.

12. Clark, "Carolyn Thomas Foreman," 372; Grant Foreman to E. E. Dale, June 17, 1931, Box 23, Folder 18, WHC-OU; Debo, "A Dedication," 216–17.

13. Carolyn Thomas Foreman, "Aunt Eliza of Tahlequah," *Chronicles* 9 (March 1931): 43; Carolyn Thomas Foreman, *Park Hill* (Muskogee, Okla.: Press of the Star Printery, 1958); Carolyn Thomas Foreman, *Indian Women Chiefs* (Muskogee, Okla.: Press of the Star Printery, 1954); Frances Rosser Brown, review of *Indian Women Chiefs*, by Carolyn Thomas Foreman, *Chronicles* 32 (Autumn 1954): 343.

14. Muriel Wright, review of *Indians Abroad*, by Carolyn Thomas Foreman, *Chronicles* 22 (Spring 1944): 121; Clark, "Carolyn Thomas Foreman," 373; Debo, "A Dedication," 216; R. L. Biesele, review of *Oklahoma Imprints: A History of Printing in Oklahoma before Statehood*, by Carolyn Thomas Foreman, *Mississippi Valley Historical Review* 23 (December 1936): 430.

15. Debo, "A Dedication," 217; Clark, "Carolyn Thomas Foreman," 373.

16. Fischer, "Muriel H. Wright," 3–29; Ruth Arrington, "Wright, Muriel Hazel," in Barbara Sicherman et al., eds., *Notable American Women: The Modern Period* (Cambridge, Mass.: Harvard University Press, 1980).

17. Joseph B. Thoburn and Muriel H. Wright, *Oklahoma: A History of the State and Its People* (New York: Lewis Historical Publishing Co., 1929); Fischer, "Muriel H. Wright," 22; Bob L. Blackburn, "Oklahoma Historians Hall of Fame—Muriel H. Wright," *Chronicles* 71 (Winter 1993–94): 451–52.

18. Muriel Wright, *Our Oklahoma* (Guthrie, Okla.: Cooperative Publishing Co., 1939); Joseph Thoburn, review of *Our Oklahoma*, by Muriel Wright, *Chronicles* 17 (December 1939): 451; Muriel Wright, *The Story of Oklahoma* (Oklahoma City: Webb Publishing Co., 1929); Loughlin, "Assuming Indian Voices," 106, 125, 136.

19. Barresi, "Howard Zinn Interview"; Joyce, *Howard Zinn*, 18.

20. Anna Lewis, "The Teaching of History," ALC-USAO; Kenneth McIntosh, "Geronimo's Friend: Angie Debo and the New History," *Chronicles* 66 (Summer 1988): 164–77; Loughlin, "Assuming Indian Voices," 115–17; Angie Debo, "An Autobiographical Sketch, Eulogy, and Bibliography," booklet (Stillwater: Oklahoma State University, 1988), 2.

21. Arrell M. Gibson in Muriel H. Wright, *A Guide to the Indian Tribes of Oklahoma* (Norman: University of Oklahoma Press, 1986), vii–ix; LeRoy H. Fischer, "The Historic Preservation Movement in Oklahoma," *Chronicles* 57 (Spring 1979): 3–25.

22. Dana Cesar, Joan K. Smith, and Grayson Noley, "Muriel Wright: Telling the Story of Oklahoma Indian Nations," *American Education History Journal*, forthcoming; Loughlin, "Assuming Indian Voices," 122.

23. Bob L. Blackburn, "Oklahoma Historians Hall of Fame—Angie Debo," *Chronicles* 72 (Winter 1994–95): 454–59; Leckie, *Angie Debo*; Richard White, review of *Indians, Outlaws and Angie Debo*, produced by Barbara Abrash and Martha Sandlin, *Journal of American History* 76 (December 1989): 1010; Debo, "An Autobiographical Sketch," 2; Loughlin, "Assuming Indian Voices," 143; Angie Debo, *And Still the Waters Run* (Princeton, N.J.: Princeton University Press, 1940).

24. Blackburn, "Oklahoma Historians Hall of Fame—Angie Debo"; Leckie, *Angie Debo*; White, review of *Indians, Outlaws and Angie Debo*; Debo, "An Autobiographical Sketch"; Loughlin, "Assuming Indian Voices"; Debo, *And Still the Waters Run*. The decisions and crises of Debo's life, especially related to her difficulties in finding work and to her decision not to marry, are ably discussed in the above-cited sources as well as *Indians, Outlaws and Angie Debo*, produced by Barbara Abrash and Martha Sandlin, (video, 58 min., Institute for Research in History, 1988); Glenna Matthews and Gloria Valencia-Weber, "Against Great Odds: The Life of Angie Debo," *OAH Newsletter*, May 1985, 8–11; Suzanne H. Schrems and Cynthia J. Wolff, "Politics and Libel: Angie Debo and the Publication of *And Still the Waters Run*," *Western Historical Quarterly* 22 (May

1991): 184–203; Richard Lowitt, "Regionalism at the University of Oklahoma," *Chronicles* 73 (Summer 1995): 150–71. Angie Debo, *The Rise and Fall of the Choctaw Republic* (Norman: University of Oklahoma Press, 1934).

25. Patricia Nelson Limerick, "Land, Justice, and Angie Debo: Telling the Truth to— and about—Your Neighbors," *Great Plains Quarterly* 21 (Fall 2001): 268, 269, 271; Angie Debo, *Prairie City: The Story of an American Community* (New York: Alfred A. Knopf, 1944); Debo, *Oklahoma: Foot-Loose and Fancy-Free* (Norman: University of Oklahoma Press, 1949).

26. Matthews and Weber, "Against Great Odds," 9; Anne Hodges Morgan, "Introduction to the Paperback Edition," in *The WPA Guide to 1930s Oklahoma* (Lawrence: University of Kansas Press, 1986), ix–xi; Birchfield, "Anna Lewis," ALC-USAO.

27. Morgan, "Introduction," 9–11; Leckie, *Angie Debo*, 87–89; Angie Debo, *Tulsa: From Creek Town to Oil Capital* (Norman: University of Oklahoma Press, 1943).

28. Debo, *Prairie City*, viii–ix. Gloria Valencia-Weber wrote, "Marshall supported her in every way that we know deeply caring people care for each other"; Debo, "An Autobiographical Sketch," 4. Sociologist Jeff S. Sharp recommended Debo's *Prairie City* as "a fully detailed historic background for understanding rural community culture and structures that persist across time and affect local change and development." See Jeff S. Sharp, "Place, Social Structure and Culture: A Review Essay on Community," *Rural Sociology* 66 (2001): 139.

29. Morgan, "Introduction," xi; Debo, *Oklahoma: Foot-Loose and Fancy-Free*, vii–viii.

CHAPTER 2

Three Oklahoma Women

Carole Jane Joyce

In the previous essay, Linda W. Reese describes the four historians she writes about as having "expanded the range of subjects by including people outside political and social power structures." Carole Jane Joyce writes of three such people in the following essay.

Joyce is retired after a lifetime as a dancer, dance teacher, and choreographer. She has also taught conversational English (in Hungary) and creative writing (in the Continuing Education program at East Central University). She is one of the few repeat contributors in this volume, having written on the Oklahoma Religious Coalition for Abortion Rights in its predecessor, *"An Oklahoma I Had Never Seen Before": Alternative Views of Oklahoma History.*

Joyce has been conducting in-depth interviews with women from every walk of life for many years now. In this essay, she draws on those interviews to tell the story of "Three Oklahoma Women." They were born in different eras, and have had very different life experiences. Alvin O. Turner (represented elsewhere in this volume) has called such people "non-elite." There is no value judgment there; the suggestion is simply that they come from the ranks of the common people rather than the wealthy and powerful. In short, they are like most of us. As Reese has helped us to realize, if the label "people's history" means anything, it surely means that people such as these belong in our history books along with presidents, kings, queens, generals, and the rich.

MAURINE

A da, Oklahoma, where cotton was once king, is where I first met Maurine Harper. My husband and I were new to the city. He had a professorial job in the history department of East Central University. I soon joined the Women's Club of the university, and some months later, by invitation, I joined the Fortnightly Club, a nationally known association that was well into its seventy-fifth year. The club, formed in 1913, had originally been known as the Delphian Society. "Believing that only a comprehensive course could meet the requirements of the day and prove acceptable to a large number of people, the Delphian Society has included those subjects which are still offered in the curriculums of leading colleges and universities—history, literature, philosophy, poetry, fiction, drama, art, ethics, music."[1] The Fortnightly Club adopted five of these curricula as its basis.

In Ada, Fortnightly's departments included Music, Modern Books, and Poetry; I chose the department of Progressive Drama. At my first meeting, I was introduced to Maurine and other members of the club who shared my desire to know more about literature. Literature drew us together and for many years kept our souls and spirits alive with knowledge of playwrights known and unknown—and also, at times, with classical music, modern books, and current events.

The Progressive Drama department read a new play every two weeks during its session, which coincided with the university's academic year. One member would be in charge of each meeting, and one would act as hostess. The one in charge would have been chosen at the previous meeting, and thus would have spent the subsequent two weeks in the library doing research on the play that had been chosen at the same time. She would be expected to know all about the play and its author. Most of the professors at the university in Ada were men at that time, and the wives were eager to start their own studies, which they were able to do through the Fortnightly Club. The club kept them abreast of what was going on in the world.

The moment I met Maurine, I was fascinated, not only by her knowledge but also by her green eyes, her brown shoulder-length hair streaked with white, and her red pants suit. However, there was something else that set her apart from the rest of the members: her chin and neck seem to float above her straight, upright body. Maurine and I were always more in agreement on local issues than most of the other members. She was always upbeat and eager to talk about her life in southeastern Oklahoma, and after some time went by, I told her that I had been doing interviews with women over the past fifteen years, and that I would like to interview her. Without hesitating, she said yes.

My initial interview with Maurine was in 1987. It covered the early years of her life. She was born on March 30, 1909, so she was in her late seventies at that time, and in her nineties the last time I interviewed her. She lives across the road from her only sister, Rosemary, in a nice neighborhood just east of downtown Ada. Rosemary, like her sister, is well informed on political issues; she is tolerant of other people and loves their company. Early in life, both girls were aware of what was going on globally and in their own community, because of the care their parents took to include them in every part of their lives. Theirs was a liberal family. In 1912, when Maurine was only three, Oklahoma's Socialist Party was the strongest in the country, and her parents were deeply involved in it. That same year, Woodrow Wilson and the Democratic Party were elected to the White House. Wilson was sworn in as president of the United States in 1913.

Maurine and her family were not poor, but they were by no means well off, either. During World War I, they were given a telephone because of the work her father did. As the county agricultural agent, he traveled by horse and buggy throughout the entire state of Oklahoma. Then when cars began to make their appearance, the state bought him one. Maurine remembers that the car was to be used only for federal business; she recalls that few people at that time had a car or a telephone. "Father was a county agent," Maurine says. "I remember being concerned for my father during wartime." In the early hours one morning, their telephone rang with the news that the war had ended. Her father was instructed to rouse the town by whatever means. He grabbed his shotgun and fired shots into the air, and soon the whole town was awake. While the newspaper began to prepare a special edition, the citizens all gathered downtown. By that afternoon, Kaiser Wilhelm was being burned in effigy in the town square. Maurine's mother took the girls downtown and bought each of them miniature flags of all of the United Nations; she explained the reason for each flag and the reason for the stuffed Wilhelm.

As a young girl, Maurine was aware that she could not ask for anything that was not reasonable. But, she was quick to add, "Sister and I were never deprived." The girls spent some of their summers with one aunt in St. Louis, while others were spent in Sherman, Texas, with the other aunt. The sisters were fortunate to have a railroad worker in the family who afforded them Frisco passes. Maurine has been making her own clothes since her school days. After learning early how much money a painter charged for painting a room, she decided to do that work herself, too. Soon she taught herself to upholster furniture and make her own curtains, and later she did her own floor design for her three-bedroom home. She decorated her home with pictures she painted—in pastels—that fit into the decor. Dollhouses were also a specialty.

Maurine has been married twice. Her first husband had an ice route, but was not interested in any kind of daily work. He only wanted money for cigarettes and beer. She was attracted to him because of his good looks and charm; in fact, she described herself as having been crazy about him. She said that he was wonderful at playing the piano, but worthless at being a husband. Before long, he moved back in with his father and brother; he and Maurine were divorced, and she did not know much about him after that.

In 1939, Maurine married for the second time. Herman Francis Harper, or "Tex," as he was known, soon became the love of her life, and he remained so until his death. He was born in Germany, and soon after was brought over to the States by his parents. He lived in California and parts of Oregon. In Oregon, he was a star football player in high school. It was his job that brought him to Oklahoma. The international oil tool company that he worked for moved him to Ada, and that is where he and Maurine met. He shared her love for Oklahoma. The two of them were full of ideas and hopes, not only for themselves but also for the town of Ada, "Queen City of the Chickasaw Nation."[2]

Ada was founded in 1890 by men who had driven their cattle into the Nation from Texas. Cattle were thus the primary business, but oil soon entered the picture. The town's post office was named for the oldest daughter of one of its earliest settlers, postmaster Jeff Reed. The first industry was the Ada Milling Company, which opened in 1901. Now the downtown area has huge Protestant churches, some occupying a full city block. Maurine attends the Episcopal Church, a few blocks south of Main Street. Ada was not Maurine's birthplace—she was born somewhere around Shawnee and Route 66—but she received all her schooling there, including a B.A. in Art from East Central University. East Central, which was founded as a normal school, now has well more than three thousand enrolled students. Maurine continued to learn, and took postgraduate classes in creative arts.

Maurine feels that she has tried to do her best in life. She was taught to be honest, and she has always tried to keep that in mind. Her parents were a good example of what citizens should be—her father always had a job, and her mother kept busy with civic affairs and continued to study her religion. They were instrumental in teaching their daughters the right things to do. "I grew up knowing that you had to be responsible for your life. I knew what the finances of my family were, and I had no idea that everyone was not so fortunate." I asked her what her technique was for handling problems during her life. "I like for my life to be open and as free as possible," she said. "I deal with a problem as fast as I can."

Maurine worked after college as a clerk and legal secretary. With her talent for fashion, she joined some other women in running a dress shop in the downtown area. She loved the creative hats with all their different styles, colors, and sizes. When Prohibition was finally repealed in 1959, she and Tex opened the first liquor store in the town. The two were involved in many endeavors through their marriage.

Maurine gave birth to three children, two girls and a boy, but one daughter died of pneumonia before she became a teenager, and the other died after graduating from college. Her son is the only one who has survived. He helps Maurine in her home these days.

Maurine's green eyes were thoughtful as she told me the following story: She was at home alone one afternoon early in her marriage when someone began pounding on her front door. Opening the door, she came face to face with a stranger, who immediately started asking her questions about her husband, calling him by his full German name. As she tried to close the door, she told the man that he would have to come back later because Tex was at work. She was not about to give him any information about anything—although he seemed to know more than she understood. Suddenly he pushed the door open, walked right past Maurine, and entered the house, continuing to ask questions about her husband and apparently looking for something. Then he bolted down the hallway, into each bedroom, and into the bathroom. Viewing the stranger as an invader in her home, Maurine yelled, "See here, what do you want?" The man, who was now in the kitchen with her, answered, "Your husband—if he is your husband." With that, Maurine ordered him to leave. He turned away from her and headed back into the living room, grabbing a small transistor radio from the bookshelf on his way out.

Once he was gone, she locked the front door for the first time in her life, something she had never thought she would have to do. The man's actions had made no sense to her. In the evening, as soon as Tex arrived home, she told him what had happened. "Well," he said, "I guess I'll have to apply for a green card first thing in the morning." Shocked, Maurine said, "You are here illegally, and I was never aware?" Tex answered, "I don't know if I'd put it that way, but I just never felt the need for the green card. You know I've always been able to work here, and no one, until now, has been the least bit interested in me. I've been here over forty years! And I served my time in World War II." Nothing else was said that night. Both of them realized how good their lives in Oklahoma had been. The next morning they drove into Oklahoma City, and he applied for a green card. Freedom is vitally important to Maurine, and she knew that she wanted her husband to experience it for the rest of his life. They never saw or heard anything more from the stranger, and to this day, Maurine is not sure what the man wanted. When I asked her how she felt while he was charging around her house, she said that she was frightened at first, then realized that she had to make a stand. "I did think about my welfare. I finally realized that I was in the middle of something that did not make any sense and certainly was not going to improve. Of course, I replayed that day many times."

In the 1980s, Ada had several companies that were doing well, including Solo Cup and Pre-Paid Legal Services, and the former railroad town was finding its way into the twenty-first century. As part of this process, the town was called during this period to join in the fight to keep *Roe v. Wade* legal. *Roe v. Wade* is the 1973 Supreme Court decision that legalized abortion. Maurine was quick to join a group called Adans for Choice. More than two hundred members strong, they spent time with local representatives and made several trips to the state capital to stay abreast of developments. Sometimes they would invite pro-choice speakers from different parts of the state to visit the town and get to know the group and what it was doing.

"Has your life met your deepest needs?" I asked Maurine. "I suppose," she replied. "One of the greatest thrills of my lifetime was taking my first airplane ride. The strip was just south of town, and after I paid the pilot one dollar, I was seated just behind him, and then we took off down the dirt runway and then into the air." As she finished this story, she took a small bow as though to indicate that she was finished with the interview.

I have since moved from Ada, and I miss Maurine and the Fortnightly Club. If you could have a conversation with only one woman in Oklahoma, I would suggest this one, Maurine from the town of Ada.

PAULA

Broken Arrow is located on the edge of Tulsa in Tulsa County. The Broken Arrow Expressway and a south loop called the Creek Turnpike join the city to Tulsa. Paula Showman Bridges lives in this town. Her home is only a few blocks from where she grew up. Paula's mother, Thelma, still lives in Paula's childhood home. The legacy that Paula brings to these pages is remarkable. If I had to choose one word to characterize her, it would be "family." She is steadfast in her belief that nothing is more important than being able to help when the family needs her. And need her they have. Before her father's death last year, she made sure that he got to do what he did best right up to the end. Paul Showman was a mechanic of the highest order and was listed in *Who's Who of Mechanics*. He invented the coil spring compressor and had it patented. But he is also in the *Guinness Book of World Records* for being the "oldest competing boat racer in the world."[3] He was so successful that his 1949 Garform racing boat came to be known as "The Legend." He modified it many times over the years. In 1949, Paul built a garage on College Street at the back of his lot. It was there that Paula gained the knowledge of motors that has stood her in good stead ever since. The garage was where everyone in the community came to get their car fixed and to learn about cars from the best. (At the time of Paul's death, it had been in continuous operation longer than any other individually owned business in Broken Arrow.) Paula learned early about cars and was never intimidated by them the way that most teenage girls were. She could talk to people about their vehicles almost as well as her father.

Paula's mother, Thelma, is a dance instructor. Paul built Thelma a dance studio in the early 1950s, also on the back of their lot. They named it Thelma Showman's School of Dance. There was never any need to wonder where the Showmans were; they were always at home. Paula learned to dance alongside her mother. They took classes in Tulsa and Oklahoma City. Paula's strength in choreography shined brightly as she aged and took on more and more responsibility for the dances created at the school.

When I first interviewed Paula, she was fifty-one years of age; fifteen years later, the interviews were finished, but my friendship with her was not. She has been a steadfast friend since we were both in our early teens. We have enjoyed each other all these years, connected through the art of dance. We began taking dance classes together as teenagers; we are both still active as choreographers. We are both 5'3" tall and weigh about the same. She has brown hair, which at various times has been long, short, shagged, pinned into a bun, and drawn up into a ponytail, and now is showing a little bit of gray. Her face, oval in shape, has high cheekbones; her eyes are gray-blue. Unlike most Oklahomans in her town, she never uses slang words or contractions. She is in tune with her world and tries to be in tune with yours.

I have always found Paula intriguing, even unique. At the age of fourteen, she got her own horse, Booger. He was pastured close by and sometimes spent the day in her yard. Booger and Paula were a winning team at the rodeos, competing in the barrel races. (Booger's sire was owned by Oklahoma's famed Johnny Lee Wills.) While Paula was still in high school, she and Booger were part of the Tulsa Mounted Troops. Horses, mechanics, and dancing were only some of Paula's interests. In 1956, she entered Tulsa's drag races with her black-and-white-pinstriped '56 Chevy. She was the only female among the racers, and she was almost barred for just that. At the same time, her father, in another class, raced his 1954 Oldsmobile and won many trophies. In 1957, Paula took part in an occasional illegal street race across Tulsa's 51st Street Bridge. The quarter-mile-long bridge was perfect for dragging, and in those days no one was on it after midnight, when people were out testing their cars. Paula usually won those races; she even beat out a brand-new 1957 Plymouth police car. In the 1960s she wanted to compete in boat races—drag boat races, that is—but was not accepted because she was a woman. Later she competed in the Powder Puff races in Ft. Gibson and in Oklahoma City at Lake Overholzer, but those races were not very frequent. Along the way, she was crowned Miss Broken Arrow in 1956, and she was queen of the Shamrock Saddle Club and the Oil Capital Round-up Club. She won blue ribbons and money for her many efforts.

At the early age of four, Paula made her debut as a performer. She sang solos in her church and on Tulsa's KVOO radio. She began dancing at Broken Arrow's famous Rooster Day festival in 1952 and continues to write routines for her mother's students to perform on that day.

Paula later became engaged to Jess Thomas, a singer with Channel 8 in Tulsa. He was on the *Big Red Jamboree,* and soon the two of them were singing and dancing together. She took a job in Tulsa to be closer to him and maintained an apartment there for a while. She worked for an electric company five hours a day, five days a week. The next year she took a job at Pan American Lab as a telephone operator. That job lasted a little over ten years. The engagement to Jess Thomas did not last that long. In 1959, Paula fell in love with a boy named Carl Bridges from Bixby, Oklahoma, and they were married the same year. They bought a home in Broken Arrow just a few blocks from her parents and only twenty miles away from Bixby, so that he too could be close to his parents. This is the home where they still reside today. Paula was an only child; in 1967, her own only child, Valerie, was born. Today Valerie, too, likes living close to her parents and grandparents. She has some involvement with the family tradition of dance, but she has built herself another kind of life.

In 1987, Paula and Carl took a vacation to Mexico. They visited the town of Puerto Vallarta and were instantly fascinated by the people and beauty. They soon purchased a condo two blocks from the Gulf of Mexico. When they returned to Oklahoma, Paula enrolled in a Spanish class at Tulsa Community College, which she finished with straight A's. That plus her annual visits to Mexico soon gave her complete control of the language, so she began to teach English to the natives of Mexico. She enjoyed teaching and soon ended up with many Mexican friends. The locals trusted her and always treated her well; they liked her and her approach to learning their language and culture and the way she shared her own language with such passion. The apartment in Mexico gives Paula a chance to get away with Carl for a few months out of the year and relax, but she always returns to Broken Arrow for Rooster Day and for the Showman recitals that her mother puts on for the town every other year. Paula writes most of the dances for those recitals, and she makes sure to teach them to the students and her mother before she goes back to Mexico.

Through the years, Paula has displayed an incredible ability to learn any kind of dancing. She even found disco fun after years of teaching tap, ballet, belly, cane, and modern. With her critical eye, she also has a talent for artwork; she has painted pictures and murals for other people, and she has surrounded the windows of their apartment in Mexico with paintings of birds in flight with ribbons and flowers.

Paula plays a big part in helping her mother keep a successful dance business going. She also had a role in many of her father's successes; he was always quick to thank his daughter for her contributions to his boat racing. She was so savvy about his boat that if anything went wrong with it, she could fix it between races with him still in it. She designed T-shirts and sold them at the races in an area that she set up with the help of her daughter, mother, and husband. Whether in Arizona, Georgia, Arkansas, or Oklahoma, Paula made sure that the family arrived on time and at the right place to participate. Her father signed many an autograph, and his daughter sold many a T-shirt. He was able to race in his later years largely because of Paula.

Paula loves every member of her family, and she dearly misses her paternal grandfather, a man who showed total acceptance of everyone. He and Paula's grandmother arrived in Oklahoma in 1890, and the Showmans have lived in the area ever since. Thus he and the town of Broken Arrow are part of Paula's very being. "Give me the values passed down from ancestors who settled here," she says. "They had the opportunity for financial security, as well as job training, such as working in the oil fields." The city has changed since Paula's grandparents' day. It now has numerous golf courses, live theater, Rhema Bible College, and a campus of Northeastern State University.

The social and cultural movements of the 1960s were not an area of concern for Paula, but the women's movement has opened doors for people like her. We now have a female Blue Angel soaring overhead to entertain us, and women now compete in the Indianapolis 500. There are sports in which women have made leaps and bounds to compete with the opposite sex. Oklahoma is the perfect place for this contender—her arms full of Indian bracelets up to her elbows, her fingers dazzling with Indian rings. She says, "Being a woman in Oklahoma gets better every year." And she believes that "Oklahoma has a rich heritage that few states can equal. Instead of catering to the customs and habits of those from other areas, we should cling to our values and traditions. Let them adapt to us." Paula Showman Bridges seems to create her own environment. She gives true meaning to a "sense of place."

JULIE

Julie Tattershall lives in Tulsa, Oklahoma, where she is the artistic director at both the Heller Theatre and the Clark Theatre. She is constantly challenging the people of this city that lies in the bend of the Arkansas River with her work as an actress, director, and writer. Through her work, she has been able to give the community a better understanding of theater. She knows that the arts offer people a chance to forget, if only for a brief time, about horrible events such as the bombing of the Murrah Federal Building on April 19, 1995—the day the world discovered exactly where Oklahoma City was located. She knows that now, in our latest time of war, entertainment helps us concentrate on other parts of our lives, if only for a while.

Julie is married to another theater enthusiast, Anthony. They are natural partners and soul mates, and their marriage is a good and healthy one full of surprises and happiness. Together they travel to places they both have always wanted to see. When I first met Julie at the University of Tulsa, she was married to someone else. That marriage obviously did not work out, in part because he was so caught up in his religion and wanted the same for Julie. She was never interested and tried to tell him so. The final straw was when he began to force his views on her by leaving pamphlets about his beliefs in places where she would find them.

In our first class together, when Julie told me her last name and I saw her red hair, I knew who she was, because I had been a childhood friend of her father.

She began to ask me questions about him that suggested that he was no longer part of her life. I soon found out that her father had left the family when she was thirteen. Julie was in her twenties when she told me that, and no one, not even her paternal grandmother, had heard anything further about him.

Most thought that he was dead and buried somewhere in Little Dixie, where he and many others like him had spent time gambling. When Julie was in her thirties, however, she discovered that in fact he was still alive. Julie's paternal grandmother was getting on in age and wanted to find out what had happened to her son, so she hired a private detective, who found him and his new family only miles from his childhood home. Julie's father was not pleased when she tried to renew her relationship with him, and her struggle with this newfound truth was profound. He died not long thereafter, without giving Julie the opportunity to get close to him and have her questions answered.

Julie's mother is now happily married to a man with whom she went to school. They reunited at their fiftieth high school reunion. Some 1,000 graduates were in the class of 1954 at Tulsa's Central High School. The two of them left for parts unknown during the last night of the reunion and were married before anyone figured it out, including Julie and her siblings and her new stepfather's family. The decision they made that evening turned out to be a good one. They now live part of the time in Tulsa and the rest in California, where his work is. The two of them were involved in Julie's wedding to Anthony. Her stepfather walked her down the aisle while her mother sat proudly in the front pew.

Julie gives to the community in many different ways. She created a group called Women's Writes. As its artistic director, not only did she teach women how to write plays, poems, and stories, but she gave each one a sense of confidence. She began a workshop for children that met in the summer months when they were out of school. She teaches and directs children so that they too can learn to be individuals in their own right and not be afraid to make contributions as they mature.

"I think children should be exposed to as much as possible in order for their gifts to appear," Julie told me. "I think everyone has gifts to offer. Sometimes it takes opportunity and exposure to bring forth those gifts." She also said: "It was assumed that because I lived in Oklahoma I would never have a job in the arts. I think Oklahomans have inferiority complexes in regards to art. That somehow if you're from somewhere else, then you must be a 'real' artist. To be from Oklahoma is somehow a given for not being a 'real' artist. Art does not belong to a place. Great theater happens all over the world." Tulsa has pockets of wonderful entertainment that keep the city happy on the weekends, and during the week as well. Julie is now "somebody" in the town of Tulsa. Through the creative process, she is making a mark on this metropolitan city.

Tulsa has produced many famous people in the arts, from Jennifer Jones to Leon Russell. Many among the ultra-rich have called the city their home, including J. Paul Getty and Waite Phillips. The legacy left by Phillips, the Philbrook Museum of Art, houses Indian and European art. The Italian villa-style structure has wonderful gardens behind it. At one time, in the 1970s, visitors were allowed to bring a picnic lunch to the garden, where they could view a family movie and show off their picnic baskets and crystal ware. Once called "the Oil Capital of the World," the city now boasts the world's most comprehensive collection of American western art, the Gilcrease Museum.[4]

Tulsa is a perfect fit for Julie and Anthony's lifestyle. Both gain inspiration from the city and its many interesting places. "I think a place never defines you," said Julie, "but sometimes it can be an obstacle or a blessing. I did receive early exposure to theater in elementary school. That was a blessing. Once on stage, I felt at home."

Julie considers herself a feminist; she believes in equal pay for equal work. She is open to any kind of relationship that people might want for themselves. She would never shut anyone out because of his or her sexual orientation, religious background, or origin. She is unhappy about the history books she had to read in school that seemed to have only white men in them. She grew up with a black friend and a black relative and never understood what the uproar was all about over black and white. Although Julie was born only in 1960, the movements for peace and justice that dominated that decade have clearly influenced her; people such as Julie remind us that those ideals are still alive. She is opposed to the current (2005) presidential administration's war on terrorism and Iraq, and in my most recent interview with her she spoke eloquently and passionately against the administration's rollback of the progress we have made since the 1960s on environmental issues. Julie's worldview is inclusive of all. Her most recent focus has been on older citizens, through her support of an organization called the 'Round the Bend Players, a senior citizens' theater group that performs, among other places, at assisted living centers.

Because Tulsa was able to keep its race riot of 1921 under wraps for nearly seventy years, Julie didn't read about it in any of her textbooks. The riot is now being exposed for what it was, a horrendous act perpetrated by whites against blacks. Many Tulsans knew only what the local paper let them know: It reported that only a few black people were killed, when in reality well more than three hundred probably died. Perhaps the full truth will never be known.

The history scholars still disagree on many of the aspects of that horrible time. Julie learned more about the riot after college. She says: "The more I understood what had happened, the more appalled I became. It was like coming out of a dream to understand about oppression." She feels that in some ways she was oppressed growing up. She says: "I grew up thinking other people were important and I was not. My importance lay in making other people happy to the point of almost no longer existing." Julie knows now that her special gifts are unique, and that she has made good choices along the way. She is an essential part of Tulsa and its wonderful theater scene. Julie Tattershall will leave her own private history—a legacy of a good heart and an open mind.

• • •

Representing Oklahoma with strength and conviction, these three women continue to do good work in their respective communities, with solid family values, business sense, and talent in the arts. It was the arts that brought us all together, a reminder for me of just how much the arts improve the quality of our lives. These women have used their artistic talent to enrich their communities: Maurine through her interest in literature, Julie through her lifetime work in theater, and Paula through her contributions to dance. They certainly have enriched my life. I am in their debt for sharing their interesting, productive lives with me.

Three Oklahoma women: Born before World War I, in the 1930s, and at the beginning of the 1960s. Different times, different lives. But all very rich lives, and all a part of Oklahoma history. As history was traditionally done, with a political/diplomatic focus, such lives were usually excluded. What a loss! If the emphasis on social and cultural aspects of the lives of ordinary people that has been a part of historical writing since the 1960s has done nothing else, it is enough that it has helped us to appreciate the lives of women such as Maurine, Paula, and Julie.

NOTES

1. *The Delphian Course*, vol. 1 (Chicago: The Delphian Society, 1913), xi.

2. Marvin E. Kroeker and Guy W. Logsdon, *Ada, Oklahoma: Queen City of the Chickasaw Nation—A Pictorial History* (Virginia Beach, Va.: The Donning Co., 1998), is an excellent source of information about the town of Ada.

3. Paul Showman, *Broken Arrow & Me Growin' Up Together* (self-published, 2003), 180.

4. Danney Goble, *Tulsa! Biography of the American City* (Tulsa, Okla.: Council Oak Books, 1997), is a rich resource for information on Tulsa and its history.

CHAPTER 3

Black Oklahomans

AN ESSAY ON THE QUEST FOR FREEDOM

Jimmie Lewis Franklin

Jimmie L. Franklin holds the Ph.D. from the University of Oklahoma and has written several books about the state, including *Born Sober: Prohibition in Oklahoma, 1907–1959* and *Journey toward Hope: A History of Blacks in Oklahoma.* He retired from Vanderbilt University after a long and distinguished career as primarily a historian of the American South, including a year as president of the Southern Historical Association.

He wrote a thoughtful essay, "Black Oklahomans and Sense of Place," for this volume's predecessor; he contributes another thoughtful one here, one that he is perhaps uniquely qualified to write, on black Oklahomans and the quest for freedom. It helps us understand the meaning of the African American experience in Oklahoma, and thus the meaning of Oklahoma history itself.

P erhaps no word is more familiar to the average American than "freedom." Even when a person cannot define it precisely, it takes on an intrinsic value that practically everyone seems to comprehend. Viewed positively, the word implies the right to do or say something; importantly, it also connotes the absence of indefensible binding restrictions by government or its agents. Although people speak casually of freedom in generalized terms, it is applied specifically to a large number of phases of life, including political, economic, religious, and social matters. The idea of freedom carried in the hearts and minds of America's citizens is deeply rooted in the country's most sacred documents, and "standing on my constitutional rights" is a favorite expression among those "liberty-loving folk" who feel unjustly offended by governmental action or decree.

Even before their emancipation, black Americans embodied the same idea of freedom as other citizens. Despite years of segregation and discrimination after the Civil War, African Americans absorbed its meaning from school texts and from community and social institutions that stressed democratic values and civic responsibilities. Like most Americans, blacks did not wrestle with the intellectual foundations of American freedom. They may have known about the struggle for it during the revolutionary period of American history, or something about the subsequent struggle to perfect it. Most of them, however, were concerned about the practical impact of freedom upon their daily lives. To the black American, segregation and discrimination meant essentially an absence of the equality enjoyed by other citizens.[1]

The quest for freedom by blacks in Oklahoma during the era of segregation resembled the struggle in the American South. There were, however, notable historic developments that set the Oklahoma movement apart, that gave it greater intensity and sustained power than similar movements exhibited in other places in the country. Often these differences were subtle and went virtually unnoticed. Some of them, however, have become clearer with time, or more obvious upon closer examination through different historical lenses.

When the historian looks at black land ownership in Oklahoma, for example, even though it was comparatively small in comparison to the rate for whites, it is easy to understand why the right to possess and hold on to property and political rights helped to establish a strong foundation for the freedom fight after Oklahoma statehood. That struggle, so central to the idea of freedom in America, received support from black newspapers, of which there were more in Oklahoma than in other states of the American South. Notable efforts for freedom had their incubation in many small places in Oklahoma, especially in black towns that promoted black pride and at times a sense of black nationalism. Although historians have documented their small success but ultimate failure, the towns' contribution to the idea of freedom has sometimes escaped the attention of serious students of history. Black Oklahomans' early organized protest to gain their constitutional rights before Oklahoma statehood in 1907 laid the foundation for the achievement of full freedom in the fifty years after Oklahoma's admission to the Union.

Following the Civil War, blacks and their supporters asked the government for grants of land for the ex-slaves. Few of the 4 million freedmen received any acreage, and the promise of "forty acres and a mule" became an unfulfilled hope that left them mired in poverty. Freedmen in Indian Territory, roughly the eastern portion of present-day Oklahoma, however, have a history different from that of the ex-slaves in the Deep South. In 1866, the federal government demanded that the Indian tribes of Oklahoma (who had supposedly sided with the Confederacy) divide their communal lands and make individual allotments to their members—including the freedmen. Although the tribes disagreed with the idea of private ownership of lands, they could hardly refuse the government's dictates. Their land was allotted, and most of the ex-slaves received some acreage.[2]

When the area that became Oklahoma Territory was opened for settlement by Congress, thousands of immigrants of diverse backgrounds rushed into the region. African Americans were among them, although historians cannot say exactly how many blacks arrived in the original land rush of 1889 and in the openings that came later. Whatever their number, those who came from the South were in search of a "promised land" where they could find prosperity, where they could educate their children and live beyond the harsh racial restrictions that had characterized life in the southern states. Adventuresome and daring like other pioneers, they demonstrated an aggressive response to their surroundings as they attempted to mold their own future in what they hoped was a free and fair land.[3]

The difficult fight to maintain the land that came into their hands helps to explain the intensity of blacks' quest for freedom in the state. In his absorbing autobiography, *My Life and an Era*, B. C. Franklin recounts the fraud, deception, chicanery, and legal trickery that caused both Indians and blacks to lose the lands they had acquired through allotment or settlement in the pre- and early statehood period. The dispossession of this vital resource left many of them penniless and without the means to pay their debts or to provide adequate care for their families. The struggle to hold on to their land reinforced in blacks' minds the meaningful relationship between land, property owning, and the practical notion of freedom. Freedom was more than a theory. At the time of statehood, some blacks, including Franklin, became actively involved in the struggle against laws that restricted economic and social rights that had so much to do with the exercise of freedom in a competitive society.[4]

Land—the idea of property holding and political rights—led some blacks to seek freedom within their own all-black towns. Prior to the historic land runs in Oklahoma, some black settlements had already begun to develop when free blacks and runaways from the Indian tribes built new communities. After allotment of Indian lands, more towns came into existence. Indeed, some black leaders after the Civil War mentioned Indian Territory as a place for newly emancipated freedmen to settle, but the desire for land by whites condemned any such movement to failure. Although historians are not sure of the exact number of black towns that sprouted in Oklahoma, they have been able to document more than fifty of them. Most of those were founded in the half-century following the cessation of hostilities between North and South.

Both race and economics played a central role in the establishment of black towns. In the end, however, a weak economic foundation proved the major reason for the failure of most of them. Many blacks looked upon the towns as "safe havens"—ideal places where they could be free of white intrusion, harassment, and oppression. However, while those who harbored a separatist philosophy found essentially what they wanted, black towns still existed in a predominantly white state; moreover, the economies of the towns and villages in Oklahoma were so interlocked that hardly anyone or any place escaped the interdependence that came with organized life in the state, even when it was unequal. So complete separatism, as many envisioned it, was mostly a fiction, although some blacks managed to live a portion of their cultural existence divorced from whites.

Yet the very *presence* of whites in nearby communities had a continuing effect upon citizens in the black towns, although they may not have counted as many direct contacts with whites as fellow blacks in urban areas. In some sections of Oklahoma, whites attempted to frustrate the growth of some black towns by restricting the sale of nearby lands and by trying to force blacks into segregated sections of "mixed" communities.

Economic problems continuously dogged the black towns of Oklahoma. Black town promoters pushed hard to develop transportation facilities to provide commercial contacts with areas outside the town, but black business never succeeded in creating a viable trade with outlying areas. When success became almost impossible, residents used new and improved roads—designed in great part to deliver goods and services from the towns—to relocate elsewhere. A few towns such as Langston and the small but historically popular Boley would survive, but their existence always appeared precarious.

Financing and credit in particular frustrated black town growth. Historian Norman Crockett has explained the challenges that black entrepreneurs confronted in their efforts to build a vibrant economy that would attract progressive citizens to the towns. Obviously, capital and credit had a direct bearing on business success, but both appeared in short supply in the black towns. Credit for black farmers near the towns came high; and when some white lenders refused loans to them during the growing or harvesting season, they encountered economic disaster. Black merchants who could not secure a credit line similarly faced failure. The three places that Crockett studied in Oklahoma that depended greatly upon cotton—Langston, Clearview, and Boley—failed economically because of credit problems and a one-crop economy.[5]

Whether economic diversification of crops would have been a panacea for black towns still remains problematic for the historian. It is reasonable to assume that at the very least, diversification would have improved their chances of survival, since a one-crop failure affected not only cotton but related businesses as well, and, to a degree, some social institutions. If black town optimism seemed justified at the time, the reality was that the prospect of creating a small, competitive, agricultural community was at odds with the course of American business history during the latter part of the nineteenth and the early twentieth centuries. As Crockett and others have pointed out, the chance of any small, new town succeeding—of whatever color—was slight indeed.

This history of the black towns, so filled with failure or limited success, has important meaning relative to the idea of freedom in Oklahoma. When the careful observer examines the Oklahoma black town experience within the framework of the "separate but equal" doctrine propounded by *Plessy v. Ferguson,* irony again surfaces: overwhelming success of the black town model would have earned validity for the "separate but equal" doctrine among those who supported *Plessy.* They would have been able to contend that American democracy could achieve egalitarian ends through racial separation, and that the U.S. Supreme Court had "gotten things right" in the decree that sanctioned the inequality of one race over the other. However, even if the towns had realized economic success, it is doubtful that they could have sustained over an extended period of time the cultural isolation that many black citizens desired, without damaging the core democratic values upon which the country rested.[6]

Even as the majority of black Oklahomans realized that racial isolation was not a viable practical approach to freedom, the "Back to Africa" movement and black migration from Oklahoma to Canada in the early part of the twentieth century attested to the deep dissatisfaction among African Americans in the state. Significantly, the vast majority of them viewed freedom within an American context: They were determined not to compromise on the idea of inclusion in the American mainstream, although most of them may not have thought in terms of what people later called "integration."

And, in fact, black residents in the towns demonstrated considerable self-reliance and belief in black pride. Young blacks "held both themselves and their race in much higher esteem than black youth living in mixed communities." Although the black town experiment may have failed to reach its ultimate goal, attachment to the idea of self-government and self-reliance helped to build a leadership class that served the needs of a larger black community that believed in the possibility of real freedom in a land of diverse people.[7]

The black press found a footing in the small black towns and in some larger cities of Oklahoma. Many of those papers had only a brief life, but their existence, especially during the era near statehood, tells us something about the quest for equality that set Oklahoma apart from other southern states; collectively, they had a profound impact on how African Americans in the state pursued freedom, reflecting a strong heritage of black freedom that laid the groundwork for social change a full decade prior to Oklahoma statehood. Because of their access to a relatively large constituency that usually transcended subscription numbers, editors of black newspapers often became leaders in their communities. Like black journals elsewhere, Oklahoma papers promoted a sense of community and group cohesiveness; their advocacy for black freedom was open and often strident—even militant in tone at times. Although there did exist some ideological and political differences among Oklahoma newspapers during the fifty years of black life under Jim Crow, black editors in Oklahoma were more likely than their counterparts in the Deep South to confront their white adversaries.

Few, if any, southern states had as many newspapers that proclaimed freedom in the early years of their existence as Oklahoma. The first black newspaper published in Oklahoma, the *Oklahoma Guide,* appeared shortly after the land rush of 1889, and was followed two years later by the *Langston Herald.* Established by E. P. McCabe, a leading proponent of black migration to Oklahoma, the *Herald* served as a promoter of black settlement. By the time of statehood in 1907, some seventy black newspapers had been founded in the territories. Again, like black newspapers elsewhere, Oklahoma's papers survived basically on subscriptions, since white businesses reluctantly advertised in them. Unlike many papers, however, the overwhelming majority of them did not accept direct political subsidies and so enjoyed considerable independence from undue pressures that could compromise their stand on fundamental issues. Editors eager to provide blacks an opportunity to escape oppression wrote of economic advancement and freedom. The *Herald* proclaimed that it wanted to help blacks become "free men and women." Its task was to show the race how to obtain "more freedom, more money, a better education for your children, [and] a better and more comfortable home."[8]

If any newspaper in Oklahoma history stood as an icon of black freedom, it was the *Oklahoma City Black Dispatch*. Organized in 1915, the *Dispatch* became the eyes and ears of the black community. Its long existence and sensitivity to the idea of freedom made it the preeminent voice for equality in the state during the Jim Crow era. By the mid-twentieth century, the paper had a circulation that exceeded 2,300 subscribers, but its influence was much greater than its readership. Although published in Oklahoma's capital city, the *Dispatch* took pride in its thorough knowledge of racial issues throughout the state. By the end of the Jim Crow era, only Tulsa's *Oklahoma Eagle*, the state's second most influential journal by the mid-twentieth century, could rival the *Dispatch* in distribution and in its clarion call for freedom.

The success of the *Oklahoma City Black Dispatch* resulted from the hard work and total commitment to freedom of its founder and editor for nearly a half century, Roscoe Dunjee. So pervasive was his influence and his commitment to freedom that his biographer characterized him as the "Little Caesar of Civil Rights," a fitting description for this untiring warrior for black rights. Young Dunjee arrived in Oklahoma Territory in 1892 with his parents. At that time, race relations exhibited a fluid nature, but segregation had already begun to make its legal appearances in law and custom in some territorial localities. Just how much impact these changes had on the young Dunjee is not known, but undoubtedly the young man felt the sting of race in his early years on Oklahoma's frontier.[9]

Dunjee came of age when Oklahoma and much of the United States were undergoing notable social and political changes that expanded the meaning of freedom within a democracy. While *Plessy* began to impose its restrictive features upon black life after 1896, the so-called "progressive movement," which roughly encompassed the later part of the nineteenth century and the first two decades of the twentieth, held out some hope for changes in race relations. Unfortunately, that possibility proved disappointing when white progressives turned their backs on meaningful reforms that would have aided blacks economically and politically. However, a large number of African Americans, especially ministers, worked hard to accomplish changes in their own communities. Like white reformers, they wanted to preserve moral values, promote a sense of community, and alter social institutions to better serve all citizens.

Historians sometimes focus on white progressives and the expansion of the boundaries of American freedom without giving much attention to the contributions of blacks. Roscoe Dunjee fits perfectly the definition of a "progressive," and his philosophy mirrored that of most other progressives who worked for reform during the era. Although the establishment of his *Oklahoma City Black Dispatch* came near the end of the era, his editorials during that time and later reflected the depth of his commitment to change, to his notion of an ever-evolving democracy. A Republican (like most blacks of that era), Dunjee believed that the best chance for the achievement of unfettered freedom resided in the party of Abraham Lincoln. Despite his political allegiance, characterizing Dunjee often proved difficult except for his steadfast commitment to black freedom.

For example, he admired the conservative Booker T. Washington—leader of black America from 1895 to his death in 1915—for his emphasis on economic development and vocational training. Yet the idea of complete separation of the races repulsed Dunjee. He touted the advantages of solid vocational training in the schools, and he supported Washington's National Negro Business League. In time, however, he also gave backing to liberal arts education as a vital tool for advancing freedom.[10]

Dunjee had praise for Washington, but his search for black freedom mirrored more closely the ideas of W. E. B. Du Bois, the black scholar and activist who did so much to shape black thought and reform in the twentieth century. Dunjee, like Du Bois, believed that ultimate freedom rested with an educated black leadership, a position that did not lead him to underestimate the impact that the masses could have on the political process. He recognized that in some specific instances, conservative leaders such as Washington had promoted a spirit of progressivism by improving black life through their emphasis on self-reliance, education, and the establishment of social service institutions. But it was Du Bois's belief in the value of consistent protest that propelled Dunjee and defined his center on race reform; and it was Du Bois's spirit that led the young Oklahoma City editor to the National Association for the Advancement of Colored People, on which he pinned his hope for black liberation.[11]

Dunjee's role as a leading participant in the creation of the Oklahoma NAACP is crucial to the understanding of blacks' strategy for freedom in

Oklahoma. Organized in 1909, the NAACP represented an offshoot of the spirit of progressivism that flowered during the early part of the twentieth century. Three years after its national founding, Dunjee and other black leaders in Oklahoma City formed a local chapter of the organization; and with the growth of other associations, Dunjee led a drive to create a state group. That task proved difficult even for the articulate and highly persuasive editor.

Ultimately, his argument prevailed that a state organization could advance the struggle for freedom more than any one chapter acting alone; thus there emerged a "State Conference of Branches," one of the most powerful state groups in the national organizational structure. Whether or not Roscoe Dunjee was the father of the conference idea, as some contend, few can deny that he was among its leading advocates, or that it represented an effective tool against impediments to black freedom.[12]

The Oklahoma State Conference of Branches of the NAACP waged legal war upon the anti-freedom forces in Oklahoma and the United States. By statehood, there already existed a precedent for legal attacks on segregation laws that stretched back to territorial days. Unfortunately, however, pro-segregation forces had dealt the struggle for freedom a harsh blow when the Oklahoma Territorial Legislature passed statutes that separated blacks and whites. An even more disappointing development came when the new state elected legislators who passed Jim Crow laws similar to those in other states of the South. The Democratic Party had openly declared for segregation at the formation of the state in 1907, and Republicans had been too weak or unwilling to levy an all-out fight for black rights. While the failure of blacks to win their battle against racial proscription during this period has obvious significance, what is equally important is the heritage of protest that laid the foundation for the NAACP and other groups in Oklahoma that fought uncompromisingly for freedom in the half-century after Oklahoma's admission to the Union.

Roscoe Dunjee and his Oklahoma followers aggressively utilized the legal system to achieve their fundamental objectives. They would gain monumental success in the courts over four decades, which probably could not have come in any other state with a Jim Crow heritage. As Oklahoma's new state lawmakers made plans to establish restrictive legislation at the beginning of statehood—especially laws that limited black voting—blacks fearlessly prepared to contest those moves. White Oklahoma politicians (including progressives) believed that black voting rights had interjected an unholy influence into politics. The easiest way to "purify" the electoral process, therefore, was through elimination of the black vote. Lawmakers in the Deep South had repeated this argument on numerous occasions, and it had pleased their white constituents. In Oklahoma, it also prevailed with the passage of the so-called "Grandfather Clause," designed to keep blacks from the polls while protecting the rights of illiterate white voters.[13]

The legal fight against Jim Crow presented a difficult road to freedom for black Oklahomans, but realistically, it provided the only path available to them during an era when open protest received little public sanction. A victory over the Grandfather Clause would offer some hope, and it would reaffirm their belief in the courts as a viable mechanism for constitutional redress of grievances. Blacks knew that the right to the ballot stood as one of the most important guarantees to freedom in a democratic society, and to surrender it was, in effect, to place every other right in jeopardy. This reasoning explained the full-scale assault by black Oklahomans upon voting restrictions.

The youthful NAACP, not yet a year old at the time of the passage of the Grandfather Clause, directed its full energy toward defeat of the legislation. Although the case originated with Oklahoma, the national organization rendered advice and submitted a brief to the U.S. Supreme Court that in 1915 declared the Grandfather Clause unconstitutional in the *Guinn* case.[14]

The victory over restrictive voting rights in Oklahoma demonstrated a calculated legal approach to freedom by Dunjee and black Oklahoma leaders. Although they did not encounter the level of overt violence that too often characterized the movement for freedom in the Deep South, they did have to confront defensive arguments of whites in support of "their way of life." Southern states, including Oklahoma, confidently boosted the idea of "federalism"—a division of power between the states and the central government— to frustrate black freedom. With federalism as a constitutional shield, local and state governments repeatedly invoked their police powers and established racially restrictive laws to deny blacks access to services and opportunities normally provided to white citizens.

Oklahomans brought a number of issues before the courts during the era of Jim Crow, but the state NAACP focused heavily upon cases that involved constitutional issues. When white Oklahoma officials manipulated the judicial system to convict Jess Hollins on rape allegations, blacks and the NAACP appealed his conviction to a state criminal court and won a rehearing; the favorable 1935 decision for the NAACP decreed that Hollins must be tried in a legitimate courtroom (not a basement of a courthouse) and had the right to legal counsel who could present a case before a jury of the accused man's peers. Theoretically, the decision should have destroyed the all-white jury system that had long prevailed in the state, but justice was no kinder here than it was when black Oklahomans sued again to protect their right to the ballot: after the successful *Guinn* case, the Oklahoma legislature passed a statute designed to achieve the same ends as the Grandfather Clause. Although lawmakers neatly crafted the language of the legislation, blacks readily recognized the attempt to disfranchise them and turned to the courts. In 1931, the Supreme Court dealt Oklahoma another crushing legal defeat when it declared in the *Lane* case that the so-called Registration Law of 1916 was unconstitutional.[15]

If voting represented the most important centerpiece of democratic freedom, education did not rank far behind. At statehood, Oklahoma had provided for segregated learning, and the state successfully defeated attempts to equalize the system in the four subsequent decades. To white politicians, black education existed to train young blacks for a secondary place in a predominantly white society. Although they had to accept separation, black Oklahomans never resigned themselves to the inequality that characterized education in the state. They had long regarded quality education as an important tool for the protection of democratic freedoms and for social and economic advancement. But despite legal challenges to equalize the funding of black and white schools, little progress took place until the mid-twentieth century.

During the post–World War II period, segregation in higher education became a central concern of the NAACP, and Oklahoma blacks played a crucial role in the drive to open both graduate and professional education. Black leaders in Oklahoma adopted the view of Du Bois that freedom would come from exceptionally talented persons within the community who willingly challenged the status quo.

In 1945, the Oklahoma NAACP chose an honor graduate of all-black Langston University, Ada Lois Sipuel (Fisher), to apply for admission to the University of Oklahoma Law School at Norman. Denied entrance to the university, Sipuel went to the Oklahoma courts; after she was rejected there, her attorneys, Amos T. Hall and Thurgood Marshall, appealed her case to the U.S. Supreme Court. To the dismay of many Oklahomans and other white southerners, the court declared that the state had to provide Sipuel an education in law *equal* to that of white students.[16]

The Supreme Court's *Sipuel* ruling did not abolish Oklahoma's segregation laws. That possibility, however, had begun to loom large on the legal horizon. By 1949, the state had set aside its discriminatory admissions policy at the University of Oklahoma, but the institution had attempted to segregate black and white students in the classroom following the "desegregation" of the university. Aided by the NAACP, one of the school's black students, G. W. McLaurin, filed suit to end that practice. In a favorable (and again historic) ruling, the Court ruled that the university's policy interfered with McLaurin's ability to study, and that Oklahoma had denied him equal protection of the laws. In two cases of national significance, Oklahoma had pushed the movement toward freedom closer to reality.

Just four years after *McLaurin,* the highest court in the land brought an end to segregated public education in *Brown v. Board of Education of Topeka,* and that decision destroyed the legal foundation for separation in American life.[17]

The legal attacks upon inequality and injustice did not bring full freedom to blacks. In the 1950s, a younger generation of black reformers in Oklahoma turned to more direct and confrontational techniques. That black Oklahomans were among the leaders of the movement of protest should not have surprised anyone, given the state's history of racial protest. A national climate of racial reform in the mid-1950s and 1960s did have a direct impact on the movement in Oklahoma. But there was something equally as important that shaped the direction of the freedom movement in the state as Jim Crow began to lose legal and moral sanction. An older generation of black leaders had either retired from racial battles or passed away. Their persistent work, nevertheless, had enabled them to bequeath a legacy of legalism and skillful protest to a younger generation of new freedom fighters who now found the sojourn toward freedom too piecemeal and too slow. These new black reformers were a modified version of W. E. B. Du Bois's "talented tenth," composed principally of black professionals who felt an obligation to confront injustice and to improve the race. A number of the nonprofessional fighters were upwardly mobile youths who found the gulf between American professions of freedom and the existence of racial discrimination too hypocritical to accommodate. They greatly shaped the contours of the continuing fight for freedom during the Martin Luther King era of civil rights.

Few people understood Oklahoma's historic struggle for freedom or the need for more direct action in the new era as well as Clara Luper, director of the Oklahoma NAACP Youth Council. Luper grew up in Hoffman, Oklahoma, and did her undergraduate work at Langston University. As a student of history, she understood how American freedom had evolved, and the work that black leaders in Oklahoma and the nation had done to advance the cause of black people. Luper had done more than read about freedom in Hoffman— she had internalized it! The growth of the idea in her mind was a product of intellectual development, to be sure, but it also grew from family teaching and a Christian religion that stressed equality. In later years, when she led her little NAACP army in "sit-ins" against the giant forces of segregation and discrimination, she often wove together commentaries on freedom and biblical scripture to inspire her young warriors.

Luper possessed a strong sense of place that nourished an appreciation for her state, but it also gave her license to criticize its weaknesses. A devoted follower of Martin Luther King, Jr., and his Gandhian philosophy of nonviolent social change, she believed that direct protest should support an uncompromising attack on social and racial injustice. In 1958, Luper and the Oklahoma NAACP Youth Council set out to destroy segregation in public accommodations. Initially they targeted five restaurants in Oklahoma City that refused blacks equal service. Between August 1958 and the summer of 1963, the group succeeded in opening more than two hundred public places that previously had excluded blacks from first-class service. The Oklahoma sit-in movement appeared a year and a half before black students in Greensboro, North Carolina, staged a sit-in of their own that drew more national attention.

The sit-in strategy spread across the American South in the 1960s and became an important part of the march toward freedom throughout the United States. Indeed, it seems highly unlikely that the U.S. Congress would have adopted a civil rights bill that opened public accommodations to all citizens regardless of race without the use of the sit-in technique. Again, Oklahoma had taken the lead in helping to break down barriers that impeded racial progress toward freedom.

With the passage of the 1964 act, America had now legally closed the door on Jim Crow, although the country continued to face a number of daunting problems that the system of segregation and discrimination had created over many years.[18] At the end of the 1960s, black Oklahomans could look back on a history that had made them a part of one of the most triumphant nonviolent campaigns for freedom in the Western world. They had confronted the racial proscriptions visited upon them during the era of Jim Crow, and their responses resembled those of blacks in other states of the American South. But the freedom movement in Oklahoma had its own notable character, its own remarkable intensity. The fight for land and property, the presence of black towns, a large and aggressive black press, and a religious attachment to legal redress combined to produce fervor within the Oklahoma freedom movement that gave it a unique place in history.

The late and distinguished historian of Oklahoma Arrell Morgan Gibson often remarked that Oklahoma was a special kind of state. The history of the fight for black freedom lends considerable credence to that assertion.

NOTES

1. Eric Foner, *The Story of American Freedom* (New York: Norton, 1998), 3–100, 275–99. Freedom in the United States has drawn considerable attention from scholars and other writers. Foner's work most influenced this essay.

2. Jimmie L. Franklin, *Journey toward Hope: A History of Blacks in Oklahoma* (Norman: University of Oklahoma Press, 1982), 9–10.

3. Kaye Teall, *Black History in Oklahoma: A Resource Book* (Oklahoma City: Oklahoma City Public Schools, 1971), 139–66. For a superior study—the only one of its type—that exploits a number of disciplines in its analysis, see "The Fight for the Promised Land: The End of Indian Sovereignty," in Murray R. Wickett, *Contested Territory: Whites, Native Americans, and African Americans in Oklahoma, 1865–1907* (Baton Rouge: Louisiana State University Press, 2000), 42–66; also Danney Goble, *Progressive Oklahoma: The Making of a New Kind of State* (Norman: University of Oklahoma Press, 1980), 115–44.

4. John Hope Franklin and John Whittington Franklin, *My Life and an Era: The Autobiography of Buck Colbert Franklin* (Baton Rouge: Louisiana State University Press, 1997). Buck Colbert Franklin was John Hope Franklin's father. Born in Homer, Oklahoma, in 1879, he died in 1960 after a long career in law. In this autobiography, Franklin comments extensively on blacks and land, but students of Oklahoma history should give it a full reading, since it addresses a variety of important issues over a long span of time. Edward Magdol, *A Right to the Land: Essays on the Freedmen's Community* (Westport, Conn.: Greenwood Press, 1977), 212, offers a comparative look at black land ownership in the South during the first decade of the twentieth century.

5. Scholarship on all-black towns has been especially good during the last three decades. One of the best monographic works to appear is Norman L. Crockett, *The Black Towns* (Lawrence: Regents Press of Kansas, 1979). It treats the three Oklahoma communities noted herein (Langston, Clearview, and Boley) along with Nicodemus, Kansas, and Mound Bayou, Mississippi. Another fine study is Kenneth Marvin Hamilton, *Black Towns and Profit: Promotion and Development in the Trans-Appalachian West, 1877–1915* (Urbana: University of Illinois Press, 1991), 99–137. The reader should not ignore a fine piece by George O. Carney, "Oklahoma's All-Black Towns," in Monroe Billington and Roger D. Hardaway, eds., *African Americans on the Western Frontier* (Boulder: University of Colorado Press, 1998), 147–59.

6. On *Plessy,* see Charles A. Lofgren, *The Plessy Case: A Legal-Historical Interpretation* (New York: Oxford, 1987).

7. The quote in the paragraph is from Crockett, *Black Towns,* 185. On the Oklahoma Back to Africa Movement, the best study is William Bittle and Gilbert Geis, *The Longest Way Home: Chief Alfred Sam's Back-to-Africa Movement* (Detroit: Wayne Uni-

versity Press, 1964). Crockett discusses both the Chief Sam movement and black migration to Canada in *Black Towns*, 168–74. An effort to form an all-black state in Oklahoma is treated in Wickett, *Contested Territory*, 55–58, and Arthur L. Tolson, *The Black Oklahomans: A History, 1541–1972* (New Orleans: Edwards Printing Co., 1972), 73–88.

8. The leading student of the black press in Oklahoma is Nudie Eugene Williams, who began his investigation with "Black Newspapers and the Exodusters" (master's thesis, Oklahoma State University, 1977). A more recent study is his "Oklahoma: Genesis and Tradition of the Black Press, 1889–1980," in Lewis Henry Suggs, ed., *The Black Press in the Middle West, 1865–1985* (Westport, Conn.: Greenwood Press, 1996), 267–94. The partial quotations above are from 271.

9. No full-length published biography of Roscoe Dunjee exists. John Thompson wrote an informative study of the powerful editor in his doctoral dissertation, "Little Caesar of Civil Rights: Roscoe Dunjee in Oklahoma City, 1915–1955" (Purdue University, 1990). See also Franklin, *Journey toward Hope*, 54–57.

10. Goble, *Progressive Oklahoma*, 115–45; also Dewey W. Grantham, *Southern Progressivism: The Reconciliation of Progress and Tradition* (Knoxville: University of Tennessee Press, 1983), 231–45, for the problems of white southern reformers and race. I have written of African Americans, progressivism, and American historians in "Blacks and the Progressive Movement: Emergence of a New Synthesis," *OAH/Magazine of History* 23 (Spring 1999): 20–23.

11. The classic battle of ideas between Booker T. Washington and W. E. B. Du Bois receives superb treatment in August Meir, *Negro Thought in America, 1880–1915: Racial Ideologies in the Age of Washington* (Ann Arbor: University of Michigan Press, 1966), 161–247; see also Louis Harlan, *Booker T. Washington: The Wizard of Tuskegee, 1901–1915* (New York: Oxford, 1986), especially 359–77.

12. For the motivation behind the founding of the NAACP, see chapter 6 in Elliott M. Rudwick, *W. E. B. Du Bois: Propagandist for the Negro Protest* (New York: Atheneum, 1968), 120–50, and Thompson, "Little Caesar of Civil Rights," 71.

13. Gerald Hickman, "Disfranchisement in Oklahoma: The Grandfather Clause of 1910–1916" (master's thesis, University of Tulsa, 1967); for germane comment, see Tolson, *The Black Oklahomans*, 153–58.

14. See commentary on *Guinn v. United States* in Loren Miller, *The Petitioners: The Story of the Supreme Court of the United States and the Negro* (Cleveland: World Publishing Co., 1966), 219–20.

15. For comment on *Jess Hollins v. State of Oklahoma*, see Teall, *Black History in Oklahoma*, 198, 238, and Thompson, "Little Caesar of Civil Rights," 71–75; and for *Lane v. Wilson*, see Miller, *The Petitioners*, 297–98.

16. Miller, *The Petitioners*, 334–36. Shortly before her death, Ada Lois Sipuel Fisher published her autobiography, *A Matter of Black and White: The Autobiography of Ada Lois Sipuel* (Norman: University of Oklahoma Press, 1996). That work is useful not only for a discussion of her case, but also for its commentary on black community and family life in Oklahoma. At the time of Sipuel's application to the University of Oklahoma, George L. Cross served as the institution's president. His readable account

of the Sipuel and McLaurin cases is *Blacks in White Colleges: Oklahoma's Landmark Cases* (Norman: University of Oklahoma Press, 1975), 35–84; see also Teall, *Black History in Oklahoma*, 273–77. On the state's attempt to establish a separate law school for blacks in Oklahoma City, see Zella J. Black Patterson, *Langston University: A History* (Norman: University of Oklahoma Press, 1979), 233–37.

17. Miller, *The Petitioners*, 336–38; and Cross, *Blacks in White Colleges*, 85–114.

18. Clara Luper discusses her work for freedom in *Behold the Walls* (Oklahoma City: J. Wire, 1979). See also Allan A. Saxe, "Protest and Reform: The Desegregation of Oklahoma City" (Ph.D. diss., University of Oklahoma, 1969). As used above, "sense of place" refers to a powerful and seductive feeling that comes from knowing the natural world that surrounds a person—the fields, streams, rivers, and valleys, or the simple beauty of a sunrise or sunset. It grows, too, from understanding the positive aspects of an environment, its manners and morals, art and architecture, special foods, even its peculiar speech patterns. Such an appreciation provided a coping mechanism for blacks against many of the negative factors in their lives. For a more extended discussion of this subject, see my "Black Oklahomans and Sense of Place," in Davis D. Joyce, ed., *"An Oklahoma I Had Never Seen Before": Alternative Views of Oklahoma History* (Norman: University of Oklahoma Press, 1994), 265–79.

CHAPTER 4

Oklahoma City and the Origins of
the Modern Direct Action Movement

Amanda Strunk Frady

Amanda Strunk Frady holds the B.A. degree from East Central University and the M.L.S. from Texas Woman's University. She is currently Public Services Librarian for the Rowlett Public Library in Rowlett, Texas. In this essay, she carefully documents the fact that Oklahoma City was the site of sit-ins as a method of accomplishing integration well before the sit-in movement became a national phenomenon. This is not nearly as well known as the fact that Oklahoma was also the setting for important court decisions before the all-important *Brown v. the Board of Education of Topeka, Kansas,* in 1954.

The civil rights movement in the United States evolved through many stages. The American South of the 1940s continued to be plagued by a Jim Crow society. All public accommodations were segregated and showed little sign of change. World War II gave African American men a new sense of respect, and they were not eager to return to their homes in the South as second-class citizens after fighting for freedom and democracy overseas. The Truman administration often acted to promote racial equality, but southern Democrats in Congress were able to defeat much of its civil rights legislation. As a result, direct action was needed in the South. An argument has been made that the sit-in that took place in Greensboro, North Carolina, on February 1, 1960, marked the beginning of the new direct action movement. In his book *Civilities and Civil Rights: Greensboro, North Carolina, and the Black Struggle for Freedom,* noted scholar William H. Chafe recognizes but minimizes the importance of the similar sit-in demonstrations that occurred before the Greensboro demonstrations.[1] In reality, the sit-in movement had begun more than a year earlier, in August 1958. Taking their lead from Dr. Martin Luther King, Jr., the National Association for the Advancement of Colored People (NAACP) Youth Council of Oklahoma City took the first major step toward ending segregation of lunch counters. The success of the sit-ins in Oklahoma City by the NAACP Youth Council not only led to the desegregation of Oklahoma lunch counters, but also sparked a wave of similar demonstrations and results across the nation.

THE CIVIL RIGHTS MOVEMENT
LEADING UP TO 1958

The sit-ins in Oklahoma City followed years of progress in civil rights actions. The civil rights movement achieved a number of advances during the Truman administration. President Truman called for an end to Jim Crow segregation on the grounds that to deny anyone human rights was "an invitation to communism."[2] In 1946, Truman created a Committee on Civil Rights to advise him on ways that the government, at the federal, state, and local levels, could elevate civil rights. In 1947, the President's Commission on Civil Rights reported a need for action against segregation.[3] Southern Democrats reacted badly to the report, but it became the blueprint for civil rights legislation for the next twenty years. Truman also made an effort to desegregate the armed forces. On July 26, 1948, he declared that the military would no longer have "separate but equal" training facilities, and that it would be an equal opportunity employer.[4] President Truman launched a federal course for civil rights when others would not.

Civil rights efforts continued throughout the 1950s. In 1954, the U.S. Supreme Court handed down its landmark decision in *Brown v. the Board of Education of Topeka, Kansas.* The ruling of the Court stated, "We conclude that in the field of public education the doctrine of 'separate but equal' has no place. Separate educational facilities are inherently unequal."[5] Unfortunately, the Supreme Court allowed a great deal of leeway in the implementation of school desegregation, and southern states were thus able to continue segregating schoolchildren for years to come. After Rosa Parks refused to give up her seat on the bus on December 5, 1955, African American leaders saw an opportunity to make a statement in Montgomery, Alabama. Dr. King successfully led the Montgomery Bus Boycott between December 1955 and December 1956. Civil rights activists in Montgomery succeeded by using direct economic action against the bus companies.

In Oklahoma City, Clara Luper, the advisor of the Oklahoma City NAACP Youth Council, took notice of King's direct economic action and its success. Luper, a high school history teacher, created a play for Negro History Week entitled *Brother President*. The play was based on King's nonviolent techniques in Montgomery, Alabama. Henry Wright, the national youth director for the NAACP, was present for one of the performances. He invited Luper and the twenty-six members of the cast to New York to perform for the 1957 "Salute to Young Freedom Fighters Rally."[6] The group stopped on the way for their first of many integrated lunch counter experiences. When they returned to Oklahoma City, they decided that they would start breaking down segregation in public accommodations in Oklahoma City.

The youth began by approaching owners and managers in small groups and writing letters to city council members, the city manager, and city churches. They were unsuccessful at each attempt. Even the black churches held back. After a fifteen-month letter-writing campaign and personal visits, the group decided to take their movement one step further. The council chose the four largest segregated restaurants in downtown Oklahoma City for their demonstrations: Katz, Veazey's, Kress, and John A. Brown's.

THE MOVEMENT BEGINS

Katz Drug Store was their first target. Blacks could shop throughout the store, and they could order food to go, which would be placed in a paper sack to be eaten outside. But they could not eat inside the store. On August 19, 1958, Richard Brown, Elmer Edwards, Linda Pogue, Lana Pogue, Areda Tolliver, Calvin Luper, Marilyn Luper, Portwood Williams, Jr., Lynzetta Jones, Gwendolyn Fuller, Alma Faye Posey, Barbara Posey, Goldie Battle, and Betty Germany drove into downtown Oklahoma City, walked into Katz Drug Store, and sat down at the lunch counter. Barbara Posey, president of the Youth Council, ordered thirteen cokes and placed a five dollar bill on the counter.[7] With this action, they declared war on the system of segregation in Oklahoma City. Mr. Masoner, the manager at Katz, was outraged. "Mrs. Luper, you know better than this," he stormed. "You know we don't serve colored folks at the counter. I don't see what's wrong with you colored folks. Mrs. Luper, you take these children out of here—this moment!"[8] Luper and the children kept their seats and repeated their order. The police and the press soon arrived. White customers yelled things like "Nigger go home!" and "Who do they think they are?"[9] To keep herself focused, Luper pulled out what they referred to as Martin Luther King's Non-Violent Plans and read them repeatedly as she prayed silently. At closing, the group left quietly.

That evening, Luper received both threatening and encouraging calls from black and white citizens of Oklahoma City. The next day, all of the children came back to Katz with more friends. On the 21st, after two days of patient nonviolent protesting, Katz Drug Store gave in. According to the August 22, 1958, edition of the *Daily Oklahoman,* the youth "were finally served shortly after 5 p.m."[10] Katz, a leading drug store chain, not only desegregated the lunch counter in Oklahoma City, but also announced that all "38 outlets in Missouri, Oklahoma, Kansas, and Iowa would serve all people regardless of race, creed or color."[11] A few Youth Council members at a time were sent back to Katz the next day to ensure that the policy change was permanent.[12]

THE MOVEMENT CONTINUES

After being served at Katz, the Youth Council moved on to Veazy's Drug Store. Veazy's manager met a group of three volunteers from the Youth Council at the door. "I'm happy that you all came over. We are very proud. Our management met yesterday and decided to change our policy. Our new policy states that the eating facilities at Veazy's Drug Store are open to all people," explained the manager.[13] The students sat down, had a Coke, and tipped the waitress before moving on to the next battle. They met the rest of the group across the street. They had been waiting to stage a mass demonstration at Veazy's if it had been necessary.

S. H. Kress was the next target. At Kress, the group was again met by a smiling manager. The management there had answered the question of how to integrate their lunch counter by removing all the chairs in their restaurant section. As E. G. Gresham, the manager of S. H. Kress, explained to a reporter for the *Norman Transcript,* "The removal of stools was to 'facilitate service,'" and "the stand-up service 'will be the policy until changed.'"[14] This victory was less satisfying than the previous two, but it was progress compared to the takeout service–only policy that had been in effect at Kress.

A portion of the group moved on to John A. Brown's, the largest department store in Oklahoma, covering a block and a half. It was there that they
faced the longest, most difficult battle. The sit-in at Brown's began August 22,
1958, and continued without cessation until June 23, 1961.[15] It was the longest
single sit-in campaign in the nation. The situation was resolved after Brown's
finally agreed to end bias in the lunchroom, soda fountains, and restrooms
throughout the store. Before the sit-in at Katz Drug Store in August 1958,
African Americans had been able to order food at only two places in Oklahoma City, both of which were segregated.[16] By the time that Brown's desegregated its facilities not quite three years later, 117 stores in the city had been
integrated through the efforts of the NAACP Youth Council.[17]

A CITY DIVIDED

The African American and white communities in Oklahoma City were
both divided by the demonstrations. The Oklahoma City NAACP Youth
Council started out with fourteen members in 1958. The membership had
grown to a thousand by 1961, making it one of the largest NAACP youth
councils in the nation. They estimated that 78 percent of the African American
population of Oklahoma City took part in the John A. Brown demonstration.[18] Many volunteers offered to bring sandwiches for the children to eat
while they waited. Others offered to chauffeur anyone who needed a ride
downtown to the demonstrations. However, a small group of African Americans in Oklahoma City were unhappy with the actions of the Youth Council.
After the first day at Katz, an unidentified black man called Mrs. Luper to
chastise her for disgracing her race by acting out against the white people who
had been so nice to him and by involving innocent children.[19] Others were
upset because their white employers were threatening to fire those involved in
the lunch counter protests. Most of the calls that Luper received warned her to
be careful. She was traveling into dangerous territory.

The abuse and hate calls that came from the white community were more
violent and more disturbing. During the sit-in at John A. Brown's, shotgun
shells were left on Luper's porch along with a note from the Ku Klux Klan.
Someone broke into her home and burned some furniture that belonged to
her and her son.[20] At one point, the police met Luper at Brown's to warn her
that there was a bomb threat against her home. Luper rushed home to get the
flag that had covered the casket of her father, a World War I veteran. News of
the bomb threat was broadcast over the radio, and friends came to watch

Luper's house so that she could return to the demonstrations. Members of the American Legion and the Veterans of Foreign Wars offered their support to prevent bombings and violence in Oklahoma City. A white lady whom Luper had never met offered to keep the flag in her safety deposit box.[21]

A few white people came forward to help the Youth Council win their war against segregation. Some sent letters to the management of Brown's declaring their support for the NAACP youth. On September 13, 1960, Howard Furlow wrote Mrs. John A. Brown, the owner of Brown's, to inform her that his family would no longer shop at her store. He even mentioned some furniture he had intended to purchase and the stores he was choosing to give his business to instead of Brown's.[22] An anonymous letter to the editor of the *Oklahoma City Black Dispatch* voiced support for the sit-in movement at John A. Brown's. The author of the letter claimed to be a patron of Brown's who now planned to withdraw support because of the sit-ins. This person went so far as to say, "There is no place in enlightened Oklahoma City for your business unless your policy changes."[23] As an act of kindness and support, an elderly white man ordered ten dishes of ice cream for the children at Brown's. They declined the ice cream, saying, "He's very nice, but I don't think we'd better."[24]

The NAACP Youth Council received similar mixed results from area churches. After the first three days of sit-ins, Luper sent the children two or three at a time to twenty white churches in Oklahoma City. Seventeen of the churches welcomed the children; one, however, turned them away, and two others placed the visitors in a segregated seating area. At Kelham Avenue Baptist Church, Betty Germany, age seventeen, and Barbara Rockmore, age fourteen, were advised by the pastor not to go into the church. In his defense, the pastor told reporters for the *Daily Oklahoman,* "I told the girls that regardless of my own personal convictions in the matter, I didn't feel that their attendance in church would help their cause downtown."[25] Marilyn Luper, age ten, and Areda Tolliver, age eleven, were escorted to their seats at Capitol Hill Baptist Church. Five minutes later, the man who had seated them returned and asked them to move to a segregated section, with "God doesn't want the races to mix" as his only explanation. The girls did not give up their seats right away, but they did leave the church shortly thereafter.[26] Alice Henry, age twelve, and Lana Pogue, age six, attended the First Church of the Nazarene. They started in the rear of the auditorium, were later moved to the balcony, and finally ended up in an area where no one else was sitting, where they remained for the remainder of the church service.[27] All seventeen other churches attended by the Youth Council seated the children with the white congregation and treated them hospitably. Shortly after the visit, the Oklahoma City Council of Churches devised a plan to support local restaurant owners who were willing to desegregate. The Council of Churches wanted to aid in the improvement of racial relations in Oklahoma City.[28]

ST. LOUIS, MISSOURI

The sit-in tactics in Oklahoma City were soon duplicated in St. Louis, Missouri. In February 1959, black and white Washington University students protested the segregation of off-campus lunchrooms by staging a sit-in. One white student and three black students were arrested and fined for refusing to leave the lunchroom.[29] The NAACP chapter in St. Louis posted bail for the students and dealt with the legal issues. At the end of this battle, Santora's Restaurant near the Washington University campus was opened to African Americans.[30] The sit-in movement then lagged for a year until it was picked up again in Greensboro, North Carolina.

GREENSBORO, NORTH CAROLINA

On February 1, 1960, almost eighteen months after the Katz Drug Store sit-in in Oklahoma City, four students from the North Carolina Agricultural and Technical College at Greensboro staged a sit-in for equal service at the local Woolworth's Department Store. The next day they returned with twenty-five more students. The Greensboro students rotated in shifts so that the chairs would always be filled. Since the chairs at Woolworth's were taken care of, some of the protesters moved down the street to S. H. Kress. By Saturday, hundreds of student protesters had amassed in downtown Greensboro.[31] In late February, the protests were put on hold for a meeting between the students, local officials, and the merchant association.[32] However, they were unable to come to an agreement that the students would accept. The demonstrators in Greensboro would not yield to anything less than the desegregation of all public accommodations in the city. On April 21, forty-five students were arrested and fined for trespassing at S. H. Kress.[33] After months of declining sales at the local stores, a committee representing the protesters met with the managers of the three major department stores in Greensboro: Woolworth's, S. H. Kress, and Meyer's. The first African American was served while sitting at a table in Woolworth's on July 25, 1960.[34]

THE SIT-INS CONTINUE TO SPREAD

The protests quickly spread to other North Carolina cities. One week after the sit-ins began in Greensboro, demonstrations were held at lunch counters in Winston-Salem and Durham. A day later, they sprang up in Charlotte and then Raleigh. Before the second week had passed, students were protesting at lunch counters across the state of North Carolina.[35]

Other southern states took their cue from North Carolina. Demonstrations began in Chattanooga, Tennessee, on February 18, 1960.[36] In Atlanta, Georgia, university students gathered $1,500 for full-page ads in the *Atlanta Journal, Constitution,* and *Daily World* before staging a massive sit-in movement at restaurants, bus and railroad stations, department stores, the state capitol, and other government offices.[37] They also raised enough money to post bail for the seventy-seven people arrested during the protest. In June 1961, members of the Pensacola, Florida, NAACP Youth Council were protesting at S. H. Kress, Newberry, Woolworth's, and Walgreen's.[38] Within the next four years, teens and college students would organize nonviolent sit-in protests in every southern state.

The tactics used by the students in North Carolina and across the South were the same tactics that had proved successful in Oklahoma. The groups who organized the protests were often members of NAACP youth councils or NAACP college chapters. First, a group would target a business (not always a lunch counter or restaurant) that refused equal service to African Americans. Next, a small delegation would be sent to this business to ask for service, for which they were ready to pay cash. If service was denied, the group staged a sit-in. The next day, they would arrive en masse and refuse to leave until service was rendered. This was repeated day after day. The three-day success at Katz in Oklahoma City was not a typical time frame. The process often took months, as it did at Woolworth's in Greensboro, North Carolina, or years, as was the case at John A. Brown's in Oklahoma City. The success of the sit-in movement was due largely to its effectiveness at cutting the cash flow of a business. Even if the patrons did not sympathize with the protesters, they were either unable to find a place to sit or preferred to stay away from the demonstration sites. The targeted businesses had to decide whether to close their doors completely or provide equal service to all, regardless of skin color.

THE ROLE OF THE NAACP

After the tactics were proven successful in Oklahoma City, the NAACP was prepared to offer its full support to the movement across the South. One of the most significant forms of support came from bail money and legal aid. Shortly after the Greensboro sit-ins began, Roy Wilkins, executive secretary of the NAACP, reported that the association was "ready, upon request, to defend any of the young people who may become involved with the police or in court action as a result of their participation in this movement."[39] Wilkins was true to his word. In Memphis, Tennessee, $4,500 was raised for students who had been arrested, and in Nashville the chief counsel for 150 arrested students was Alexander Looby, a member of the National Board of Directors of the NAACP. Despite having his house bombed, which he attributed to his aid to the student protesters, Looby and other NAACP lawyers continued to volunteer their services.[40] The NAACP continued to provide monetary and legal support to students in all the southern states.

The national organization staged conventions at which techniques for nonviolent protests were taught, and it also promoted action in northern states. A conference was held at Frogmore, South Carolina, to coordinate the strategies of the southeastern youth and college branches of the NAACP. Another conference was held in Houston, Texas, for the southwestern branches. At the Southwest Youth Conference, the program included reports and evaluations of demonstrations in the Southwest, as well as discussion about creating an expanded program for civil rights in the Southwest. At the 1964 Southwest Youth Conference, Clara Luper and members of the Oklahoma City Youth Council were asked to present a workshop on direct action techniques for both youth and adults.[41] In addition, Wilkins sent out letters to the leaders of NAACP chapters, youth councils, and college chapters across the country, asking them to organize sit-in protests in their own communities.[42] In the North, he also encouraged chapters to withhold patronage to stores whose southern branches denied service to African Americans, despite their northern policies. The dollars received in the northern stores of Woolworth's and S. H. Kress helped support the discriminatory policies in the southern outlets.[43]

OKLAHOMA CITY'S PLACE IN HISTORY

These nonviolent protests revolutionized the civil rights movement. Despite lack of recognition, Oklahoma and Clara Luper's Youth Council played a crucial role in putting the sit-in movement in motion. The sit-ins, which began in August 1958, were a pilot study for the NAACP. After the Oklahoma City youth proved that a sit-in could be used successfully, their efforts were used as a model for other organizations. NAACP officials acknowledged the importance of the demonstrations being waged in Oklahoma.

In March of 1960, Herbert L. Wright, NAACP youth secretary, commended the Oklahoma City youth for "a significant breakthrough in the fight against segregation in the place of public accommodations in the South" and "for the contribution you have made towards making democracy a reality for all of our citizens."[44] Executive Secretary Wilkins said in 1963, "Your city's example in not just naming a committee, but in acting on a phase of the problem should guide other urban centers to take bold and forward steps to bring about racial justice and mutual respect."[45]

By 1963, the Youth Council had helped to open two hundred places to African Americans and was credited with conducting the longest and most successful sit-ins in the nation. By emulating the methods of the NAACP Youth Council of Oklahoma City, students and youth throughout the southern states were able to organize and conduct similar demonstrations that helped lead to the eventual desegregation of the South.

NOTES

1. William H. Chafe, *Civilities and Civil Rights: Greensboro, North Carolina, and the Black Struggle for Freedom* (New York: Oxford University Press, 1981), 71.

2. Donald R. McCoy and Richard T. Ruetten, *Quest and Response: Minority Rights and the Truman Administration* (Lawrence: University Press of Kansas, 1973), 264. As cited in Richard Polenberg, *One Nation Divisible: Class, Race, and Ethnicity in the United States since 1938* (New York: Penguin Books, 1980), 108–109.

3. Fred Powledge, *Free at Last? The Civil Rights Movement and the People Who Made It* (New York: Harper Perennial, 1991), 17–18.

4. Ibid., 28.

5. Ibid., 59–60.

6. Clara Luper, *Behold the Walls* ([Oklahoma City?]: Jim Wire, 1979), 1–2.

7. Ibid., 6–9.

8. Ibid., 9.

9. Ibid.

10. "Negro Youths 'Store Sitting' in Fourth Day," *Daily Oklahoman*, August 22, 1958, 1.

11. Luper, *Behold the Walls*, 14.

12. "Negro Youths 'Store Sitting' in Fourth Day," 2.

13. Luper, *Behold the Walls*, 14–15.

14. "Negroes Continuing OC 'Sitdown' Drive," *Norman Transcript*, August 22, 1958, 2.

15. "Nation's Longest Sit-in Drive Ends Victoriously," in John H. Bracey, Jr., and August Meier, eds., *Papers of the NAACP, Part 21: Relations with the Modern Civil Rights Movement, 1956–1965* (Bethesda, Md.: University Publications of America, 1995).

16. "Negro Youths 'Store Sitting' in Fourth Day," 2.

17. "Nation's Longest Sit-in Drive Ends Victoriously."

18. Ibid.

19. Luper, *Behold the Walls*, 12–13.

20. Ibid., 20–21.

21. Ibid., 20–22.

22. Howard G. Furlow to Mrs. John A. Brown, September 13, 1960, in Bracey and Meier, *Papers of the NAACP, Part 21*.

23. "Letter to the Editor," *Black Dispatch*, August 29, 1958, 5.

24. "Negro Group's 'Sitdown' Goes into 2nd Week," *Daily Oklahoman*, August 26, 1958, 2.

25. "Negro Group Carries Plea to Churches: Attention Called to City Campaign in Eating Places," *Daily Oklahoman*, August 25, 1958, 1.

26. Ibid., 2.

27. Ibid.

28. "Council of Churches to Seek Change Policy at Restaurants," *Black Dispatch*, September 12, 1958, 1.

29. "Role of the NAACP in the 'Sit-ins,' " in Bracey and Meier, *Papers of the NAACP, Part 21*.

30. "Special Report on Sitdowns: NAACP Staff Activity in the Sitdowns," in Bracey and Meier, *Papers of the NAACP, Part 21*, 1.

31. Chafe, *Civilities and Civil Rights*, 85.

32. Bracey and Meier, *Papers of the NAACP, Part 21*, 3.

33. Chafe, *Civilities and Civil Rights*, 94.

34. Ibid., 97–98.

35. Ibid., 85–86.

36. Bracey and Meier, *Papers of the NAACP, Part 21*, 25.

37. Ibid., 26.

38. "Robert W. Saunders, Field Secretary, NAACP to Roy Wilkins, Executive Secretary, NAACP," in Bracey and Meier, *Papers of the NAACP, Part 21*.

39. "NAACP Supports Student Drive to End Lunch Counter Jim Crow," in Bracey and Meier, *Papers of the NAACP, Part 21*.

40. "Role of the NAACP in the 'Sit-ins,' " 2.

41. "Letter to Clara Luper, 5 March 1964," in John H. Bracey, Jr., Sharon Harley, and August Meier, eds., *Papers of the NAACP, Part 19: Youth File, Series D: 1956–1965 Youth Department Files* (Bethesda, Md.: University Publications of America, 1995).

42. "Roy Wilkins Memorandum to Presidents of NAACP Branches Youth Councils and College Chapters," in Bracey and Meier, *Papers of the NAACP, Part 21*.

43. "Role of the NAACP in the 'Sit-ins.' "

44. "Oklahoma NAACP Youth Sit-Down Opens Restaurant to Negroes," in Bracey and Meier, *Papers of the NAACP, Part 21*.

45. "Desegregation of Oklahoma City Hailed by Wilkins," in Bracey and Meier, *Papers of the NAACP, Part 21*.

CHAPTER 5

Joseph Bruner and the
American Indian Federation

AN ALTERNATIVE VIEW OF INDIAN RIGHTS

Marci Barnes Gracey

Marci Barnes Gracey holds the B.A. degree from East Central University and the M.A. from Oklahoma State University—both in history.

Gracey's essay is in some ways a challenge to incorporate into these pages, where "alternative" often implies left-leaning, which is emphatically not the case with Joseph Bruner. Gracey studied under Thomas W. Cowger at East Central; he is helpful on this point. The founding of Bruner's AIF, he insists, was "a direct response by a sizeable number of Indians who feared that the Indian Reorganization Act would simply perpetuate the BIA [Bureau of Indian Affairs], which so many Indians were bent on destroying." Fearing that John Collier's IRA was "nothing more than a federal tool to keep them in bondage," they often used the word "emancipation" in their rhetoric and feared a "return to the blanket." Thus, they "advocated Indian participation in American politics and complete integration into white society."

Ironically, says Cowger, "the AIF's criticisms of the BIA, and its belief in Indian self-determination, had the opposite result, and helped contribute to the termination policies that followed." Cowger's conclusion: "While I don't agree with Bruner, he still provided an alternative voice to many assimilated Indians of his day, particularly those from Oklahoma."

As Gracey insists in her subtitle, Joseph Bruner did indeed provide "An Alternative View of Indian Rights."

I n a letter in May 1934, Indian Commissioner John Collier responded to an attack made on his Indian Reorganization Act. He wrote, "You are an interesting human and social type, Mr. Bruner. . . . You call yourself an Indian, you identify yourself as an Indian, and yet some inward compulsion makes you frenziedly active to prevent Indians from receiving the help and protection which they need."[1]

Such was the response of many non-Indians and Indians to the ideas advanced by Joseph Bruner, a Muscogee Creek from Sapulpa, Oklahoma. From his humble beginnings in Indian Territory to his national prominence as president of the pro-assimilation American Indian Federation (AIF), Bruner demonstrated his dedication to the promises of equality and complete inclusion in American society that were integral to the nineteenth-century campaign to assimilate the Indian. When legislative reforms of the New Deal era threatened the fulfillment of this promise, Bruner relied on tactics learned from his experience with the dominant society to advance his alternative view of Indian rights.

A number of historians have studied Bruner's life through his work against the New Deal reforms of Indian policy in the 1930s and 1940s. Very few, however, have attempted to understand either Bruner or the AIF. As a result, allegations of "right-wing" extremism and sensationalism have tainted his legacy. This legacy results from his persisting admiration of Commissioner of Indian Affairs John Collier, a tendency to dismiss pro-assimilation Indians as being less "Indian," and a heavy dependence on government sources.

Some historians, Laurence Hauptman and Kenneth Townsend among them, have tried to provide a much more even-handed image of Bruner and his organization. Closer studies are needed not only to change views about the two, but also to increase our understanding of Collier and his reforms. This study seeks to provide such insight and to change historical perceptions of this important period in American history.[2]

In order to understand Bruner, one must understand the goals and motivations of federal Indian policy from the mid-nineteenth century. Euro-American politicians designed policy to separate American Indians from the non-Indian populations with the hope of limiting violence and permitting unfettered expansion. An early example of this policy was the removal of the Five (Civilized) Tribes (Chickasaw, Cherokee, Seminole, Choctaw, and Mus-cogee Creeks) to Indian Territory, present-day Oklahoma.[3] This policy of separation brought Bruner's ancestors to Indian Territory. His mother, Lucy, was born in 1836 in Little Rock, Arkansas, as her parents traveled with a group of Upper Creeks en route to Indian Territory. They settled along the Arkan-sas River, establishing a village that they called Tulsey-Lochapoka, meaning "town of the turtling place."[4] The Lochapokas built a peaceful, if somewhat isolated, community in the wooded hills of present-day eastern Oklahoma, where, according to historian Angie Debo, "they were entirely unaware of the storm clouds gathering in the world outside" as the Civil War approached.[5]

The Civil War forever altered the lives of the residents of Indian Territory and would have a special impact on Joe Bruner's life. The split of the Union divided the residents of Indian Territory. In November 1861, Lucy and her first husband joined Opothle Yahola, a leader among the Upper Creeks, and his party of Indians opposed to cooperation with the South. As they set off with their belongings toward Kansas and Union protection, the refugees were attacked by Confederate regiments, including some Indian troops.[6] Joseph Bruner compared their expedition to a second Trail of Tears. When a widowed Lucy later returned to Lochapoka, she found her village in ruins.[7] In addi-tion, the federal government used the Civil War to punish the Five Tribes by taking away their lands. Those groups who remained loyal believed that the government would compensate them for their losses. Ultimately, so-called Loyal Creeks such as Lucy Bruner received no compensation for fiscal or personal losses. This would be the catalyzing factor in Bruner's campaign for Indian rights.

Following the Civil War, the policy of separation continued with Grant's Peace Policy and the establishment of a reservation system under the adminis-tration of religious organizations. By 1880, increased western expansion and violent conflict between the tribes and Euro-Americans made it clear that reservations were not the answer. The only solution to the "Indian problem," according to reformers and politicians, was total assimilation through allot-ment in severalty as outlined in the Dawes Severalty Act of 1887.[8] This legis-lation divided tribal lands among individuals with the restriction that the government would hold it in trust for twenty-five years. Reformers hoped that the Dawes Act would turn the American Indians into small farmers after the fashion of the dominant society. Once an individual Indian had demonstrated the ability to be an "American," or a Protestant farmer, his or her reward would be granted. According to Frederick Hoxie, this reward included "the extension of citizenship and other symbols of membership in American society."[9]

The policy of assimilation would dominate the lives of all American Indians in the late nineteenth century. Joseph Bruner was no exception. He was born in September 1872, in a log cabin in the woods near Lochapoka (Tulsa). In 1878, after his father's death, his mother moved her young son to Bruner family land on Rock Creek, near present-day Sapulpa, where she operated an inn, providing meals to government officials who were traveling through the territory. The comings and goings of those officials introduced Bruner to the daily influence of the government on his life. His childhood was not extraordinary for his generation, centering, for the most part, on his community and its culture. His earliest remembrances were the competitive stickball matches held during the annual Green Corn ceremonies that he participated in as a youngster.[10]

As was true of so many other Indian children, the boarding school—a crucial tool in the campaign to assimilate—became an important factor in Bruner's life. In 1884, young Joe began his formal education at the Creek National School in Wealaka.[11] As a tool of assimilation, boarding schools taught students the value of work and other ideals of Anglo society and severely punished those who retained their traditional cultures.[12] In 1888, at the age of sixteen, Joseph Bruner entered the Baptist Indian University (now Bacone College) in Muskogee. Through his limited formal education, he received an introduction to the harsh lesson of the campaign to assimilate. He also learned the English language and Euro-American politics, skills that would be useful to him as an adult.[13]

As the Dawes Commission allotted Indian Territory in the 1890s, Bruner appeared to be a promising candidate for assimilation. During 1891–92, he participated in a truly "western experience" when he worked as a "cowpuncher" on the Turkey Track Ranch. After marrying Margaret Dart, who was one-sixteenth Shawnee, Bruner returned to the Rock Creek homestead, where he continued the family tradition of farming. He used his keen intellect and knowledge of indigenous languages and English to enter the lucrative oil industry. He quickly became a respected businessperson and a member of the First Christian Church of Sapulpa. Receiving his allotment and roll number at the age of twenty-seven, Bruner was poised at the brink of complete inclusion in American society. Certainly, the rewards for his compliance with the lessons of assimilation would pay off soon, not only for Bruner himself, but also for the other "assimilated" Indians of Indian Territory. Allotment provided opportunities to increase assimilation; however, it also made way for statehood.[14]

In the first decade of the twentieth century, the "progressive" members of the Five Tribes in Indian Territory hoped to enter the Union as a separate Indian statehood. They believed that they had successfully completed their tutelage in American citizenship and deserved to be full participants in American society and politics. At Muskogee, delegates gathered to draft a constitution for a separate Indian state of Sequoyah. Already a Creek leader as an elected representative in the House of Warriors, Bruner attended the meeting as a delegate from Sapulpa. Dominated by the leading personalities of Indian Territory—particularly Charles Haskell, an intermarried non-Indian and attorney, and William "Alfalfa Bill" Murray, a Chickasaw—the delegates quickly produced a constitution. According to historian Arrell M. Gibson, the Sequoyah Convention's constitution was a "well-written document that followed closely the traditional pattern of American constitutional government."[15] Members of the Five Tribes were familiar with the political institutions of American democracy. For example, the Creeks had elected leaders, including a principal chief and second chief; the Creek Nation had a national council consisting of a House of Kings, made up of one representative from each of forty-seven towns, and the House of Warriors, with representation based on population. Bruner used these institutions to hone his leadership skills and to maintain ties to his people and culture from 1898 to the 1940s.[16]

Congress and President Theodore Roosevelt were resolute in the conviction that Indian Territory and Oklahoma Territory would join the Union as a single state. A separate Indian state was antithetical to the ideals of assimilation and its promise of inclusion. If American Indians had their own state, it theoretically could become a sanctuary for those resistant to assimilation. A joint state would allow Indians to integrate into the Euro-American society by forcing their cooperation with non-Indians and ensuring the dominance of American political institutions. While disappointed by the failure to gain a separate state, many individual Indians, including Bruner, accepted joint statehood as part of the promise of complete inclusion and equality in American society.[17]

The idyllic society envisioned by the promoters of assimilation never materialized. Allotment was a disaster, leaving Indians with little land and inadequate social services.[18] Attitudes about assimilation had changed. Suddenly, the promises of equality and complete inclusion in American society were off the table. By 1920, according to Hoxie, the Indians were a "peripheral people," trapped in a static position in society as dependents. They were just another minority group relegated to a specific role and expected to remain in it. Although the federal government lived up to the legal promise of citizenship with the Indian Citizenship Act of 1924, most individuals in the mainstream society did not consider the Indian equal to the Euro-American.[19]

In the twentieth century, the challenges facing American Indians in the modern society created a group isolated by assimilation from their traditional communities. Many individuals sought to renew their ties with their people and turned to organizations that transcended tribal lines. According to Hazel Hertzberg, modern pan-Indian movements began during the Progressive Era, when certain American Indians began to recognize a common identity based on shared experiences in the institutions of assimilation. Improved communication, the growth of the English language, and better education helped to unite these individuals. Leaders of pan-Indian movements wanted to retain their "Indianness" while adopting the desirable aspects of Euro-American society.[20]

One of the earliest of these movements was the Society of American Indians (SAI), which was established in 1911. The group succeeded in establishing common ground but was unable to effect real change in policy. This inability created tension among its members and exacerbated differences over the abolition of the Bureau of Indian Affairs (BIA), native religious practices utilizing peyote, and the role of the organization in tribal politics.[21] One of the earliest leaders of the SAI was Carlos Montezuma, a Yavapai physician, who led a faction proposing the abolition of the BIA. In the 1920s, the organization disbanded in response to the tremendous pressure created by the different attitudes in the movement.[22]

Pan-Indian movements were particularly popular among members of the Five Tribes, whose "Indianness" was often questioned because of their level of assimilation. According to W. David Baird, pan-Indian movements attracted these individuals because they promoted "a single ethnic identity rather than one reflecting tribal diversity."[23] He continued, "Nothing set the Five Tribes people apart quite so much as their outspoken advocacy of assimilation . . . they had the endorsement of reformers and government policy makers who continually exhibited them as proof that assimilationist programs worked."[24] As the SAI fell apart in the 1920s, a regional expression of pan-Indianism developed in Oklahoma.

The Society of Oklahoma Indians (SOI) introduced Bruner to pan-Indian leadership. His efforts in the movement built much of the philosophy that he used in the AIF. In 1923, the SOI claimed to be "founded by a small number of patriotic Indian citizens . . . to organize the poor, uneducated and unorganized patriotic Indian Peoples of Oklahoma." Its leaders included Bruner, Frank Cayou, Delos K. Lonewolf, O. K. Chandler, and W. W. LeFlore; all would play an important role in the AIF.[25]

The 1920s built Bruner's experience as a pan-Indian leader and molded his ideas about the role of the Indian in the twentieth century. He developed his leadership skills in tribal politics and demonstrated his aptitude for the responsibilities of citizenship with his personal and professional successes. He served his people by assisting others in legal matters and maneuvering through the complex language of federal law.[26] He was the personification of the advocacy of assimilation. As a leader in the SOI, he stressed an idea that would become his anthem as AIF president: Indians were citizens— American citizens. At the February 1924 SOI convention in Tulsa, Bruner stressed "Americanism" in his address: "We are one hundred percent Americans, our boys volunteered as soldiers. . . . Why aren't we one hundred percent American?"[27] This would be a familiar sentiment expressed by Bruner in the 1930s and 1940s through the AIF.

In the 1930s, the campaign to assimilate the Indians suffered a damaging blow with the introduction of a new policy that celebrated and protected indigenous cultures. This new policy began with the confirmation of the eccentric John Collier to the post of commissioner of Indian Affairs. A former progressive reformer in New York, Collier dedicated himself to reversing the disastrous allotment policies. He set out to write new legislation, such as the Indian Reorganization Act (IRA), also known as the Wheeler-Howard Act, and the Oklahoma Indian Welfare Act, or Thomas-Rogers Bill. He hoped to bring other New Deal programs to Indian communities to improve economic, health, and social conditions. He adopted a policy of cultural pluralism that allowed Indians to maintain their cultural heritage while adopting the beneficial aspects of the dominant society.[28] Cultural pluralism contradicted the policy of assimilation—contradictory to those lessons ingrained in Bruner and others from their earliest days in boarding schools, enrollment by the Dawes Commission, participation in statehood, and pan-Indian activism.

With this new reform spirit, Bruner and other veterans of the pan-Indian movement in Oklahoma felt the need to reorganize. In 1933, Bruner and other individual members of the Five Tribes formed the Indian National Confederacy. According to its bylaws, the Confederacy sought cooperation, harmony, and the preservation of the "noblest traditions and ideals of the Red Man . . . to cultivate the new ideals of an enlightened and awakened citizenship." In addition, it called for the advancement of "American citizenship and civilization," the core values of the campaign for assimilation. Essentially, the leaders wanted greater involvement of Indians in the development of federal policies.[29]

Initially, Bruner was hopeful that Collier would work with the Confederacy to change Indian policy. That cooperative spirit quickly developed into acrimonious bickering as it became clear to Bruner that Collier's programs did not protect assimilation.[30] When Collier traveled to Muskogee for a meeting with members of the Five Tribes, Bruner was hostile, posing many objections and calling for the meeting to be dismissed.[31] This hostility did not dampen Collier's enthusiasm for his legislation.[32]

The measures of the IRA were written by staffers of the BIA and Interior Department with direction from Collier and advice from anthropologists. In January 1934, Collier met with members of non-Indian reform organizations at the Cosmos Club in Washington, D.C., to seek additional input. In February, the measure was introduced in the House of Representatives, and Collier announced that he would meet with Indians during a series of congresses throughout the spring.[33]

After the bill was introduced in the House of Representatives in February, Congress debated its tenets and made many revisions. The original version had four sections: "Indian Self-Government," "Special Education for Indians," "Indian Lands," and "Court of Indian Affairs." Once congressional committees finished with the draft, the provision for a Court of Indian Affairs was abandoned completely, and many other changes were made, including the exclusion of Oklahoma Indians that Senator Thomas favored.[34]

The IRA provided for many of Collier's ideas. To promote self-government, Congress appropriated funds to establish tribal corporations and for a revolving economic credit fund. New tribal governments and constitutions were authorized, as were elections to approve charters. To advance education, the bill created an annual appropriation for vocational training, with a limited amount designated for higher education. To protect Indian land, several measures were approved; however, they fell well below Collier's expectations. Allotment was ended and the trust period extended. The government agreed to return surplus land and to allow the Interior Department to authorize voluntary land exchanges on the reservation. A $2 million fund was established for the purchase of land for the landless and to add land to existing reservations. Additional measures instituted forest protection and preventive soil erosion programs. Finally, the measure authorized a hiring preference for American Indians in the BIA.[35]

The measure excluding the Oklahoma tribes was a result of opposition in the state to the measures dealing with land ownership. Many individuals like Bruner had embraced the idea of private ownership and were leery of government involvement with property. In addition, there were a number of non-Indians who had become wealthy as a result of the vulnerability of allotments.[36]

In 1935, Thomas was made chair of the Senate Indian Affairs Committee, and Representative Will Rogers of Moore was made chair of its counterpart in the House. Believing that Oklahoma tribes could benefit from some of the measures of the IRA, the two men set out in early 1935 to draft a bill that would address the needs of Oklahoma Indians.

As introduced in February 1935, the Thomas-Rogers Bill divided Indians into two groups on the basis of their "degree of Indian blood." The first group, with a blood quotient of half or more, would have their property held in trust. The second group, with less than half Indian blood, would have restrictions removed as soon as a competency commission gave its approval. Like the IRA, the bill gave the secretary of the interior the authority to buy land for tribes. It also gave the president the authority to extend the trust period; however, the trust could be lifted if it was requested with the secretary of the interior's approval. The secretary gained the authority to regulate the estates of second-degree Indians, as well as the additional power to approve the appointment of guardians, a right formerly given to state courts. The Thomas-Rogers Bill, like the IRA, extended social services and established corporations for Oklahoma's indigenous groups and established a credit association.[37]

Opposition to the first bill killed it in the House of Representatives. Thomas worked with Collier to revise the bill before it was reintroduced in August, but the House did not act on it before the session expired. In June 1936, the bill was reintroduced in the Senate, and the previous amendments were discarded. New provisions developed in the House were adopted. In June 1936, the final bill was signed by President Roosevelt, and Collier's New Deal reforms came to Oklahoma.[38]

The final provisions of the Oklahoma Indian Welfare Act gave the secretary of the interior authority to manage inheritance and land issues, but the wealthy Osages of Osage County were excluded. The secretary also had the authority to purchase land. Like the IRA, tribes and bands could form corporations and adopt constitutions and bylaws. Loans were authorized for individuals and groups. The act failed to provide for continuing restrictions or for property protection. In addition, the state judiciary maintained its jurisdiction over inheritance and guardianship.[39]

The American Indian Federation was a union of like-minded individuals who gathered in Washington, D.C., in June 1934 to protest the passage of the IRA. The AIF argued that Indians "were the only race held in a position of slavery and involuntary servitude."[40] Like the Indian National Confederacy, the AIF sought to unite individuals across tribal lines, to promote "American citizenship and civilization," and to encourage the hiring of Indians by the Bureau of Indian Affairs. The tenets of the AIF constitution were identical to those of the Indian National Confederacy.[41] The AIF differed from the Confederacy in that it extended membership to individuals outside of Oklahoma. In addition, the AIF had three informal goals that were never part of the Confederacy's agenda: abolition of the BIA, repeal of the IRA, and the removal of John Collier from the office of commissioner.[42] The AIF was a national organization that made Bruner a national figure.

In their assault on the Indian New Deal, the leaders of the AIF opposed the Wheeler-Howard Act and the Thomas-Rogers Bill through written letters of protest, the publication of articles in popular journals, and appearances at congressional hearings. The campaign would be an extensive one, designed to discredit Collier and his reforms. This effort would demonstrate the influence of the dominant society on the AIF's leadership by its use of the language of anticommunism.

The earliest technique used was a letter-writing campaign targeting Congressman Rogers as well as other politicians. AIF leaders successfully persuaded Rogers to provide the AIF with an opportunity to present a number of charges to Congress in February 1935.[43] Their complaints included charges of subversion in the BIA; the irregular election procedures outlined by the Wheeler-Howard Act, which required only individuals who opposed the measures of the IRA to vote; and BIA use of oppression against opposition.[44]

In February 1935, Bruner began AIF testimony before a House committee. He claimed that the IRA's preservation of indigenous cultures and reversal of the policies of assimilation "handicapped" American Indians. He also provided evidence to support charges that Collier was bitter toward opponents of the IRA and refused to approve the expenditure of tribal funds for opponents to travel to Washington, D.C., to testify against the Indian New Deal. He recounted the stories of individuals who had lost their BIA jobs because they called for people to reject the IRA.[45] Other AIF leaders reiterated the charges made by Bruner. Obviously their testimony was ineffective, because the Oklahoma Indian Welfare Act became law.[46]

AIF leaders realized that to build a national movement, they had to have popular support. Two examples of efforts made in this regard were a memorial written by Navajo activist Jacob C. Morgan of New Mexico in October 1934, and a pamphlet written by Alice Lee Jemison and O. K. Chandler in 1936 called "Now Who's Un-American? An Exposé of Communism in the United States Government."[47] Bruner participated in these efforts to publicize the AIF campaign by contributing an article to the *National Republic* in 1935 titled "The Indian Demands Justice."[48]

The goal of "The Indian Demands Justice" was to inform mainstream society about injustices inflicted by the federal government on American Indians. It was a rational narrative outlining AIF complaints. Bruner glorified the efforts of the Indian to fulfill "his duty toward the white man." He used cooperation with colonists, efforts to become farmers and participants in the dominant society, and voluntary military service in World War I to illustrate the American Indian's desire to be part of mainstream society.[49] Bruner called treatment of Native Americans by the government disgraceful. Instead of the freedom the government had promised, he argued, the Indian New Deal limited freedoms as the BIA destroyed individualism and denied rights to citizenship. By creating new tribal governments and increasing the authority of the secretary of the interior, Bruner felt that the government had erected new hurdles between individuals and their land. With the emphasis on tribal identity, the accomplishments of the individual were overshadowed by the cultural achievements of the group. For a "self-made man" such as Bruner, the idea of greater government involvement in his affairs contradicted the promise of full inclusion in American society that the policy of assimilation had granted.[50]

For the most part, Bruner used the article to attack the bureaucracy, not specific individuals. He claimed that the BIA controlled Indian property and forced individuals to surrender the right of self-government. When he did target Collier specifically, it was to charge the commissioner with taking too much authority. In addition to calling for the repeal of the IRA, Bruner used the article to call for equality for American Indians, a demonstration of the lessons he had learned from the policy of assimilation.[51]

In 1935, Bruner extended his efforts to discredit Collier in public, but instead of rational arguments, he used nativism and fear of un-Americanism to advance his charges. In an "open letter" to "The American Citizenship of the United States," Bruner portrayed Collier as a communist seeking to "sovietize" Native Americans.[52] John Collier, according to Bruner, was "an associate and admirer of radicals, liberals, free thinkers, and communists" and under the influence of the American Civil Liberties Union (ACLU).[53] Bruner opposed Collier's cooperation with other nations, including the influence of Mexican programs in the development of community centers in New Mexico, Chinese medical advisers, Canadian anthropologists, and South African ethnologists.[54]

Particularly offensive to Bruner was the employment of non-Indians in the Indian Bureau. As an example, he offered the case of Esherf Shevky, a Turkish biologist. As a student at Stanford University in the 1920s, Shevky had conducted a survey of the Pueblo Indians that Collier utilized in his reform campaigns. Shevky, who came to the United States in 1913, did not apply for citizenship until he went to work for the BIA in the 1930s. Bruner and other AIF leaders objected to his employment because he filled a position that they believed an Indian should fill. Although historians have cast the attack on Shevky as unfair and xenophobic, the main motivation of the AIF leaders in this pursuit was the desire to see Indians in control of the BIA. Essentially, it was part of an effort to empower Native Americans.[55]

Unlike the *National Republic* article, this piece brutally attacked Collier as an atheist and a communist trying to force Indians into his ideology. Bruner called for Collier's removal and for repeal of the IRA. The intended audience for this letter was not specified; however, judging by its inflammatory, nativist, anticommunist rhetoric, it probably was intended for the non-Indian dominant society in addition to like-minded Indians. The AIF may have distributed it to what Bruner called "patriotic organizations," such as the American Legion or the Daughters of the American Revolution. Most likely, the AIF provided copies to its members and sympathetic politicians. Whatever its audience, the intent of the piece was clear. Bruner had designed it to draw attention to Collier's policies and to raise questions about his motivations.[56] The charges of communism brought the AIF to the forefront of a wider debate about Americanism. The red-baiting brought attention to the cause of Indian rights, but it would ultimately lead to the downfall of Bruner's organization.

Bruner viewed himself and other Indians as loyal, patriotic Native American citizens dedicated to the United States and Christianity. The AIF's mission, much like that of the Euro-American Christian reformers of the late nineteenth and early twentieth centuries, was to protect the "helpless" and "uncivilized" by demonstrating the value of American citizenship and assimilation. Unlike those early reformers who saw danger in the persistence of indigenous religion and culture, the leaders of the AIF had a new perceived enemy, communism. In their relentless assault on the influence of communism, the AIF leaders made real enemies in John Collier and Secretary of the Interior Harold L. Ickes. In response to AIF charges, Collier retaliated with charges of fascism. Between 1938 and 1940, these adversaries exchanged accusations, each trying to prove that the other was "un-American," while claiming to be the protector of "American" ideals.

The Great Depression encouraged political extremism on both the right and the left. In the 1930s, Congress turned its attention to this phenomenon, with particular emphasis on domestic fascism. According to John Hayes, "All virtues and vices that would later mark post–World War II congressional investigations [on communism] were first played out by investigations of domestic fascism in the 1930s."[57] The AIF was drowned out by this movement that would destroy it as a legitimate voice in Indian affairs. The House Un-American Activities Committee (HUAC) was established in 1937 and quickly came under the influence of Representative Martin Dies of Texas, a conservative, anti–New Deal Democrat. He used HUAC to investigate both domestic communism and fascism. His favorite targets were New Deal liberals such as Ickes and Collier.[58]

In November 1938, Dies eagerly gave the AIF an audience with HUAC. Alice Lee Jemison, the federation's representative in Washington, provided a one-hundred-page statement to outline the AIF's charges against Collier and other BIA officials. Her testimony detailed BIA connections with the ACLU and the Communist Party of the United States of America (CPUSA). She criticized textbooks used in reservation schools for advancing communism, much as Christian reformers utilized textbooks to advance assimilation.[59] Jemison's testimony was critical of Collier's legislative reforms. Ultimately, she demonstrated the AIF's dedication to assimilation and its promise of citizenship and equality.[60]

When the AIF began its attacks on Collier and the Indian New Deal, Collier's initial response was one of disinterest. He did not even attend AIF appearances before Congress until Representative John McGroarty of California warned him to take the proceedings seriously.[61] It quickly became apparent that he should not ignore the AIF, so he resorted to bitter personal attacks. He claimed that Bruner sought the "exploitation and injury of his own peo-

ple" and was intoxicated by his "momentary apotheosis."[62] Once, in testimony, Collier said that Bruner was "good natured and not too intelligent."[63]
By 1938, Collier and Ickes had developed a new plan of attack against AIF
leaders. In his "secret diary," Ickes indicated that Jemison worked with domestic Nazi groups. At his request, the FBI investigated and infiltrated the AIF.
Ultimately, the investigations led to charges that Bruner and others were pro-
fascist, "fifth-column" subversives.[64]

The roots of domestic fascism lay in a German propaganda campaign that
began in the United States in 1936. According to Sander A. Diamond, the Ger-
mans used any anticommunist and right-wing organization in their "American Enlightenment" program to educate the American public.[65] The primary
organ of this movement was the German-American Bund, led by Fritz Kuhn,
a German veteran and immigrant. The Bund allied itself with most anti–New
Deal factions and often infiltrated such groups.[66] The Bund was interested in
the American Indian, and according to author Harold Lavine, it used American abuse of Indians to terminate "all talk about Jews in Germany."[67]

In May 1939, Collier informed the president of the National Association of
Indian Affairs, Oliver LaFarge, that the BIA had proof that the AIF associated
with pro-fascist groups.[68] In 1940, Collier took his evidence to the House
Committee on Indian Affairs and charged that the AIF was part of the fascist
movement in the United States.[69] His most damaging evidence was the case of
Elwood A. Towner, who had called for Bund members to provide support for
the AIF. Towner, according to historian Kenneth Townsend, was a Hoopa
Indian from Pendleton, Oregon, and an attorney who "offered himself as a
model for Indian youth to emulate."[70] He was also a member of the Bund, an
indication of his mixed heritage. According to Collier, Towner appeared at
Bund meetings as Chief Red Cloud, "adorned in Indian dress and wearing
swastikas on both arms and his headband." In addition, Collier claimed that
Towner was a member of the AIF.[71] The commissioner also relied on Jemison's
cooperation with another group, the James True Associates, and payments
made to her by the Bund to discredit the AIF.[72]

Bruner and Jemison relentlessly denied Collier's claims that the AIF associated with fascist groups. Bruner wrote that Towner was in "no way connected
with us in membership or otherwise in our organization."[73] Jemison testified
that Towner had come to an AIF convention and wanted to speak; however,
she said that she and other leaders had dismissed him as "a troublemaker,
trying to break up the federation." She added, "Consequently, we thought he
was an agent of Mr. Collier, we did not pay any attention to him."[74] She also

denied that she was a fascist, but she admitted to having received payment from the Bund and other organizations for the use of articles that she had written.[75] Their efforts to defend the AIF and to restore its tarnished image were unsuccessful. The accusations of subversion prevailed. Those charges continue to tarnish its legacy and its leaders today.

Faced with increasing suspicion of un-Americanism from HUAC, Bruner launched a campaign designed to obtain compensation for injustices and to achieve complete inclusion in American society. In his effort to empower Native Americans, he called for Indians to take charge of their future and to assume an active role in shaping federal policy. In 1940, Senator Elmer Thomas of Oklahoma, as chair of the Senate Committee on Indian Affairs, gave Bruner and other leaders an opportunity to argue the merits of a proposed Settlement Bill.

The Settlement Bill was an ill-conceived and selfish attempt to mold federal Indian policy for the benefit of AIF members. It grew out of a 1935 AIF resolution, reaffirmed in 1937, that called for Congress "to stop introducing any Bills . . . pertaining to Indian Affairs except such Bills as shall be specifically requested by the Indians themselves." To justify this resolution, AIF leaders argued that Indians were controlled by a plethora of BIA regulations, which governed "every act of Indian life . . . which an Indian may do from the first breath of life which he draws at birth to the one with which he makes his exit."[76] "Resolution No. 20," in 1937, marked the birth of the legislation. Unanimously the delegates agreed to authorize Bruner, as national president, "to prepare or to have prepared a comprehensive program of Indian legislation which will accomplish the purpose of the American Indian Federation [and] shall become the legislative program" of the organization. After approval of the draft, AIF leaders were to present it to Congress. The resolution read, "Our claims against the Government on account of broken or violated treaties remain unsettled, and the time for the emancipation of the Indian and his complete establishment as an American citizen in all that the word applies, is as far removed from accomplishment today as it was 100 years ago."[77]

In 1938, Bruner and leaders of the Oklahoma contingent of the AIF set out to accomplish their task of formulating a viable Indian legislative program. They continued to harass Collier with charges of communism; however, direct attacks by the executive committee decreased. In 1939, Senator Thomas and Representative Usher L. Burdick of North Dakota introduced the Settlement Bill. The proposed legislation called for a voluntary final settlement of all individual claims against the government for those who were willing to join the federation by paying $1 for themselves and any deceased relative. Payment of these "dues" entitled the individual and any ancestor to inclusion on a roll and to a $3,000 payment for "full, final, and complete settlement of all their rights, equities, or interests in and to all past, present, or future claims."[78] By accepting final settlement, individuals agreed to relinquish tribal allegiance and to surrender all rights to treaty provisions or government services. In addition, the legislation called for state courts to settle estate disputes and for the secretary of the interior to retain supervision over the rights to tribal property.[79] The Settlement Bill specifically represented the interests of Bruner, who viewed it as an opportunity to gain compensation for his mother's, and other Loyalists', losses during the Civil War.[80]

Collier reveled in the opportunity to discredit further the AIF, and along with Ickes, he used his influence in Congress to stifle support for the proposed bill. The two called the bill the "Indian Racket" and tried to persuade its sponsors to withdraw their support. In a letter to Congressman Burdick, Ickes warned that the AIF had malicious intent and sought to "victimize" Native Americans with their "cynical scheme" targeting "ignorant and needy Indians."[81] Persuaded by Ickes's and Collier's arguments, Burdick withdrew the bill in the House of Representatives. He justified his action by stating that "the attitudes and the operation of the American Indian Federation has [sic] been called in question . . . and very grave charges were made against this organization by the Department of the Interior."[82]

Bruner and other AIF leaders denied claims that the Settlement Bill was part of a scheme to defraud Indians. In a letter to Congressman Burdick, they responded to the charges made by Ickes and Collier by continuing to question the men's "Americanism" and claiming that they had communist sympathies. In this letter, AIF leaders Bruner, O. K. Chandler, and N. B. Johnson argued that Ickes had misrepresented the group and its intent. The AIF also resented Ickes's calling Indians "dupes" and "ignorant." If the plan were to be accepted by all of the American Indians in the United States, the federation argued, it would cost slightly more than $1 billion.

The AIF argued that this was less than it would cost to administer Indian affairs through the bureau over a twenty-year period. The federation also defended the $1 fee for inclusion in the settlement roll by arguing that this was an amount fixed by the AIF for dues before the development of the bill. In addition, the AIF denied charges that its leaders profited from the fees; however, they failed to provide an explanation of how the federation used the money. They claimed that Collier and Ickes had attacked the AIF because of its campaign to repeal the Indian Reorganization Act. Specifically, the group pointed to the influence of the ACLU and "foreign-born" individuals in the Interior Department. Finally, the AIF denied any connection with "any group objectionable to a loyal patriotic citizen."[83]

Senator Thomas agreed to give the AIF an opportunity to present its legislation; however, he disapproved of many of the aspects of the Settlement Bill and opinions of AIF leaders. He was uncomfortable with the per capita payments, fearing that they would create greater economic problems. A final settlement implied the loss of the federal advocate to protect the Indians from fraud. Although such an idea was not expressed in the bill, Thomas opposed the federation's desire to close Indian schools, fearing that most Indians would then remain uneducated. His concerns about the repercussions of the Settlement Bill were admirable and valid. Nevertheless, they also reflected a persistent attitude of paternalism. Like many of his colleagues, Thomas was uncertain about the abilities of American Indians to succeed in the dominant society. He was afraid that without the BIA and government supervision, Indians would be unable to compete with non-Indians.[84]

AIF representative O. K. Chandler addressed Thomas's concerns. He claimed that separate Indian schools perpetuated a feeling of inferiority and prevented the Indian from becoming "a resourceful, independent, self-supporting citizen." He believed that the institutions under the New Deal administration taught "Indianness," not citizenship. Chandler argued that Indians were capable of managing their own money, and that failure to do so was a social problem, not a cultural one.[85] Collier's and Ickes's opposition and Thomas's concerns killed the Settlement Bill. More important, the bill transformed the AIF.

Following the debate over the Settlement Bill, the federation transformed from a national movement into a regional one, as reflected in changes in its structure and leadership. By 1940, Oklahoma county districts had replaced most of the national districts. In 1938, the national leadership of the AIF included many Oklahomans as well as individuals from New York, Idaho, Nevada, California, and Arizona. By 1940, the number of non-Oklahomans had decreased dramatically. Most of those remaining members had been founding members of the group. More important, Oklahomans dominated the administrative board that handled the business affairs of the group. It never included more than two non-Oklahoman members.[86] The most impor-

tant change in leadership was the resignation of Jemison because of her opposition to the Settlement Bill. She believed that the legislation contradicted
the AIF's goals to fight the Indian Reorganization Act and abolish the BIA.[87]

Additional shifts in leadership after 1940 continued to weaken the AIF. In
the early 1940s, Bruner faced personal tribulations, including the death of his
wife and his own declining health. He spent much of his time with his daughter in Window Rock, Arizona, leaving the administration of the AIF in the
hands of the others. O. K. Chandler dominated the organization until 1943,
when Bruner became aware that Chandler had abused the powers bestowed
upon him. Bruner unsuccessfully appealed to Jemison to return to the organization. Bruner then turned to Napoleon B. Johnson to assume the dominant
position in the AIF. In 1944, however, his influence was diminished further
when he became the first president of the National Congress of American
Indians (NCAI).[88]

Because of the emphasis on final settlement and abolition of the BIA,
historians have characterized the Settlement Bill as "an early version of termination legislation, which dissolved tribal entities and liquidated tribal assets."[89] Central to termination was a belief in assimilation, a call for the end
of government supervision, and hostility toward the BIA. Neither the AIF
nor its leaders were the first to advocate such ideas. They had been part of
Carlos Montezuma's campaign through the Society of American Indians in
the early twentieth century.[90] Ideas about termination were also evident in
Congress before the Settlement Bill. For example, in 1935, as Collier defended
the Wheeler-Howard Act, Representative John McGroarty of California announced his desire to see an end to the BIA and termination of the trust
relationship.[91]

After 1940, Bruner tried to maintain his campaign for Indian rights. World
War II drew attention and resources away from that cause, and particularly
the AIF. Military service and defense industry growth provided additional
economic opportunities for Indians away from reservations. Congress di-
verted funds from the BIA to support the war effort. Senator Burton K.
Wheeler, an early sponsor of the IRA, launched attacks on the legislation and
called for its repeal. Congress no longer needed Indian opposition to Collier
to justify their attacks on the BIA; the war provided a much better excuse.[92]

The emergence of the NCAI further weakened the AIF. Formed in late
1944, the NCAI, according to Thomas Cowger, was a moderate organization
that attempted to appeal to the full spectrum of Indian society. Most of
its early efforts concentrated on repealing the termination legislation of the

1950s.[93] Bruner found the NCAI to be objectionable from its inception. Its creation made the AIF unnecessary because it appeared that there was room for only one national Indian movement. The NCAI also removed Napoleon Johnson from the AIF and its causes.[94]

Joseph Bruner's opinions were controversial and were often characterized as non-Indian. However, if his ideas are examined as those of an individual taught to emulate the dominant society and to deny the significance of his indigenous culture, he becomes a product of his environment. His ideas about the importance of Indian control of the BIA foreshadowed the self-determination movement in the latter half of the century. His was a message of empowerment, although the method for such power was questionable. From his efforts and rhetoric, it appeared that he believed Indian culture to be inferior to Anglo culture; however, he never denied that he was an Indian. He was proud of his heritage throughout his life. In 1957, his crusade to protect Indian rights ended with his death in an Indian hospital in Claremore. It was an ironic twist, considering his former campaign to close such institutions, but by the end of his life he had revised many of his opinions about the usefulness of many institutions for Indians.[95]

NOTES

The information presented in this article is based on the author's master's thesis. See Marci Barnes Gracey, "Attacking the Indian New Deal: The American Indian Federation and the Quest to Protect Assimilation" (Oklahoma State University, 2003). The author would like to express her gratitude to the faculty and staff of the history department at Oklahoma State University, Dr. Thomas W. Cowger of East Central University, and the staff at the Oklahoma Historical Society, the Carl Albert Congressional Research and Studies Center, and the Sapulpa Historical Society.

1. John Collier to Joseph Bruner, May 9, 1934, John Collier Papers, 1922–1968, Oklahoma State University, Stillwater, Oklahoma (microform).

2. Laurence M. Hauptman, "The American Indian Federation and the Indian New Deal: A Reinterpretation," *Pacific Historical Review* 52 (November 1983): 378–402, and Kenneth William Townsend, *World War II and the American Indian* (Albuquerque: University of New Mexico Press, 2000). For additional works about John Collier and the Indian New Deal, see Lawrence Kelly, *The Assault on Assimilation: John Collier and the Origins of Indian Policy Reform* (Albuquerque: University of New Mexico Press, 1983); Kenneth R. Philp, *John Collier's Crusade for Indian Reform, 1920–1954* (Tucson: University of Arizona Press, 1977); Elmer R. Rusco, *A Fateful Time: The Background and Legislative History of the Indian Reorganization Act* (Reno: University of Nevada Press, 2000); Robert Fay Schrader, *The Indian Arts and Crafts Board: An Aspect of New Deal Indian Policy* (Albuquerque: University of New Mexico Press, 1983);

82 MARCI BARNES GRACEY

Graham D. Taylor, *The New Deal and American Indian Tribalism: The Administration of the Indian Reorganization Act, 1934–1945* (Lincoln: University of Nebraska Press, 1980).

3. Frederick E. Hoxie, *A Final Promise: The Campaign to Assimilate the Indians, 1880–1920* (Lincoln: University of Nebraska Press, 1988), 2, 10.

4. Interview with Joseph Bruner by Effie S. Jackson, February 28, 1938, *Indian-Pioneer Histories*, Indian Archives, Oklahoma Historical Society, Oklahoma City, 89:267. For more information, see Angie Debo, *Tulsa: From Creek Town to Oil Capital* (Norman: University of Oklahoma Press, 1943). Creeks divided into factions called the Upper and Lower Creeks. Lower Creeks were predominantly of mixed ancestry and were highly assimilated individuals who had agreed to come to Indian Territory in the 1820s. Upper Creeks were more conservative and traditional and had resisted efforts to remove them until 1835. For more information, see Arrell M. Gibson, *Oklahoma: A History of Five Centuries* (Norman: University of Oklahoma Press, 1981), 49–51.

5. Debo, *Tulsa*, 23.

6. Ibid., 29; Gibson, *Oklahoma*, 121.

7. Debo, *Tulsa*, 36; interview with Joseph Bruner, *Indian-Pioneer Histories*, 77:325.

8. Hoxie, *A Final Promise*, 2, 10; Francis Paul Prucha, *The Great Father: The United States Government and the American Indians* (Lincoln: University of Nebraska Press, 1988), 2:616, 631.

9. Prucha, *The Great Father*, 15, 219; Hoxie, *A Final Promise*, 15.

10. Interview with Joseph Bruner, *Indian-Pioneer Histories*, 89:266.

11. *Sapulpa, OK 74066* (Sapulpa, Okla.: Sapulpa Historical Society, 1981), 1:217.

12. Ibid.

13. For discussion of boarding school experiences, see David Wallace Adams, *Education for Extinction: American Indians and the Boarding School Experience, 1875–1925* (Lawrence: University Press of Kansas, 1995).

14. Interview with Joseph Bruner, *Indian-Pioneer Histories*, 89:271. For a discussion of the allotment and statehood processes, see Gibson, *Oklahoma*, 194–202.

15. Gibson, *Oklahoma*, 196. Bruner's involvement was documented in a photograph of the town's delegates housed at the Sapulpa Historical Society.

16. Gibson, *Oklahoma*, 137; interview with Joseph Bruner, *Indian-Pioneer Histories*, 77:325; 89:271.

17. For information about Bruner's activities and businesses, see the Bruner Collection at the Sapulpa Historical Society Museum.

18. Prucha, *The Great Father*, 2:808, 896. Members of the Five Tribes received citizenship with statehood; however, many other groups had not been extended citizenship before 1924.

19. Hoxie, *A Final Promise*, x, xi, 236, 242.

20. Hazel W. Hertzberg, *The Search for an American Identity: Modern Pan-Indian Movements* (Syracuse, N.Y.: Syracuse University Press, 1971), 5–6.

21. Ibid., 6.

22. Ibid., 7. Other important leaders were Dr. Charles Eastman, Thomas L. Sloan, Gertrude Bonnin, and Henry Standing Bear. Hertzberg provides the most comprehensive study of pan-Indian movements, including the SAI. For more information

about Montezuma, see Peter Iverson, *Carlos Montezuma and the Changing World of American Indians* (Albuquerque: University of New Mexico Press, 1982).

23. W. David Baird, "Are There 'Real' Indians in Oklahoma? Historical Perspectives of the Five Civilized Tribes," *Chronicles of Oklahoma* 68 (Spring 1990): 12.

24. Ibid.

25. "Society of Oklahoma Indians," program from Fourth Annual Convention, June 1927, in Pawhuska, Oklahoma, Harriette J. Westbrook Collection, 2000.020, Box 22, Oklahoma Historical Society; interview with Bruner, *Indian-Pioneer Histories*, 77:325; 89:271.

26. *Sapulpa, OK 74066*, 2:217–19; interview with Bruner, *Indian-Pioneer Histories*, 77:325; 89:271.

27. "Address of the Honorable Joseph Bruner," at Society of Oklahoma Indians February 1924 Convention, S. W. Brown, Jr., Collection, Oklahoma Historical Society, Box 15, Society of Oklahoma Indians file, 7–8.

28. Donald L. Parman, *The Navajos and the New Deal* (New Haven, Conn.: Yale University Press, 1976), 30.

29. Joseph Bruner to John Collier, September 7, 1933, John Collier Papers.

30. Bruner to Collier, September 16, 1933, John Collier Papers. "Proceedings of the Conference for the Indians of the Five Civilized Tribes at Oklahoma," March 22, 1934, John Collier Papers, 4, 7.

31. "Proceedings of the Conference for the Indians of the Five Civilized Tribes," 39, 43, 52.

32. M. K. Sniffen, ed., *Indian Truth* 11 (April 1934): 1.

33. Vine Deloria, Jr., *The Indian Reorganization Act: Congresses and Bills* (Norman: University of Oklahoma Press, 2002), vii.

34. Ibid., xi, xv.

35. Ibid., xv, xvi; See also Philp, *John Collier's Crusade for Indian Reform*, 159; Kenneth R. Philp, "John Collier, 1933–45," in Robert M. Kvasnicka and Herman J. Viola, eds., *The Commissioners of Indian Affairs, 1824–1977* (Lincoln: University of Nebraska Press, 1979), 278; Hauptman, "The American Indian Federation and the Indian New Deal," 389.

36. Deloria, *The Indian Reorganization Act*, xv.

37. Peter M. Wright, "John Collier and the Oklahoma Indian Welfare Act of 1936," *Chronicles of Oklahoma* 50 (Autumn 1972): 362–63.

38. Ibid., 367, 368, 370.

39. Ibid., 370.

40. "Statement of Joseph Bruner, President of the American Indian Federation," House Committee on Indian Affairs, Indian Conditions and Affairs, Hearings on H.R. 7781, 74th Cong., 1st Sess., February 11, 1935, 14–15.

41. Ibid.

42. Joseph Bruner, "The Indian Demands Justice," *National Republic* 20 (March 1935): 31.

43. Joseph Bruner to Will Rogers, January 30, 1935, House Committee, Indian Conditions and Affairs, 23.

44. Ibid.

45. "Testimony of Joseph Bruner" and William C. Knorr to Bruner, December 15, 1934, House Committee, Indian Conditions and Affairs, 27.

46. "Testimony of Alice Lee Jemison," ibid., 37–38; "Testimony by Winslow J. Couro," February 12, 1935, ibid., 68; Wright, "John Collier," 370.

47. Jacob C. Morgan, "To All Indians and Friends," October 25, 1934, Bruner Collection, Sapulpa Historical Society; O. K. Chandler and Alice Lee Jemison, "Now Who's Un-American? An Exposé of Communism in the United States Government," 1936, Lee Harkins Collection, Oklahoma Historical Society.

48. Bruner, "The Indian Demands Justice," 23–24, 31.

49. Ibid., 23.

50. Ibid., 24.

51. Ibid., 24, 31.

52. Joseph Bruner, "To the American Citizenship of the United States," April 1935, 1–2, John Collier Papers.

53. Ibid., 1.

54. Ibid., 2.

55. Ibid.; Philp, *John Collier's Crusade for Indian Reform*, 44, 172; Parman, *The Navajos and the New Deal*, 100; "Statement by John Collier," House Committee, Indian Conditions and Affairs, 717.

56. Bruner, "To the American Citizenship of the United States," 3–4.

57. John E. Haynes, *Red Scare or Red Menace? American Communism and Anticommunism in the Cold War Era* (Chicago: Ivan R. Dee, 1996), 64.

58. Ibid., 66.

59. Statement by Alice Lee Jemison, House Special Committee, Un-American Activities and Propaganda, 75th Cong., November 1938, 2437–39, 2441–42, 2443, 2444.

60. Ibid., 2446–2447, 2502.

61. House Committee, Indian Conditions and Affairs, 27–28.

62. "Statement by John Collier," ibid., 768, 771, 774, 775, 776.

63. "Statement by John Collier," House Committee on Indian Affairs, Wheeler-Howard—Exempt Certain Indians, Hearings on S. 2103, 76th Cong. 3rd Sess., 1940, 468.

64. Harold L. Ickes, *The Secret Diary of Harold L. Ickes* (New York: Simon and Schuster, 1953–54), 2:506–507.

65. Sanders A. Diamond, *The Nazi Movement in the United States, 1924–1960* (Ithaca, N.Y.: Cornell University Press, 1974), 193–94.

66. Ibid.

67. Harold Lavine, *Fifth Column in America* (New York: Doubleday, Doran and Co., 1940), 207.

68. Collier to Oliver LaFarge, May 10, 1939, John Collier Papers.

69. "Statement by John Collier," House Committee, Wheeler-Howard Act—Exempt Certain Indians, 68, 69, 70.

70. Townsend, *World War II and the American Indian*, 42–43.

71. "Statement by John Collier," House Committee, Wheeler-Howard Act—Exempt Certain Indians, 68.

72. Ibid., 100, 106, 118.

73. Bruner to Mrs. S. S. Severson, February 17, 1942, Bruner Collection.

74. "Statement by Alice Lee Jemison," House Committee, Wheeler-Howard Act—Exempt Certain Indians, 166.

75. Ibid., 153, 156, 165.

76. "Resolution No. 7 of 1937," July 30, 1937, Folder 93, Box 34, Subject Series, Elmer Thomas Collection, Carl Albert Congressional Research and Studies Center, University of Oklahoma.

77. "Resolution No. 20," July 31, 1937, Folder 93, Box 24, Legislative Series, Thomas Collection, Carl Albert Center.

78. Senate Committee on Indian Affairs, Final Discharge, Certain Individual Indians, Hearings on S. 3750. 76th Cong., 3rd Sess., June 20, 1940, 1, Bruner Collection, Sapulpa Historical Society.

79. Ibid.

80. Bruner to S. W. Brown, Jr., January 24, 1939, Brown Collection, Box 13, AIF File. The Brown Collection includes a number of boxes concerning Brown's efforts to bring about a settlement. Unfortunately, there has not been a comprehensive study of the efforts of Loyal Creeks and their descendants to gain compensation.

81. Harold L. Ickes to Usher L. Burdick, April 18, 1939, Congressional Record, May 1939, Harkins Collection, 82.105.194.

82. "Statement of the Hon. Usher L. Burdick of North Dakota in the House of Representatives," May 1 and 19, 1939, ibid.

83. American Indian Federation to Usher L. Burdick, May 15, 1939, ibid.

84. "Statement of Elmer Thomas, Chair," Senate Committee on Indian Affairs, Final Discharge, Certain Individual Indians, Hearings on S. 3750, 76th Cong., 3rd Sess., June 20, 1940, 10–12.

85. "Statement of O.K. Chandler," ibid.

86. "AIF Constitution," House Committee, Indian Conditions and Affairs, 15. These changes were evident in the letters and resolutions of the AIF after 1940. See Senate Committee, Final Discharge, Certain Individual Indians, 27; and letters from Bruner to Brown in the Brown Collection. Typically, the non-Oklahoman board members were Winslow J. Couro, John E. Curran, and Lorena Burgess.

87. Alice Jemison to Joseph Bruner, July 10, 1939, Bruner Collection. For information about Jemison, see Hauptman, "Alice Jemison: Seneca Political Activist, 1901–1964," Indian Historian 12 (Summer 1979): 60–62. Based on the claims of John Collier, some scholars argue that Bruner and others forced Jemison to resign because of her connection to fifth-column organizations; however, there appears to be no proof to back up this argument. Bruner and Jemison remained friends after her resignation and continued to correspond with one another, especially after Bruner and Chandler ended their friendship. See Jeré Bishop Franco, Crossing the Pond: The Native American Effort in World War II (Denton: University of North Texas Press, 1999), 31.

88. Bruner to Brown, June 17, 1943, Brown Collection, Box 12; Bruner to Brown, August 2, 1943, Brown Collection, Box 12; Sapulpa, OK 74066, 1:219; Rita F. Newton to Alice Lee Jemison, June 28, 1943, Bruner Collection.

89. Hauptman, "The American Indian Federation," 399. For additional discussion of termination policy and the influence of the AIF, see Kenneth R. Philp, Termination

Revisited: American Indians on the Trail to Self-Determination, 1933–1953 (Lincoln: University of Nebraska Press, 1999).

90. Iverson, *Carlos Montezuma and the Changing World of American Indians,* 67, 94, 105, 107.

91. House Committee, Indian Conditions and Affairs, 55–56.

92. Townsend, *World War II and the American Indian,* 170, 196, 215–17, provides an excellent discussion of American Indian experiences during World War II. For additional information, see Alison R. Bernstein, *American Indians and World War II: Toward a New Era in Indian Affairs* (Norman: University of Oklahoma Press, 1999); Donald L. Fixico, *Termination and Relocation: Federal Indian Policy, 1945–1960* (Albuquerque: University of New Mexico Press, 1986); Franco, *Crossing the Pond.*

93. For a discussion of the early efforts of the NCAI, see Thomas W. Cowger, *The National Congress of American Indians: The Founding Years* (Lincoln: University of Nebraska Press, 1999).

94. Bruner to Thomas, February 3, 1945, Bruner Collection; Bruner to Ms. Sunflower, Secretary of the National League for Justice to American Indians, Inc., January 10, 1946, Bruner Collection; Bruner to Mr. Millima M. Newton, December 30, 1944, Bruner Collection; "National Congress of American Indians: An Indian Bureau Organization, How It Was Formed," June 1, 1947, Bruner Collection.

95. In an unidentified news article discussing the upcoming AIF convention in Tulsa, Bruner is quoted as saying that the only beneficiaries of Collier's legislative reforms were Indian hospitals and schools. See "Indians Pave Way to Go after Collier Scalp Again in August," Folder 5, Box 7, Legislative Series, Lyle Boren Collection, Carl Albert Center. For information on Bruner's death, see "Joseph Bruner, Indian Rights Champion, Dies; Believed First Male Born in Tulsa," January 1957, Sapulpa Historical Society.

CHAPTER 6

Getting Along

WOODY GUTHRIE AND OKLAHOMA'S
RED DIRT MUSICIANS

Thomas Conner

After chronicling the rise of Red Dirt music in articles as the pop music critic at the *Tulsa World* newspaper, Thomas Conner served a 2000–2001 fellowship with the National Arts Journalism Program at Columbia University, during which he researched Woody Guthrie's life and legacy at the Woody Guthrie Archives in Manhattan. In 2002, music producer Bob Kline hired Conner to conduct interviews for a DVD companion to his next music compilation, *Red Dirt Sampler, Vol. 2,* a live concert follow-up to his previous and well-received roundup of the difficult-to-define Red Dirt music native to north-central Oklahoma. Conner conducted many hours of interviews; some of these were excerpted between musical performances on the DVD, which is still in post-production, and the rest of the material was tapped for this article, which explores the connections between Guthrie's Oklahoma roots and the development of this musical—or is it spiritual?—genre called Red Dirt. Conner is now a features editor at the *Chicago Sun-Times.*

> *"Americana" is a new one on me, but when these fellers hire out to write a column every day they ain't no telling what kinds of words they'll fall back on to make a living.*
> —WOODY GUTHRIE'S SCRIBBLED RESPONSE TO A 1940 NEWSPAPER
> REVIEW, WHICH INCLUDED HIS *DUST BOWL BALLADS* LP
> UNDER THE HEADING "AMERICANA."[1]

Yellow Dog Studios is hidden on an exposed-brick block of downtown Tulsa that has thus far, and likely forever, escaped "revitalization." But on three typically steamy nights in June 2002, a small audience found this hidden recording studio and gathered to witness live recordings by some of the region's most notable purveyors of a relatively young genre that has come to be called Red Dirt music. Nearly twenty acts were recorded in three days for a CD compilation titled *Red Dirt Sampler, Vol. 2: Songs in the Spirit of Woody Guthrie,* a live follow-up to an influential studio outing recorded with many of the same musicians in 1997 in Stillwater. The performances at Yellow Dog Studios included songwriters such as Bob Childers, Tom Skinner, and Mike McClure, as well as groups like the Red Dirt Rangers, Medicine Show, and the Farm Couple. Most of the acts could be united loosely under umbrella terms such as "alt-country," "roots music," or "Americana," but there also were performances by Local Hero, a popular Tulsa-based reggae band, and Steve Pryor, widely acclaimed as one of the greatest blues guitarists undiscovered by the music industry. The resulting recording is a *mélange* of music—folk, country, bluegrass, reggae, rock, and blues—that seems to have few commonalities. Just by listening to the music itself, it's not easy to determine exactly what connects these Oklahoma-native artists and why they fly under the same banner of Red Dirt music. But when you begin to listen to the words—to the stories being told—the simple and rather practical method to the music begins to crystallize. By the end of the recording session, for instance, not only had several dozen songs been recorded, but several dozen stories had been told, nearly all of them about Oklahoma—its history, its spirit, and its character.

One of the songwriters that week, Greg Jacobs, held the audience rapt with what has since become a signature song for him, "Farmer's Luck," from his 2001 disc *Reclining with Age* on Binky Records, a Louisiana-based label that has released several recordings by Red Dirt musicians, including Childers and Skinner. Jacobs is a teacher, regardless of which of his two professions he is practicing. By day, he's illuminating Oklahoma history for a captive audience of teenagers, his students at Checotah High School. By night and during school vacations, he's playing area nightclubs and festivals, singing much of the same history for audiences who are aren't captive as much as captivated.

"Farmer's Luck" relates the creation of Lake Eufaula, the state's largest man-made lake, from the perspective of Jacobs's grandparents, whose family farm now lies underneath its muddy waters. The U.S. Army Corps of Engineers, as a result of the River and Harbor Act of 1946, began constructing the dam on the South Canadian River in 1956, for flood control, water supply, hydroelectric power, and navigation resources. Citing "eminent domain," the state forced hundreds of property owners to give up their land—mostly farms—in the area to be flooded. It was a promising economic venture for the state and a severe economic hardship for those forced off their land.

"You know, when they build a lake like that, a lot of people don't take into account that the best farmland is bottomland, along the river," Jacobs recalled several months later in a 2002 interview for the *Tulsa World*.[2] "The Corps of Engineers comes in and says, 'We're going to buy your land. Period.' You have no choice but to sell, because they have eminent domain. There's a stipulation where if you invest that sale money back into land, you don't get taxed on it. Well, there was no land to buy back then, and what there was went sky high. So the farmers couldn't reinvest their money, and the government then came and took a third of it back in taxes."

That's the class lecture, anyway. Here's the chorus of Jacobs's eight-verse song:

> They're gonna dam the Deep Fork River, they're gonna build
>   themselves a lake
> They're gonna dam the South Canadian, whatever else it takes
> They're gonna bring in here some tourists, they're gonna make
>   themselves some bucks
> They're gonna dam the Deep Fork River, and damn the farmer's luck.[3]

"That one's a true folk song," Jacobs said. "It meets all the qualifications for a folk song. One, it's long. Two, it's about folks. Three, it's got a story and a moral." He chuckled to himself, then sighed. "Everything I've been writing lately is in that vein. I guess I'm a folkie, after all." He continues this style in many of his other songs, telling tales of the state's history in "Okie Wind" and "A Little Rain Will Do." He recounts the 1918 Green Corn Rebellion in the title song to his 1997 album *South of Muskogee Town*.

Shortly after Jacobs performed "Farmer's Luck" at Yellow Dog Studios, another acclaimed Red Dirt figure presented a few of his populist songs. Stocky, muscled, bald, and inked with several colorful and snaky tattoos—looking like a bouncer at a nightclub door, not one of the carefully coiffed musicians on stage—Brandon Jenkins sang three alternately fierce and delicate songs about his Oklahoma upbringing in a style of music he describes in his own promotional material as "Red Dirt, bluegrass, Green Country, white trash" ("Green Country" being the catchy tourism department label for the region of northeastern Oklahoma around Tulsa).

One of the songs was his own signature ballad, "Refinery Blues," about his childhood growing up in Sand Springs near the cluster of oil refineries on the west bank of the Arkansas River. The song reflects on three generations of Jenkins patriarchs, each of whom worked hard toward a goal of saving enough money to move out of the "three-room shack" and away from the illnesses allegedly caused by the nearby refinery emissions:

> My back yard's a refinery
> My daddy passed away and left the place to me
> Nobody lives past 53
> Livin' next door to this refinery[4]

Later that night, after Jenkins and others had performed, several of the artists sat down to talk about what they were doing together on this project and what qualified them to wear the Red Dirt label. They discussed musical forms, their own musical discoveries, even styles of guitars, but what united the various musicians' definitions of Red Dirt music was the influence— conscious and otherwise—of a long-gone singer-songwriter and fellow Oklahoman: Woody Guthrie.

That was, indeed, the goal of the project. *Red Dirt Sampler* producer Bob Kline said he had set out to gather together musicians and songwriters who "exemplified the spirit of Woody—in their own work, not just by covering his songs." In searching for such artists, he also wound up with a roster of singer-songwriters who each struggle with the little-understood and ill-defined Red Dirt label. Does that mean that any musician inspired by Guthrie can be called Red Dirt? No—but if the musician hails from Oklahoma and claims Guthrie as a chief influence, it's likely, for Red Dirt musicians tend to be those who revere Guthrie not only for his accomplishments but for his origins as well.

Jenkins defended his motives: "We're all inspired by Woody in that way, by his music and his being here in Oklahoma. The way I'm most inspired by him is that when I write a song now, I try to keep the common man in mind. . . . That song I sang tonight, 'Refinery Blues'—that whole area over there is full of people who've been diagnosed with cancer. If Woody found out about that, he'd have tried to write a song about it, to draw attention to it. In a lot of my music, I try to do that, to speak for those people who can't speak for themselves."

"He was a storyteller, and we see ourselves that way," Jacobs said. "He wrote stories of substance. Woody said, 'Write what you see.' I like to write story songs. I was lucky enough to grow up with my grandparents and hear their stories, and it's often their stories I tell. 'Farmer's Luck' is their story. It's not an environmentalist song, it's a family song. It's about families, and every time I play that song, somebody comes up and says, hey, I'm from Eufaula or Checotah and I know all about that. Then they tell me their own family story."

Family, storytelling, getting along—these are the hallmarks of a lot of folk music. But they are the themes of everything that has been called Red Dirt music, and they were the driving force of Woody Guthrie's life and career. The tunes that fall into the freely applied Red Dirt category bring these elements together in a new way. Red Dirt music is, in a sense, a delayed reaction to Guthrie's life and legacy, a loose musical movement with the potential to focus and synthesize the entire heritage of Oklahoma and its music.

THE COMPOSTING OF RED DIRT

The phrase "Red Dirt" has a loose, nearly thirty-year history as a label for a particular kind of music native to the Oklahoma landscape, specifically the open land consisting of crimson iron-oxide clay that stretches between Stillwater and Okemah and points west; however, the use of the identifier has proliferated widely in music circles and in the media within the last decade. I'm partly to blame for thrusting it into the common regional language. As a music journalist at the *World* for nearly eight years, from early 1995 to late 2002, I seized upon the Red Dirt Rangers' self-titled 1996 debut CD and began writing articles about the band in which its members broached the subject of a regional musical identity and struggled to define themselves amid their Red Dirt classification, which they helped establish by incorporating it into the name of their band. (I had been a fan of the Rangers since my university days in the early '90s, driving from Norman to downtown Oklahoma City to see them perform at a delicious dive—with a dirt floor, if memory serves—called the Rock Island, back before the city's warehouse district became today's gentrified Bricktown.) Once the term was in print, other acts came forward eager to expound on the nebulous genre. Our newspaper coverage of them mushroomed (colleague John Wooley had written about Red Dirt long before I came along, and together we expounded on the music throughout the '90s), and by 1999, when the *Tulsa World* launched the first Spot Music Awards, an annual readers' poll and ceremony honoring regional musicians, there was no question as to whether we should include a category for Best Red Dirt Act, which the Red Dirt Rangers won handily for the first five years. By 2003, the *Tulsa World* had even revised its newsroom stylebook with an entry specifying that the phrase "Red Dirt" be capitalized "when referring to the music genre."

During the last decade, though, Wooley and I have spilled countless gallons of ink attempting to describe accurately and discuss rationally exactly what Red Dirt music is. We have heard as many definitions of Red Dirt music as there are practitioners of it. Our own attempts have involved a lot of hyphens and conjunctions, usually along these lines: country-roots music with a decided storytelling folk ambition and a classic-rock edge. Rogers State University assistant professor Dr. Hugh W. Foley, Jr., adds a lyrical component to the definition in his entry on Red Dirt music in the *Oklahoma Music Guide,* cowritten with Oklahoma State University professor Dr. George O. Carney. Foley writes that Red Dirt music is "often delivered with lyrically sardonic humor that is often dry as the red earth. . . . When humor is not the object of the song's lyrically focused intent, subtle and melancholy appraisals of rural and small town society's decay fill the verses of red dirt music, and, occasionally, a song about love lost or gained creeps or weeps its way into the mix."[5]

We at the *World* have, as have others—even those who wear the label proudly—occasionally doubted that Red Dirt is, indeed, a unique and identifiable "sound." All music is regional, really, but what made these Oklahoma musicians different from the countless alt-country and roots-rock players fueling other scenes across America? But just as our skepticism began to take shape, we would see a Texas newspaper article mention those Red Dirt boys from Oklahoma, or something like the Red Dirt Music Awards would spring up, as they did in 2003, and we would realize that Red Dirt was viewed by most area musicians and many fans as an identifiable genre unique to north-central Oklahoma.

In every interview, we would ask these artists about their influences. Who did they listen to, and who inspired their own songwriting efforts? These are horribly clichéd queries, but they began to paint a clear picture. Without fail, each answer came back a mixture of classic country (George Jones, Hank Williams, Willie Nelson), classic rock (the Eagles, Doug Sahm, even Led Zeppelin), and both old (Pete Seeger, Bob Dylan) and modern (Townes Van Zandt, Steve Earle) folk music. Numerous Oklahomans have been mentioned as influences, spanning many styles and decades, from Leon Russell and J. J. Cale in the early 1970s (pioneers of the Tulsa Sound, an equally slippery label applied to regional rock music with a certain shuffle and a laid-back approach) to the early days of both Merle Haggard and Garth Brooks. But Woody Guthrie's name is mentioned more than all the others. In a 2004 search of the *Tulsa World*'s electronic story archives (dating back to 1989), 272 full-length articles used the phrase "Red Dirt" as a musical form, and 143 of those mentioned Woody Guthrie.

The story of what came to be called Red Dirt music begins just a few years after Guthrie's death in 1967. The first use of the term in a musical context, Foley wrote, likely was the "Red Dirt Boogie, Brother," a tune about "plain old rock 'n' roll" on Kiowa-Comanche-Muscogee guitarist Jesse Ed Davis's 1972 album *Ululu*.[6] But the proliferation of the music known as Red Dirt focuses on three songwriters, none of whom were born in Oklahoma, but each of whom settled in the Stillwater area.

Around the same time as Davis's album in 1972, an album was released by a Stillwater band called Moses. An independent release, *Moses Live* required a record label name for its cover, so the band's leader, Steve Ripley, made one up: Red Dirt Records. The album's liner notes, by journalist Mike Dugan, described Moses's music as "a hue of funk, a shade of sound, a basic spirit," and acknowledged its debt to "the color of the earth surrounding Enid and nearby Stillwater, Moses' home base."[7]

Ripley, who was born in Boise, Idaho, and had grown up on his family's Payne County farm, eventually made a successful career of this vaguely described musical essence. He has worked for Leon Russell both on record and behind the scenes, produced such Oklahoma stars as Roy Clark and Johnny Lee Wills, and played guitar with Bob Dylan (including on the 1981 *Shot of Love* album). He settled in Tulsa in 1987 and soon after took over Russell's famed recording studio, the Church, before founding the million-selling, Grammy-nominated Tulsa-based country band the Tractors in the mid-'90s. ("Baby Likes to Rock It" was a Top 10 hit from the band's No. 1 self-titled 1994 debut disc.)

"When we had Moses back in Stillwater, it was kind of a precursor to what I'm doing today," Ripley told John Wooley for a 2000 article in the *Tulsa World*. "It was that mix of Hank Williams, Chuck Berry and Bob Dylan, that blend of country and rock 'n' roll—I don't like the term 'country-rock'—that people like around Stillwater. I don't want to claim that I'm the father of the movement, but I do think we kind of coined the name for it back then."[8]

In Ripley's 2002 publicity bio, which describes his music as "neo-traditionalist, retro-whatever, country-something," he touches on the disparate musical influences he sought to synthesize not only in the Tractors but in all the music he's been a part of: "The Beatles listened to the same music I did growing up. I've been to George Harrison's house, and all he could talk about is James Burton ('Suzie-Q,' 1957). There was a time when country was a rockin' thing, when you could hear on one radio station Hank [Williams] and Chuck Berry, Jerry Lee [Lewis] and Merle [Haggard], Buck [Owens] and Johnny Cash and Ray Charles. That's the kind of music I wanted to make again. But it wasn't easy to get at what that would actually be."[9]

When most current Red Dirt musicians relate the history of the genre, they tell the story of Moses, and then invariably move to the genesis of Jimmy LaFave and a song he wrote called "Red Dirt Roads at Night." A native of Wills Point, Texas, east of Dallas, LaFave moved with his family to Stillwater in the early '70s , when he was a teenager. A fan of Bob Dylan, LaFave suddenly found himself in the home state of Dylan's godhead, Woody Guthrie. "I started playing around with my guitar and with other musicians when I was still in high school in Stillwater, and people kept playing me Woody Guthrie songs," LaFave said following his participation in a panel discussion titled "Made for You and Me: Woody Guthrie's Dust Bowl Legacy" at the 2002 South by Southwest music conference in Austin, Texas. "I really tuned into them because I knew this was the music that inspired Dylan. Then I got completely swept away in Woody's music itself, not just as a source for Bob but as a source for about everything I was into and listening to at the time—and still, really. His music had this sense of humanity that sounded so much like what I had grown up hearing people talk about in rural Texas and Oklahoma."[10]

LaFave spent his formative years in Stillwater, learning how to play music in the rural college town and even operating his own venue, Up Your Alley, just off "the Strip" (Washington Street) in Stillwater. But, like Guthrie, he is known more for the Oklahoma-bred musical influence that he took elsewhere than for anything he actually produced while in the state. In 1985, LaFave moved to Austin to ensconce himself in the Texas capital's thriving music industry. For the next eight years, he hosted an open-mike songwriters' event at a coffee bar called the Chicago House. In 1992 he released his first album, and although it was titled *Austin Skyline,* it marked the beginning of a success-ful writing and performing career in which LaFave would consistently discuss the Oklahoma roots of his music—to the point that, as the biography from his label, Bohemia Beat Records, says, "many people think of him as being from Oklahoma because of his strong musical ties to the state and what he often refers to as his 'Red Dirt music.' "[11]

LaFave speaks often of his reverence for the years he spent in the Stillwater area, but his songs themselves often address the regional inspiration clearly. In songs that can be raucous rock 'n' roll, twangy balladry, or naked folk music (sometimes within the same composition), LaFave frequently refers to the Oklahoma land and locales that were his touchstones—the "farm down in red dirt country" he envisions underneath a "Ramblin' Sky"; the Mother Road "cities that never made the first song," such as "Chandler, Oklahoma" and the specific memories there—a '62 Corvette and a "girl that done me wrong"—in "Route 66 Revisited"; the "red dirt on the rise" in his easygoing cover of "Early Summer Rain" by Kevin Welch (another Oklahoma native); his frequent and heartfelt covers of Leon Russell's "Home Sweet Oklahoma" and Guthrie's "Oklahoma Hills"; and the driving country riffs of what many Red Dirt musicians hail as their anthem, "Red Dirt Roads at Night," in which LaFave begins his recollections with "My heart still lies on those windswept plains / where poor dirt farmers used to pray for rain," before recounting the mobile parties that he and his buddies had in trucks as they aimlessly drove the red-dirt county-line roads after dark. As a result, LaFave has been a popular draw at Oklahoma venues, including his yearly performances at the annual Woody Guthrie Folk Festival in Guthrie's home town of Okemah.

The third songwriter in this triumvirate is local legend Bob Childers, commonly referred to as the godfather of Red Dirt music. John Cooper, singer-mandolinist of the Red Dirt Rangers, extends that title, calling Childers "the poet laureate, the Bob Dylan of Red Dirt music." A leader of a weekly Stillwater Reunion Jam off and on throughout the '80s and early '90s at a Stillwater bar called Willie's, which featured regular guests such as LaFave, Greg Jacobs, and Garth Brooks, Childers was a struggling songwriter when LaFave met him in 1978 and encouraged him to perform, booking his first gigs at LaFave's Up Your Alley club. Born in West Virginia, Childers moved to Ponca City when he was very young; he spent much of his adult life moving from place to place, yet he always wound up back in Oklahoma, particularly around Stillwater. "I was hitchhiking my way back to Ponca City (from California)," Childers told the music Web site TexasTroubadours.com in an undated interview, "and these guys picked me up in Oklahoma City and said they'd take me to Ponca but that they had to stop off in Stillwater. When we did, I ran into a guy that I played music with in high school, and he told me about a party going on that weekend, and one thing or another happened, and I wound up going to hear a guy named Chuck Dunlap play."[12]

Childers eventually met LaFave, who produced Childers's debut album, 1979's *I Ain't No Jukebox*. In 1986, Childers moved to Nashville; Garth Brooks lived with him for a while as the two songwriters tried to push their talents on the country music industry. A few years later, Childers was in Austin, Texas, working with LaFave again. In between these travels, he was back in Stillwater, and he settled there in the early '90s. His songs—their laid-back approach, storytelling habit, and stylistic jumble—ignited and inspired the entire Red Dirt family; pick up almost any album by an artist classified as Red Dirt, and there's likely a Childers song on it. Jason Boland, for example, insists on recording at least one Childers song on every record he makes with his band, the Stragglers.

Childers's songs are recognizable by their natural imagery, above all. "When Our Work Is Done" considers the lilies of the field and their inherent—and infectious—happiness, while several of his songs mention soaring eagles and inviting deserts. Most of his characters are nameless, almost abstract—the "Babe" he addresses in "Buffalo Thunder," the unnamed family of "Mexican Morning" living "out in the dirt streets" where "simple wisdom runs so deep," the "gypsy princess" who provides such crucial company in "The Drifter's Dream," the faceless muse of his most popular song, "Restless Spirits"—save the subject of "Wile E. Coyote," whom Childers defends with a populist, positively Guthrie-esque perspective on the economics of the situation:

> All those near misses
> They ain't your fault
> The Acme Company's been rippin' you off
> Sendin' you dynamite that won't detonate
> and jet roller skates without any brakes[13]

Also, Childers sings about a lot of "old cowboys"—the one knocked off his feet in "Buffalo Thunder," the gypsy roamer subject of "Kind of a Cowboy," the carefree drifter "Cowboy Bob." Never, though, do these songs possess any of the usual country music clues to such subjects: the rhythms mosey more than they gallop; the guitar riffs reflect more than they rush. Childers's cowboys are in no hurry. They are all wanderers, like himself, like the subject of "Pathfinder," an unknown figure who sits "tall in the saddle" and waits "for the signs."

One song in particular has become a hallmark of Red Dirt concerts and a virtual anthem at the Woody Guthrie Folk Festival. It's called "Woody's Road," named by *No Depression* magazine as one of the best songs written about Guthrie. After years of his own cross-country rambling, Childers wrote the chorus:

Woody's road was rough and rocky
Woody's road went everywhere
I guess everywhere's where
He felt most at home
Just a ramblin' friend of man
Reachin' out his hand
That's why I went walkin' Woody's road.[14]

At the 2002 Guthrie festival in Okemah, Childers recalled his inspiration for the song: "In the movie *Alice's Restaurant,* Arlo gets somewhere and says, 'I'll bet Woody's road passed through here.' That phrase stuck in my mind, and four years later Greg Johnson was having one of his Woody Guthrie tributes in Austin, and I wasn't assigned one of the better-known songs, and I wasn't able to learn it very well. In self-defense, I said, 'Woody would want me to write my own damn song.' So I did, walking in a field one day." The song became a centerpiece of 2003's Ribbon of Highway Tour, a concert series organized by LaFave to present Woody's songs—and to illustrate his influence—to audiences around the country. Childers narrated the tour and performed his signature song on its stops throughout the country.

Stillwater had its share of beer halls and nightclubs where local musicians honed their chops, and the local music certainly took shape in those venues. But the crucible of Red Dirt music was just outside of town. When Childers found himself back in Stillwater in 1990, he needed a place to live, and he wound up where most Stillwater-based Red Dirt musicians either lived or spent countless hours hanging out and playing music—at the Farm. Just to the northwest of Stillwater was a piece of land LaFave first mentioned in "Red Dirt Roads at Night," the spot where his rolling gang would sometimes stop for a spell: "Those younger years never did me no harm / Always seemed to be a party at the farm."[15]

The farm mentioned in "Ramblin' Sky" is this same specific patch of land, which he goes on to endow with mystical properties:

I know a farm down in red dirt country
where magnetic properties reside
and there may be a pathway into the hollow earth
underneath that big old ramblin' sky.[16]

Like the Red Dirt genre itself, the Farm became its own capitalized capital of a particular culture. The Farm was an unused land-run claim in the floodplain of Stillwater Creek owned by a family named Schroeder. For at least two decades, the 149-acre property sat for sale—too expensive to bring up to commercial code—with a six-bedroom house and a few outbuildings in which more than sixty people, mostly musicians, lived over the course of two decades. When the Rangers' John Cooper moved into the house in 1979, the monthly rent was $100; when his roommate Dan Pierce moved out of the house in 1999, the rent had not changed. It was cheap and remote—a haven for freethinking, freewheeling musicians for the better part of two decades until it was sold to a Stillwater church at the turn of the millennium. "It was so cheap, so big, and so accessible," remembered Cooper in 2004, "and it was far enough out of town that the cops wouldn't bother us . . . pretty much. We were able to do what we wanted—play music till all hours, party, become this crazy, close family."

The Farm was a gathering place, a makeshift commune, where mostly musicians congregated to talk, drink, and play songs, and it was there that these musicians played for each other the wide variety of music that had inspired them individually. Childers lived there throughout the '90s, in a converted garage he called the Gypsy Café, named partly to be humorous, but also because he frequently opened it up as a performance space and rehearsal venue. In an undated interview at TexasTroubadours.com, Organic Boogie Band leader Stoney LaRue described the Farm as "like a hippie commune where you could dance around the fire and play music until the sun came up, or went down, and just be at home with anyone who had the same drive. There was a lot of diversity there."[17]

Brad James, of the Red Dirt band Medicine Show, remembered the diversity during a 2002 interview: "Around the fire at the Farm, you'd hear Guy Clark and [Little Feat's] Lowell George. Everyone brought what they heard and played it for each other. That's why you get so many different styles under this Red Dirt label. It just all came together into something unique, something there but not really there, like a ghost." Cooper continued, "I can't count the nights or the number of Stillwater bars where, when it hit 1:45 A.M., the rallying cry would go up: 'Party at the Farm!' And sure enough, about 2:30 in the morning, here came this procession of headlights, a crazy mix of people coming out to finish the party at the Farm. And someone had to pick up guitars, and everybody would play. It was Red Dirt music school."

Stillwater itself already encouraged this kind of interaction. "It was George Jones meeting the Rolling Stones," Cooper said during the 2002 interview. "It was Woody Guthrie meeting Bob Wills. It was, simply put, the city kid coming into contact with the country kid." The players gravitating to the Farm were mostly students at Stillwater's Oklahoma State University, a land-grant institution with the state's largest agricultural programs. This was also the early '80s, when popular culture was exerting greater influence through FM radio and cable television. Kids who had grown up listening to AM country radio were now lying around dormitory lounges watching MTV. Those especially interested in music were going to clubs and hearing tales of Stillwater music figures, from Hoyt Axton (who was at OSU in the late '50s on a football scholarship) to Gary Busey (who was a musician in the area before his acting career, which included a 1978 film role as Buddy Holly), and hearing a lot of songs being covered in nightclubs, songs by Waylon Jennings, Willie Nelson, Kris Kristopherson, and other pillars of a national movement that by then was referred to by its own often-debated and loosely applied term: "outlaw country." These players recorded albums throughout the '70s with a defiantly anti-Nashville stance—recordings with rough and unpolished edges, arrangements with a clear reverence for rock 'n' roll and the honky-tonk side of country—and by the end of the decade, their music had become a fixture of small-town jukeboxes and bar bands.

Cooper continued: "So you've got these kids who come to the school who are farmers—earth people, people who understand the country, the land—and other kids who come in from Tulsa or Oklahoma City for some of the other programs, who've got a lot of rock 'n' roll and, back then, maybe disco music. And they're all getting to be inundated with TV and modern music, so the ones who try to make their own music wind up trying to make this big stew, just trying everything imaginable, because—in many ways—college is the last place you can try that before you enter the 'real world.'"

Out of this scene and the nightly jams at the Farm came the Dylan–Bruce Springsteen mixture of LaFave; Cooper's laid-back, country-rocking Red Dirt Rangers; the earthy, back-porch country of LaRue's Organic Boogie Band; the intense fiddle playing of Randy Crouch; the old-timey bluegrass harmonies of the Farm Couple (singer Monica Taylor lived for several months "under a tarp" at the Farm); the Grateful Dead–inspired jams of Medicine Show; the straightforward folk of Greg Jacobs; the harder-rocking bar band sound of Jason Boland & the Stragglers; and the national successes of the bands Cross Canadian Ragweed and Great Divide. Regionally revered songwriter Tom Skinner also was a regular at the Farm. He played in a Stillwater band called Santa Fe, featuring a young singer named Garth Brooks, who would go on to enormous success in the '80s and '90s with a more well-heeled, Nashville-friendly approach to country music, all the while maintaining his home north of Tulsa.

Stillwater's nightclubs also were instrumental to the development of these musicians. Brandon Jenkins fondly remembered the Wormy Dog Saloon during an interview: "The Wormy Dog was awesome. A lot of guys would go there and be exposed to some of these people we're talking about. There were all kinds of music big back then in the late '80s, but one of the reasons country became such a big deal again was the Wormy Dog. They jumped on country and shoved it down people's throats, which made it hip again."

Stoney LaRue was part of that effort. Shortly after he had reached the legal drinking age and was able to go to the club, LaRue was called onto the Wormy Dog stage one night by Cody Canada of Cross Canadian Ragweed. He played one song, stepped off the stage, and was offered a job performing there. "This scene could only have developed in a small town like Stillwater," LaRue said. "You can't get away from each other; you just keep running into people. If someone's getting known, you run into them lots of places, and you can get to know them and maybe play with them. I've run into Cody (Canada) and Jason (Boland) at parties and played songs with them. And I mean, a lot. That's why everybody here plays each other's songs. I just don't think that happens to players in Nashville, which probably explains a lot of Nashville's problems."

Bob Wiles, former bassist for the Red Dirt Rangers, told the *Tulsa World,* "Every one of these acts has a songwriter in it, and no songwriter says 'hands off.' Playing someone else's song is in no way diminishing your own songwriting talent. We all play each other's songs. I remember going to see Greg Jacobs once and ending up learning a Bob Childers song from him."[18]

Randy Crouch, a versatile musician who can play fiddle and guitar simultaneously, gravitated to a club called the Bar Ditch and then to the Farm, for the same reasons: "The Bar Ditch was great. It's where Alvin Crow used to play and a lot of other Texas bands. People would go there and really listen to the music. Same thing at the Farm—whoever was playing something, people would listen to what they were doing. There were all these little cosmic moments where everyone would be listening, and getting it, and in their minds you could see they were learning from it and figuring how they were going to make it part of their own thing. I was, anyway. And pretty soon the whole bunch were friends, pulling for each other, helping each other out, just wanting what's best for each other. It made a togetherness you don't see as much in Texas and other places, other scenes. It's what makes the music different."

So the music that took form in Stillwater was characterized not only by a synthesis of musical styles, but also by a melding of personalities. The musicians who found a place in the Red Dirt circle formed a common, almost sibling, bond. They each desired to make music and to make it on their own terms, but this desire was not exclusive to helping each other succeed in performing and songwriting. It's not that the Stillwater scene has been somehow absent of cliques, infighting, and jealousy, but the overriding purpose for making music for most of these musicians was to get together, hang out, and make a peaceable environment. That transcended most other concerns, and the result has been a tightly knit, mostly friendly and fraternal group. "In a word, we're all brothers," Boland told TexasTroubadours.com. "I guess that's more than one word, isn't it?"[19]

GUTHRIE AND THE MUSIC OF
THE OKLAHOMA LANDSCAPE

Like Ripley, LaFave, and Childers, Woody Guthrie was an Oklahoman who spent much of his life moving around, often in and out of his home state. Of course, it may be ironic that the figurehead of Red Dirt music was a rascally wanderer who lived in Oklahoma for only the first seventeen years of his life— and who wrote few songs while actually in the state. In 1929, with his mother packed off to the mental hospital in Norman (long before doctors understood her Huntington's disease as a physiological, not psychological, deterioration) and his father nursing severe burns in the care of relatives in Pampa, Texas, Guthrie hitchhiked from his splintered Okemah home to the Texas coast. Soon after, he joined his father in Pampa; five years later he moved to Los Angeles; and by 1940 his home base—as much as a restless roamer like Woody could maintain a permanent address—was Manhattan. There were occasional stints up and down the valleys of California, a productive month along the border of Washington and Oregon, and several lengthy stays in the backwoods of northern Florida. But after leaving Okemah, Woody returned to Oklahoma only a handful of times for brief family visits or, in the case of a 1952 return to Okemah, a bit of bitter, self-pitying soul searching.

But throughout his life, Woody was an Oklahoman, almost to a fault. His formative years in Okemah marked him indelibly and fashioned the identity, or the basis for a persona, that he would employ for the rest of his life—and which eventually would inspire the regional pride of the Red Dirt family of musicians. Guthrie dressed like a country boy, chewed his native accent, and emphasized his well-trained folk wit. His Los Angeles radio show in the early 1930s billed him as "Oklahoma Woody." The radio show he started in August 1940 on CBS in New York was called "Back Where I Come From." Before he wrote "California Stars," one of the songs made popular on the *Mermaid Avenue* CD by Billy Bragg & Wilco in 1998, the lyric began as "Oklahoma Clouds" ("How I'd like to rest my weary bones tonight / on a bed of Oklahoma clouds").[20]

He spent much of his time writing songs about what he remembered—"Oklahoma Hills," one of his bona fide hits, co-written with cousin Jack Guthrie; "Down in Oklayhoma," in which he still used inclusive pronouns, as if he were still a resident defending his homeland:

> Some say we're first in everything worst
> Down in Oklayhoma
> I say we're first in everything best
> Down in Oklayhoma.[21]

Even specific folk tales such as the Oklahoma exploits of "Pretty Boy Floyd" or the tragedy recounted in "Don't Kill My Baby and My Son," a song he wrote in 1948 from Coney Island, New York, about the lynching of a black family by a white mob west of Okemah one year before Guthrie was born, fit this profile. (Joel Rafael, a California singer-songwriter and a regular performer at the annual Woody Guthrie Folk Festival in Okemah, put this lyric to new music on his 2002 *Woodeye* album.) By 1952, when the permanency of his hospitalization began to become obvious to him, his notebook scribblings turned not only to religion but to the other comfort to his soul: memories of home. One of his legal pads from the Brooklyn State Hospital features a short poem, "Okleye Homeye Home," complete with a small sketch of a house in a field with swirling clouds—of dust?—on the horizon:

> Take me back to my Oklahomy!
> Right on
> Back to my Oklahomey!
> Tote me back
> To my
> Okleye homeye home![22]

Guthrie, however, was not like the people he traveled with and celebrated in his songs. The hands that strummed his small-body guitars had seen little hard labor. As Harry Menig carefully illustrates in his essay "Woody Guthrie:

The Oklahoma Years, 1912–1929," Guthrie's father provided well for his family throughout Woody's early years. Although often identified as a character like those in *The Grapes of Wrath*, Guthrie states on the 1940 Library of Congress Recordings interview with musicologist Alan Lomax, "I wasn't in the class of people John Steinbeck calls the Okies. My dad was worth $40,000."[23]

The issues that Guthrie put into his songs, both the peaceable and the protest, were not so much about class as they were about community. The friendliness and cooperative spirit of his hometown and home state—the very attributes of Oklahoma celebrated by the national media in the aftermath of the 1995 bombing of the Murrah Federal Building in Oklahoma City—were what inspired him and fired the can't-we-just-get-along spirit of the majority of his songs. "Okemah was, in a sense, Woody Guthrie's foster parent," Menig says. "From its people he learned music, charity, hatred, violence, but most of all, a sense of 'getting along'—a need for self-survival through cooperation."[24]

"Everything he did and fought for had to do with the basic values he learned in Oklahoma," said Woody's daughter Nora in a 2002 interview prior to the Smithsonian traveling exhibit of her father's artifacts. "When I lecture in Oklahoma, I tell people, 'You think he's talking about other people's rights and other people's problems, but he was talking about your grandfather'— and I point at them—'and your aunt and your cousin. These were his people. Everything he wrote, especially the early songs, was about your family.' He wasn't that expanded back then. What did he know from America? All he knew was that someone's grandmother lost the farm or someone's cousin was done wrong. Everything he cared about came from his love for Oklahoma and then became explained and justified by the rest of his life. When he finally traveled to other places, he found that they were having the same problems, so he could become this spokesperson for America—the people, not the land or the landscape."[25]

And that may be an important distinction—or a misunderstanding. In my conversations with many people about Guthrie's connection to Oklahoma, and especially about Red Dirt music, there have been frequent mentions of "land" when I believe that the speaker really meant "people" or "culture." But in Oklahoma, land, people, and culture are not easily separated. Just as southern gospel music sounds the way it does because of the call and response the singers used over the distance of large fields, much of the music born from this breadbasket sounds the way it does because of the rhythm of the threshers, the steadiness of the plows, the slow threat of thunderstorms, and the great distances from here to there. If Hoyt Axton, for instance, had been born in Chicago rather than in Duncan, Oklahoma, you can bet his hit song "Never Been to Spain" would lack the dramatic spaces and subtleties that so eloquently echo a prairie boy's landlocked wanderlust.

"The unifying theme in Woody's music is that he wrote about the land he loved," said Guy Logsdon, retired director of libraries at the University of Tulsa and noted Woody Guthrie scholar, in a 2002 interview. "He played the melodies and music that came from the land he loved, from Oklahoma, one of the most culturally diverse places in America. Let's also say he modified it. He used the music he heard as a foundation and built upon it. That's what these Red Dirt guys are doing. The Garth Brookses and Jimmy LaFaves and Tom Skinners . . . they use their heritage as a foundation and build their own sound on top of it. It just happens to be a very broad foundation."

"We all live in the country," said John Cooper of his bandmates in the Red Dirt Rangers during a 2002 interview outside his trailer home on a patch of land near Glencoe. "Ben [Han, guitarist] lives in a geodesic dome. His house is not just on the land, it's in it. We spend time isolated and with the land, and that makes a difference when we get together. The other night we sat down to jam just to sit down and play, to fill the space with some music. Brad [Piccolo, singer-guitarist] and I are working on a song called 'I Live in the Country.' When you live in the city and create music, the energy of the place you're in makes it come out a certain way. That's why punk is an urban music. It's the same for the country. The fact that you're out here makes the music come out a certain way. It would be hard to write some of our laid-back, folky music in New York City. You could do it—Woody did it, but it was far different from the music he wrote on the road. Where you're at has something to do with the music you make."

BANDS OF BROTHERS

In the case of Red Dirt music, however, it's not just location, location, location. It's also the company the musicians keep. Brandon Jenkins, Yellow Dog studio owner Dave Percefull, and I were sitting in the studio control room late one night after one of the 2001 *Red Dirt Sampler* recording sessions when Jenkins said something I found startling at the time. Jenkins has seen both sides of the music industry; he was snatched up by a small Alabama-based record label, Rainy Records, in the early '90s and toured the country's boot-scootin' nightclubs in a cowboy hat and long sleeves. He eventually moved back to Oklahoma, where he "shed the hat, rolled up my sleeves [to show off his tattoos], and got back to my roots." I pressed him further for, if not a definition, at least an explanation of Red Dirt music. He had been running through the usual Stillwater country-meets-rock, city-kids-vs.-country-kids explanations, and then he was quiet for a few minutes. Eventually, he shifted forward in his chair and said, "I think that Red Dirt music isn't about music at all."

He continued, "When we talk about Red Dirt music, we always kind of go past the fact that most of us who are described as Red Dirt really don't sound anything alike. I mean, I thought about this earlier tonight listening to Brad James [& the Organic Boogie Band]. I don't sound anything like him, and neither of us sounds like the kind of upbeat, free-spirited stuff the [Red Dirt] Rangers do, and no one in this whole category does the kind of harmony and bluegrass the Farm Couple does. When you think of a musical category like bluegrass, you know immediately what just about anybody called 'bluegrass' will sound like. But you can't say that about Red Dirt, because it's not the music that binds us together. It's the communal thing, a bond that we have together, more than anything we're actually doing as singers and songwriters. It's our purpose for songwriting, not the songs themselves, that brings us together."

This is why Woody Guthrie is the figurehead of Red Dirt music, because like these modern-day Okies sitting around barrooms or camp sites—whether they be at the Farm or on the "Pastures of Plenty" Festival Stage at the annual Woody Guthrie Folk Festival in Okemah—all Woody wanted of his music was to bring common people together, regardless of what the music sounded like or what it spoke to directly. The issues he sometimes tackled in his songs were merely means to the end of all great art: uniting people with a common bond, if only for the length of a performance or as long as there was wood for the fire. The fact that this unifying notion of "great art" could be employed among ragtag Okies and dirt farmers was nothing short of revolutionary in Guthrie's day, and it's the reason Guthrie is viewed not only as the figurehead of a regional music such as Red Dirt, but as an early influence on rock 'n' roll itself.

In Guthrie's 1940s heyday, he was not usually referred to as a folk musician. Many radio disc jockeys and media writers called him a "hillbilly" musician. Art Satherley, a music producer who discovered and distributed the music of both Oklahoma native Gene Autry and Texas bandleader W. Lee O'Daniel (whose Light Crust Doughboys included Texas-born but Tulsa-famous fiddler Bob Wills), explained in a 1944 article in the *Saturday Evening Post* that "although all hillbilly music sounds monotonously alike to the urban ear-drum, it includes many types of music."[26]

The writer of the article, Maurice Zolotow, summarized Satherley's explanation of the popularity of "hillbilly" music in the early 1940s: "He explains that most Americans either live on farms today or came from farms, and that the strains of a hoedown fiddle or a cowboy plaint are their own native folk music and the one they will always respond to, no matter how far they have gone from the farm."[27]

Indeed, this fact is what endeared Guthrie to the thousands of Okies he encountered while hitchhiking and rail-hopping through California in the '30s. Displaced from their homes and farms, they almost universally welcomed Guthrie and his guitar, singing and playing the songs they had sung while working their fields in Oklahoma, Texas, and Kansas and throughout the Great Plains. As Joe Klein wrote in his 1980 biography, *Woody Guthrie: A Life:*

> They always wanted to hear the old tunes—there weren't many requests for fox trots in the box cars—and Woody was amazed by the impact the songs had. Sometimes grown men would get all misty-eyed when he sang them, and their voices would catch when they tried to sing along. The whiny old ballads his mother had taught him were a bond that all country people shared; and now, for the migrants, the songs were all that was left of the land. . . . It wasn't just entertainment; he was performing their past. They listened closely, almost reverently, to the words. In turn, he listened to their life stories, and felt their pain and anger. An odd thought began to percolate. He was one of them. The collapse of his family wasn't all that unique; these people had seen hard times, too.[28]

Guthrie's amazement at "the impact the songs had" cannot be overstated. Watching people experience the same emotions, even the same memories, as he strummed his guitar established his mission for the rest of his chaotic and troubled life. Klein's observation that Guthrie linked this experience to his own family history is not mere psychobabble, either. Born into a comfortable existence in Okemah, Guthrie grew up to see his family torn apart by financial misfortune and disease and to witness the explosive growth and crushing demise of Okemah during and after the oil boom. But as Menig wrote, Guthrie "never forgot his origins, never gave up the desire that all people might begin to live in harmony."[29]

So he set out to create that harmony, both literally and figuratively. By the time he reached New York City, after seeing so many field workers struggling in California, he took up the cause of factory workers struggling in the boroughs. Their desire to form unions fed his personal more than his political desires. The word "union" for Woody Guthrie possessed a deep well of meaning. After a youth spent in libraries in Okemah and Pampa, Texas, reading Eastern philosophy and Kahlil Gibran (Klein wrote of Woody reading Gibran's *The Prophet* and how he was "amazed to find in it a philosophy that mirrored his own exactly . . . the idea of the unity of all things"[30]), Guthrie sought to form a union of all mankind, not just machine workers or textile specialists. By the mid-'40s, as Klein points out, Guthrie was writing a series of letters from his merchant marines vessel in the Atlantic Ocean to his wife Marjorie, tracing the concept of the word "union" from the Buddha to the C.I.O. Klein claims that this was a moment of discovery for Guthrie, that he "found a spiritual rationale for his politics," and quotes a song Guthrie wrote from the boat called "Union's My Religion," in which he synthesizes his spiritual and political goals:

> I just now heard a salty seaman
> On this deep and dangerous sea;
> Talking to some Army chaplain
> That had preached to set him free:
> "When I seen my union vision
> Then I made my quick decision;
> Yes, that union's my religion;
> That I know."
> (And, that I know)[31]

In an essay Guthrie wrote about that same time, a ten-page wartime piece titled "War Songs and Work Songs," he explained how these ideas specifically related to music: "You sometimes get to wondering how many other folks feel just exactly the same about things as you do, and this is one of the things you turn on your radio for, to get to feeling like you're in touch with everybody else. . . . This makes you feel like you're 'united.' " He continues his discussion with an examination of wartime morale, then delves into why he's really fighting so hard against fascism. It's not so much the political ideas themselves that have him stirred up, it's the division they have caused. The war itself—people divided, not united—was the real cause of his agony and anger. And since he wasn't eager to fire bullets, he fired words. His songs—anyone's songs—would bring unity and peace:

A song tells you we're all the same color under our skin, and in a blood bank, the color is all the same. Hitler would like for me and you to fight each other all over the place just because we're a little different color, or shape or size, or something; but songs had ought to tell me how to like you and work with you and be your friend, and fight side by side with you. He'd like for me to fight you because you happened to be born in a different town than me, but we can make up songs and shake hands and get together and like each other a heck of a lot more because of the fact that we do come from different parts of the country. I've seen people fight just because they didn't like each other's looks or dialect or the curve of your nose; but songs have got to make us like each other more. This is getting together. This is what we mean when we say we've got a "United States" of America, it means we're "'united," that we're to-gether, and that we can work together and sing together and talk to-gether, and win this war against fascism together. And if there is such an animal anywhere in the hills of the human mind called by the name of Morale, this is what it is. Getting together.[32]

COMING TOGETHER BACK HOME

If anyone in the Oklahoma music community can speak to how we're all the "same color under our skin" and to how widely the net of Red Dirt can be spread, Doc James can. Nearly six and a half feet tall and wearing his massive dreadlocks in a huge woven cap that hung on the back of his head like a beehive, James, the Caribbean-born leader of the Tulsa-based reggae band Local Hero since the mid-'80s, certainly seemed out of place among the many cowboy boots and prairie blouses at the recording sessions for the Red Dirt Sampler. He didn't feel out of place, however.

"People are asking me how we fit in this or are in the spirit of this project, but you know, we're all alive and on the same journey. We just do them a little different," James said in an interview in a back room of Yellow Dog Studios that week in 2001. "I heard about Woody a long time ago. I didn't know he was from Oklahoma. I liked what he stood for as a musician and a person and a family man. Back in the day when he wrote songs about talking to the poorest man—that's a tradition in any culture all over the world. He did it, and he's legendary. Bob [Marley] did it. Dylan did it. Speaking to the little man, making sure he's part of the conversation, keeping the people together on some level—that's what Woody was about. . . . People think that to unite we have to agree. That's not necessarily true. We can unite when we just come to an understanding. We listen to each other, though we might not agree. We can come from different places politically, spiritually, even geographically, but we can stop and listen to each other and then be united. Music facilitates that better than anything, and Woody understood that. That's why we're here tonight. That's what all these people are trying to do."

Across the country and around the world, similar musical projects have taken place. As Guthrie deteriorated in the Brooklyn State Hospital, musicians in the burgeoning New York City folk scene organized Woody Guthrie tribute concerts. (The fact that a new generation of folk singers began mining and celebrating Guthrie's limitless legacy after he was too incapacitated to enjoy it and be properly honored in public was just one of many crushing ironies in his life.) Almost immediately after his death in 1967, two highly publicized tribute concerts were organized on the coasts—at New York's Carnegie Hall in 1968 and the Hollywood Bowl in 1970, featuring performances of Guthrie's songs by Bob Dylan, Judy Collins, Oklahoma native Tom Paxton, Odetta, Pete Seeger, and others. In 1988, Guthrie was inducted into the Rock and Roll Hall of Fame as an "Early Influence"; that same year, musicians of varying styles recorded his songs for *A Vision Shared: A Tribute to Woody Guthrie and Leadbelly,* an album that raised money for the Smithsonian Institution's efforts to buy the catalog of Folkways Records, founded a half-century earlier by one-time Guthrie producer Moe Asch. By the mid-1990s, Guthrie had been cited as an influence on rockers from Bruce Springsteen to the Clash; Springsteen and members of the Clash attended a Guthrie tribute concert at the Rock and Roll Hall of Fame in 1996—Springsteen even performed Guthrie's "Ridin' in My Car" and "Plane Wreck at Los Gatos (Deportee)."

In Guthrie's home state, however, celebration of Guthrie's legacy—and especially pride in his Oklahoma heritage—was slow in coming. In the early '50s, when McCarthyism was rampant, the Federal Bureau of Investigation started looking into Guthrie's activities, suspecting that he might be a communist. But Guthrie never joined the Communist Party; he wasn't a card-carrying anything. He played a lot of union rallies sponsored by American communists because they were supporting the workers he was singing about. Guy Logsdon, who himself has suffered accusations of being a communist simply for studying and supporting Guthrie's legacy, said, "Woody couldn't have been a communist as such because he had too good a sense of humor. . . . [Richard] Reuss, who did a great bibliography of Woody, came to Tulsa once and said he'd heard a story about Woody going to a communist meeting in

New York and asking where someone was. A man answered, 'He's not in the party anymore. We kicked him out.' 'Why?' Woody asked. 'He was diversionary.' Woody said, 'If you ask me, this whole party could stand a little diversion.' That's not diehard communism."[33]

But by the time the FBI got around to investigating him, Guthrie was so ill that, according to his declassified FBI file in the Woody Guthrie Archives, he was deemed no threat, and the investigation was dropped. His alleged communist affiliations, however, poisoned his reputation back home, particularly in the hometown in which his father, Charlie, had built a local political career decades earlier on speeches and newspaper essays bitterly denouncing the evils of socialism. Many Okemah residents became ashamed of their hometown son, and for decades they fought any attempt to celebrate his legacy. The old Guthrie home site in the southeastern part of town fell into ruins because no one would keep it up or restore it; instead, its crumbling walls have been adorned with graffiti ranging from "Damn communist" to profound poems praising his work. (Part of the reason little of the house remains is that hundreds of folk musicians from elsewhere in the country and the world have made pilgrimages to see it—and they've taken stones with them as souvenirs.) An effort to name a wing of the local library after Guthrie was rejected in the late 1960s. The city of Okemah did manage to paint "Home of Woody Guthrie" on its new water tower in 1969, but requests from the city council to have it removed continued as late as 1988, when one councilman, Bart Webb, made a motion to replace it with an American flag. The motion died for lack of a second.

It was also in 1988, however, that anti-Guthrie sentiment in Okemah and throughout the state began to wane. The same week that the Okemah City Council heard the motion to remove Guthrie's name from the water tower, a tribute concert had been given in his honor at the old Crystal Theater, where Guthrie and his mother had watched shows nearly seventy years before. The concert was led by Minnesota native Larry Long, a folk singer who had been working for four months with Okemah schoolchildren as an artist-in-residence through the Arts Council of Oklahoma and the Oklahoma Department of Education. Long had talked with the kids about Woody and about how he wrote songs about anything and everything around him; he then helped the children write their own songs about Okemah, their families, religion, and more. The event was successful enough that Long, despite some complaints and threats, was invited back for a second year. He then recorded an album: *It Takes a Lot of People* by Larry Long and the Children of Oklahoma. The following year, Arlo Guthrie performed in Okemah for the first time. "That simple little residency changed everything for Woody in his home state," said Larry McKinney, an Okemah resident who helped Long organize his events. "It opened the door to this festival."

Long and Arlo both performed at the first Woody Guthrie Folk Festival in 1998, along with LaFave, Tom Paxton, Peter Yarrow and Paul Stookey (of Peter, Paul & Mary), the Kingston Trio, and British folk rocker Billy Bragg, who opened the Okemah festival to a standing-room-only crowd in the Crystal Theater, just a few blocks away from a stretch of state highway 27 newly renamed Woody Guthrie Street. Bragg had been selected by Nora Guthrie, who had just opened the Woody Guthrie Archives in New York City, to interpret some of the hundreds of songs that Guthrie had left behind without music. The result was an album Bragg had cut with the American roots-rock band Wilco, *Mermaid Avenue,* and the fact that he was in Okemah to open the festival resonated with all involved. The distance to which Guthrie's music had traveled and the impact it had had was made clear in Bragg's performance, which, like Woody's, mixed stories and songs to relate a common idea of unity and brotherhood. It was the return of the echo to the sound's point of origin.

Red Dirt performers dominated that first festival and have been a major focus of each event since. Many of these same performers also were gathered together at Yellow Dog Studios for the 2002 *Red Dirt Sampler* sessions. Childers played "Woody's Road." Promising newcomer Jared Tyler performed "Boy From Oklahoma," a song about Woody Guthrie written by Willis Alan Ramsey. Medicine Show delivered "The Ghost of Wiley Post." The Red Dirt Rangers sang "Idabel Blues." The DVD of the event opens with footage of Jimmy LaFave introducing the Oklahoma-flavored series by singing Woody's "Down in Oklayhoma" underneath the Guthrie statue now standing in a downtown Okemah park.

"I'm just overwhelmed and in awe of Woody's contributions to my music, to all this music," Tom Skinner said after his Yellow Dog performance. "I'm happy as hell to be caught up in this. It's a certain pride, probably—pride in singing songs about Oklahoma and what people here believe in. . . . There just wouldn't be Red Dirt music if not for what Woody did. God bless him."

NOTES

1. Woody Guthrie, handwritten on a scrapbook page of Ralf Munster and Melvin Oathout, "Music on Review," *Durham (N.C.) Herald,* July 7, 1940. Clippings file, Woody Guthrie Archives, New York City.

2. Thomas Conner, "Hot Spots: Unflinchingly Folk," *Tulsa World,* January 18, 2002.

3. Greg Jacobs, "Farmer's Luck," from *Reclining with Age* (Binky Records, 2001).

The performance I am citing directly is Greg Jacobs, "Farmer's Luck," from *Songs in the Spirit of Woody Guthrie: Red Dirt Sampler, Vol. II* (Bone-Tone, 2005).

4. Brandon Jenkins, "Refinery Blues," from *Unmended* (self-released, 2002).

5. Hugh W. Foley, Jr., and George O. Carney, *Oklahoma Music Guide* (Stillwater, Okla.: New Forums Press, 2003), 410.

6. Ibid.

7. Mike Dugan, liner notes for Moses, *Moses Live* (Red Dirt, 1972).

8. John Wooley, "Headed in a Red Direction," *Tulsa World,* May 21, 2000.

9. Media bio of Steve Ripley for *Ripley* (Audium/Koch Records, 2002).

10. Author interview.

11. Bio of Jimmy LaFave for Bohemia Beat Records, http://www.bohemiabeat .com/JimmyLaFaveBio.htm.

12. From an interview posted on TexasTroubadours.com, author unknown. The site was gone as of March 2006.

13. Bob Childers, "Wile E. Coyote," from *Nothin' More Natural* (Binky Records, 1997).

14. Ibid.

15. Jimmy LaFave, "Red Dirt Roads at Night," from *Highway Angels . . . Full Moon Rain* (Jimmy LaFave, 1989).

16. Jimmy LaFave, "Ramblin' Sky," from *Road Novel* (Bohemia Beat, 1997).

17. TexasTroubadours.com, author unknown.

18. John Wooley, "Ground Swell," *Tulsa World, Spot Magazine,* January 4, 2002.

19. TexasTroubadours.com, author unknown.

20. Woody Guthrie, "Oklahoma Clouds," SONGS-3, Notebook 7, p. 74, Woody Guthrie Archives.

21. Woody Guthrie, "Down in Oklayhoma," SONGS-1, Box 1, Folder 7 (Do-Dy), Woody Guthrie Archives.

22. Woody Guthrie, "Okleye Homeye Home," SONGS-2, Woody Guthrie Archives.

23. Harry Menig, "Woody Guthrie: The Oklahoma Years, 1912–1929," in *"An Oklahoma I Had Never Seen Before": Alternative Views of Oklahoma History* (Norman: University of Oklahoma Press, 1994), 164; Woody Guthrie, *Library of Congress Recordings* [1940] (Rounder, 1992).

24. Menig, "Woody Guthrie," 163.

25. Thomas Conner, "Woody Comes Home," *Tulsa World,* February 3, 2002.

26. Maurice Zolotow, "Hillbilly Boom," *Saturday Evening Post,* February 12, 1944.

27. Ibid.

28. Joe Klein, *Woody Guthrie: A Life* (New York: Knopf, 1980), 78.

29. Menig, "Woody Guthrie," 163.

30. Klein, *Woody Guthrie,* 68.

31. Ibid., 280–81.

32. Woody Guthrie, "War Songs and Work Songs," Box 3, Folder 22, Woody Guthrie Archives.

33. Richard A. Reuss, *A Woody Guthrie Bibliography, 1912–1967* (New York: Guthrie Children's Trust Fund, 1968).

CHAPTER 7

Vietnam Veterans Against the War

ONE OKLAHOMAN'S EXPERIENCE

Gary Dotterman

Gary Dotterman was commended by the City Council of Boston, Massachusetts, on his sixtieth birthday for the "life-long sacrifices he has made to support
the philosophy of justice for all." In addition to his role in the Vietnam War—
and his subsequent activism against that war—as recounted in this essay, Dotterman has been a journalist, a trade unionist, a television host, Director of
the Center for Marxist Education in Cambridge, Massachusetts, and an active
member of the Communist Party, USA.

This has certainly been an interesting life for a Roman Catholic boy from
Tulsa, Oklahoma! Gary attended Holy Family, Horace Mann, Bishop Kelley, and
the University of Tulsa; later he also did graduate work at Goddard College.
Among the Oklahoma political campaigns he worked in were those of J. Howard Edmondson, George Nigh, and Fred R. Harris.

It is common in Oklahoma, as across much of the nation, to honor veterans.
And that is as it should be. But surely it is appropriate also to honor—and in this
case to simply tell the story of—those who, out of deep convictions, struggled
against wars, those who worked for peace.

I was born early on the morning of June 11, 1944, at St. John's Hospital in Tulsa, Oklahoma, to Joe and Pansy Dotterman. My sister, Mary Jo, was born four years later. She still lives in Tulsa, and designs and makes fabulous costumes for ballets, theatrical productions, and operas all over the world. Pansy was born into a rural Baptist family in Arkansas; her father was a union organizer, and she went on to become a meticulous and highly accomplished seamstress. Joe grew up in a Catholic foster home in North Dakota; he rode the rails as a teenager, ending up in Arkansas. Joe and Pansy met, married, and moved to Tulsa, and Joe began a long career as a union barber at the National Bank of Tulsa. They are both gone now. Our family lived in a wooden tenement building in a multiracial working-poor neighborhood on the edge of the business district of the Oil Capital of the World, Tulsa, Oklahoma.

Mary Jo and I grew up poor, although like many kids in those postwar years we were not aware of how far down the economic ladder we really were. Both of our parents worked very hard to make sure we had what we needed. Our mother sewed and sewed and sewed. Our father cut hair and fixed bicycles to pay the bills. Our clothes were handmade, without labels, and we wore them with pride—well, most of the time, anyway. Our parents made sure that we didn't use the racist language we heard all around us. They made sure that we understood that a racial slur was as bad as taking the Lord's name in vain. We were Catholics in a Baptist state, not an easy label to carry around, and not the stuff that friendships with the rich kids "across the tracks" were made of.

The Catholic Church and the Boy Scouts were my springboard into politics. I was a much-sought-after altar boy, probably showing my talents in organizing early to the priests in my church. I moved up the ranks in the Boy Scouts, becoming an Eagle Scout, and winning the coveted "God and Country" award. My father's connections to local politicos also helped me get into the loop early. In 1952, Dad introduced me to J. Howard Edmondson, a young and promising assistant district attorney. I spent hundreds of hours with him handing out flyers, stuffing envelopes, and doing anything I could to be close to the center of power. Becoming somewhat of a campaign mascot, I began to meet those folks from the other side of the tracks who had shunned me in the past. Politics began opening up new worlds to me in Tulsa, and I loved the work.

In 1958, when I was fourteen, J. Howard was elected governor of Oklahoma. I became his "hat man," a flunky position, but at fourteen it felt like a cabinet appointment to me. My new status brought me into contact with folks who were really doing things in Tulsa and in Oklahoma. In 1959, I began branching out to issue campaigns and worked on the campaign to repeal Prohibition. (Oklahoma was the second-to-last state to allow liquor sales.) I also worked on the American Federation of Labor–Congress of Industrial Organizations (AFL-CIO) campaign to stop the so-called "right to work" law. It was at this point that I began to fantasize about someday becoming governor of Oklahoma. My world kept getting better. In 1960, Governor Edmondson nominated John F. Kennedy for president at the Democratic Convention in Los Angeles. It was amazing to have been a small part of this history-making campaign. How many sixteen-year-olds organize their lives around a goal to become governor of their state? This one did!

I put together a plan: I already had experience working with the labor movement, but I needed experience in the black community, and a military record. I enlisted in the Naval Reserves, and joined the National Association for the Advancement of Colored People (NAACP) Youth Council and the Tulsa chapter of the Congress of Racial Equality (CORE). I spent days working with other teenagers, predominantly black, to integrate restaurants in Tulsa under the leadership of a Reverend Roberts. For the first time in my life, I stared into the face of racism, and learned the language of hate. It was with Homer Johnson of CORE that I worked on the preparation for Freedom Summer in Mississippi and Georgia. I attended nonviolence training for organizers that taught me the lessons of Dr. King and others. During this period of frantic activity in the South, I came into contact with amazing people, including Lorraine Hayes of the NAACP; Ed Goodwin, editor of the *Oklahoma Eagle;* Homer Johnson, from CORE; and John Lewis, with the Student Nonviolent Coordinating Committee (SNCC), who would go on to become a long-term congressman from Georgia. Not only did I learn solid organizational skills, but the seeds were sown for a new interpretation of the politics that I had learned as a boy in Tulsa. Not long after that heady summer, President Kennedy was assassinated. It took me months to recover my energy and determination. I was pleased the next year when Lyndon Johnson gave the country a huge victory, or so it seemed, in the Voting Rights Act of 1964.

Another chapter in my life began in 1964 when I received an activation notice for the U.S. Navy, and I volunteered to go to Vietnam. I was assigned to the USS *Leonard F. Mason,* homeport of Yokosuka, Japan. Our mission was to patrol the coast of Vietnam and conduct search-and-destroy missions on rural villages. I started on the ship as a lowly deckhand, but quickly made my way to a desk job as a personnel specialist. Although I was a paper-pusher, I

also, like everyone aboard, had a combat station, assigned to a 50-caliber
machine gun. Since we were told that anyone might be the enemy, I was
ordered to destroy local fishing boats and kill their crews. Our search-and-
destroy missions were intended to count the bodies of villagers, and of other
beings that had walked on the earth, after shore bombardments and boost the
body count for Secretary McNamara's war. My last shore mission in 1965 was
called "Dagger Thrust." I counted bodies and shot anything that wasn't already dead.

I spent a lot of time writing home. I came up with the idea of sending a
newsletter to family and friends. My messages home became more and more
critical of U.S. involvement in Vietnam. One of those letters, which was
published in the *Tulsa Democrat,* was entitled "What Is the United States
Facing in Vietnam?" It read as follows: "A quote I read in *U.S. News and World
Report* stunned me, 'In the few months following the rainy season we will have
about 250,000 troops in Vietnam.' The Viet Cong have no ships, or highly
trained military troops, but they do have something that is causing us to lose
this war! To understand the Viet Cong methods may be hard to do for many
people, because they are using the politics of this war against us! A good
example is given in September's issue of *Readers' Digest.* The article, entitled,
'This is Guerrilla Warfare,' points out how just 'three or four Viet Cong can
turn a village against us without the use of force!' They use facts against us,
drawing a picture of the U.S. Troops as destroyers, and that they are the
teachers, etc. We are on the wrong side! Please tell the people at home to tell
the President that we need to change our tactics to win the Vietnamese."

These were just a few of the thoughts I sent back to Tulsa in October of
1965. In December of that year, just before Christmas, we returned to Japan
for rest and relaxation. I took leave, and left for two weeks in Tokyo. I had a
wonderful time getting to know Tokyo; it was a great city, and I took full
advantage of everything it had to offer. I made many friends in Japan, and the
U.S. Navy did not welcome some of them. Those friends became a problem
for me with our government, and because of the statements I signed upon my
discharge from the Navy, I cannot talk more about them. When I returned to
the ship, I was greeted at the door to my office by a man in a black suit. He
asked me every question in the book about my time in Tokyo. I had nothing to
hide, so I answered them all. When he finished asking questions, he said that
we were going to his office. I complied. On the way off the ship, we picked up
six Marines with guns. They put me in a gray pickup truck, in a steel box in

the back. My things were packed, and I was sent to the brig. I never saw my ship again.

When we arrived at the office of the man in the black suit, I was interrogated for another fifteen hours. The room was green, with acoustic tiles on the wall, a green-shaded 150-watt bulb hanging from the middle of the ceiling, and a two-way mirror on the wall. There was a hard, straight-backed chair in the center of the room, a desk with a lie detector, and a sailor at a typewriter in the other corner. He typed everything I said. I requested a lawyer and a priest. I was told, "No way; you need to know that I can shoot you in the head, and report you as a casualty of war. You are the property of the U.S. Navy, and have NO right to shit! You can go on a hunger strike, but no one knows where you are! Understand?" I was told that I would be held for safekeeping without a charge or trial. I was placed in maximum security in the brig. I lived in a metal box, with a light on twenty-four hours a day. There was no chair, no bed, no blanket, no reading materials, and no window. I was boxed in with a light, nothing more. Food was pushed under the door twice a day, and I ate with my hands. I was there for two weeks before being moved to a cell that was near the other sailors. Although I was securely separated from everyone, I could see people, but not talk to anyone. I remained there for two more weeks. I was allowed to go to mass at the base chapel with some fellow prisoners, but at 3:30 in the morning, so that we wouldn't mix with other sailors. The guards watched every move we made, and held guns on us when we received communion.

I continually asked for a meeting with the commander, and one day I got one. Miraculously, he allowed me to be moved to a secure dorm, and I was put to work in a discipline office as a personnel clerk. My job was to deal with the records, and the reassignment of prisoners. The relative freedom of working in the office allowed me to steal time away to work on my defense. I was never charged with anything. They told me I was being held pending an investigation. In late May of 1966, out of desperation, I sent a request for a court-martial to President Johnson. I was in a holding pattern, and nothing was being done to clear, charge, or free me. My actions caused the government to take action in two weeks. Later, orders were delivered for me to return to the States on the first flight out of Japan. I literally ran to the plane. When I arrived in San Francisco, I was given an honorable discharge. I had volunteered to go to Vietnam, but I returned to the States feeling like a war criminal—not because of my friendships in Tokyo, but because of my complicity with the heinous crimes we committed in Vietnam.

My dilemma in attempting to reconcile what had happened in Vietnam and my part in it was that I had believed that we were there for the "land of the free and the home of the brave"—that Americans did only good things for people around the world, and the thing that made us better than any other country was that we were a free nation with rights and laws that protected those rights. If there were problems, we just needed to change our leaders, or at least inform them. I returned to "the world" with a new view of my country and my government. I had the feeling that the president and the Congress were betraying us, and the knowledge of what was happening ten thousand miles from our home. I knew that lies were the truth and the truth lies. A soldier was something for the military to use and then throw away, and was not worth a deposit. I knew that my brothers in 'Nam were killing and being killed for someone else's ego, as well as profits, not for freedom. The odor of burning human bodies is something that will stay with me for the rest of my life, along with the memories of women and children crying for help in their homes that we had set fire to. I must force the visions from my mind every night before I can sleep.

I returned to Tulsa in June of 1966. I was drunk much of those first few months at home, trying to obliterate the memories I had carried back with me. Folks would want to buy me drinks, find out what it was "really like in 'Nam," but they didn't want the facts. They didn't want to hear the truth of what Uncle Sam was really doing. Eventually I found a job, and enrolled at the University of Tulsa. Folks on campus began to probe, asking real questions. 'Nam vets started to appear on campus, and I was not alone. In July of 1966, a few of us decided to organize a peace vigil at City Hall. The Saturday after the Fourth of July, eight people stood for two hours holding signs: "Stop the War," "Think," "Support Our Troops—Bring Them Home." Mine read "I am a Vietnam Veteran—Help Stop This War." Most people yelled at us, calling us traitors and worse. Two Vietnam vets approached me tentatively, quietly, and they wanted to talk. We did, and decided to meet to talk some more.

I needed to return to my roots. I drifted back to my old buddies in the Tulsa Democratic Party. They asked me to be the chair of the Tulsa County Democratic Party, and to provide leadership in the governor's campaign. I was asked to help advance President Johnson's trip to Oklahoma in late August of 1966. This was the beginning of my double life in Tulsa. By day I walked the walk and talked the talk of the Tulsa Democratic Party, and by night I met with a small group of people from the civil rights movement, some All Souls Unitarian Church students, and others from Temple Israel to plan the antiwar campaign in Tulsa. The irony of my position was great. At the LBJ rally later that week, I watched as my peace movement friends were beaten on the picket line at the rally that I had helped organize. The peace movement in Oklahoma had begun.

We started small, two or three of us traveling around the state, visiting campuses and churches, and singing and talking about the war. I told the truth about what was really happening in Vietnam. Some listened, some didn't. Some yelled, and yelled, and yelled some more. These efforts began attracting others. On the campus of the University of Tulsa, a larger antiwar presence was taking shape. Vietnam vets began to gather and organize. The very beginnings of the Oklahoma Vietnam Veterans Against the War (VVAW) were germinating in October of 1966.

The peace effort began to flourish on other campuses as well. The University of Oklahoma at Norman was the site of a large and powerful movement. Because I was a newly returned vet, I was asked to speak at rallies and meetings. My stories seemed to have a great impact on people. It was difficult speaking about my experiences in Vietnam. I remember the first big demonstration in Tulsa, in June of 1967, on Tulsa City Hall Plaza at the new work of public art entitled *Amity*. The crowd was made up of a dozen vets, along with students, Quakers, Unitarians, Catholics, and other people from the Tulsa activist community. We hung a combat flag from World War II on the side of City Hall. Speaking in front of a cardboard coffin, we planted a tree for peace, and vets testified to what we were doing in 'Nam. This demo drew more than two hundred people from across the northeastern parts of Oklahoma. That was a lot of people for Oklahoma! Tom Flowers, from Houston, Texas, spoke for the War Resisters League; it was later revealed that he was an FBI agent.

Those small, informal groups of Vietnam vets that came together in Tulsa, Claremore, Norman, and other communities provided the early support for the formation of veterans' centers and for improved health care for vets in Oklahoma. The groups were loosely connected, unaware that they were part of a national movement of Vietnam vets that was forming across the country. The national organization of Vietnam Veterans Against the War was born at a 1967 demonstration in New York City. Our little group in Oklahoma joined them, and sent a small delegation to a national meeting in Denver, Colorado.

As we made appearances around the state, other vets started to speak with us. We all had similar feelings and stories, so it felt better to be with each other. No other veterans' groups in Oklahoma made us feel a part of them. It was as if we were from different worlds. Groups such as Veterans of Foreign Wars and the American Legion would ask Vietnam vets to come in, but hanging around telling sanitized war stories was painful, and certainly not what we needed to work out our anger and guilt at the time.

The movement continued to grow. In 1970, VVAW, with a membership of about six hundred, confronted the national convention of the American Legion in Portland, Oregon. Later in the year, vets gave public witness to their experiences in Vietnam on a walk from Morristown, New Jersey, to Valley Forge, Pennsylvania. The growth of the movement led to the founding of a national action called the "Winter Soldier Investigations," in which groups of vets gathered in locales across the country to speak out about their experiences in 'Nam. Congressional hearings and a march of thousands of vets followed in April of 1971. John Kerry from Massachusetts emerged as a visible leader at this rally, and later testified at a quickly organized congressional hearing. My Oklahoma vet buddies helped to organize a contingent from the region. There were more than two hundred of us from Oklahoma, Kansas, and Arkansas. The trip to Washington energized us as a group. Our voices as vets grew louder in the heartland, bearing witness to the fact that this war was wrong, and that our country had lied to us and was continuing to lie to the American people. Our work helped to bring more Oklahomans into the antiwar movement. Our voices, along with many others, had a direct effect on our junior senator from Oklahoma, Fred R. Harris. When he declared himself against the war, and started to vote that way, things in Washington began to change. Senator Harris looked to the Oklahoma vets for support with his constituents at home, and collectively as a driving force in Congress.

All was not without problems as vets began to gain power and recognition in the antiwar movement. J. Edgar Hoover was still a dark presence in the country, and made sure that the FBI infiltrated the VVAW. It took time to figure out, but we discovered that the FBI had been paying a VVAW coordinator from Oklahoma, Arkansas, and Kansas. He would try to provoke violence in the rank and file of the vets. He would corner some vet, then talk about a need to collect weapons and train for a rebellion. He spoke to vets about how it might be a good idea to kill a senator and congressman. In some cases he was successful in convincing a brother to take up more violent ideas, but that didn't stop the progress of the VVAW.

In the end, when I look back on those early days of organizing the VVAW, I can see that the core of what was going on was the connecting of small groups of vets with each other. We were connected for life by our horrible memories. Those memories could not be shared with family, friends, or lovers. Combat vets banded together at home in the same way they had banded together in Vietnam. Many of us spent years pushing those memories away with booze and drugs. Some of us were totally unable to have healthy relationships with anyone, let alone a loved one. The hurt took many years to subside. For some of us it will last forever, but we must remember that our fight to end the war was important and played a major role, not just in Oklahoma but in the United States as a whole, in moving the people to end the Vietnam War. This battle was the best of the worst, and we as vets must not forget that when we began to speak, the heartland of America began to listen.

CHAPTER 8

Nonviolent Civil Disobedience
in Oklahoma

THE CAMPAIGN AGAINST NUCLEAR POWER

Elizabeth D. Barlow

Elizabeth D. Barlow has lived in an intentional community in Snow, Oklahoma, for twenty-five years, where she is a yoga instructor and massage therapist. She has spent much of her life working for causes she believes in, including the prevention of domestic violence, which she wrote about in this volume's predecessor, and the prevention of nuclear power, which she writes about here.

Carrie Dickerson and her organization, CASE (Citizen's Action for Safe Energy), get a lot of credit for stopping the nuclear power plant proposed near Inola by Public Service Company of Oklahoma in the 1970s. An article by Russell Ray in the *Tulsa World* on May 11, 2003, almost made it sound as though she had done it all alone. (Carrie Dickerson "is credited with stopping Black Fox," wrote Ray; further, "She delayed the project for years through numerous legal challenges.") There is no need here, and certainly no desire, to diminish Dickerson's accomplishment; she did indeed play an important role in the struggle, and it is admirable that even into her eighties, she continued speaking out about the dangers of nuclear power and the importance of emphasizing alternative energy sources such as the wind. But she did not stop Black Fox alone.

Elizabeth Barlow tells here of the role played by the Sunbelt Alliance, a group of predominantly young, nonviolent direct action advocates; especially she tells the personal/historical story of her role in that organization.

Nonviolence appeals to a universal law that transcends the legalities of any particular nation or State. The movement to abolish slavery, the struggle of women to achieve equal rights, and the mobilization to end the Indo-China war are all examples of people organizing nonviolently to end social injustice.

—*Sunbelt Alliance Handbook, p. 1*

W hen I was eleven or twelve years old, I remember riding in the car with my mother and asking her about nuclear power plants. Her answer was simple: "I don't think it's smart to build something they don't know how to tear down." Although it was the first argument I had heard against these power plants, that logical answer remains prominent in my mind.

I was nineteen when the Public Service Company of Oklahoma (PSO) began the construction of the Black Fox nuclear power plant near Inola, Oklahoma. It was the fall of 1978, and I was a student at the University of Tulsa. I first heard of the nuclear power plant while attending a Students' Progressive Caucus meeting. Linda Overbey spoke that day, informing us about the upcoming nonviolent civil disobedience training planned at her house. Training was required for anyone who would be attending the nonviolent direct action planned in October. Linda explained that there were two options for participants: you could break the law, trespass, and get arrested, or you could elect to stay at the camp and help with whatever activities were needed to support those choosing to trespass.[1] Either way, all participants were required to take the seven-hour nonviolent civil disobedience training. I decided that day, at nineteen years of age, to become involved with the Sunbelt Alliance.

As I write this, I am forty-five years old. Sitting here surrounded by my teenage journals and newspaper articles from twenty-five years ago, it becomes clear that I am also interpreting history. I was only one of hundreds of people who made the Sunbelt Alliance happen.[2] I am not one of the founders; I did not design the original structure. This cannot be a complete history of the Sunbelt Alliance, or a complete history of the proposed Black Fox nuclear power plant. Rather, it is a history of my personal involvement in the Sunbelt Alliance during a nine-month period in 1978 and 1979.

Specifically, this is the story of three separate acts of nonviolent civil disobedience that were carried out during those months. Remarkably, there were
704 arrests in protest of nuclear power in Oklahoma during that short span of
time. Numerous events are omitted from this essay—rallies, legal proceedings,
and corporation commission hearings, city council meetings, neighborhood
canvassing, speaking engagements, and lots of leafleting, activities that kept
the Alliance busy and were necessary to a successful campaign.[3] I am choosing
to focus on the civil disobedience and to discuss the precepts of nonviolence
incorporated by the Sunbelt Alliance that may be of relevance and unique to
Oklahoma sociopolitical history.

The civil disobedience campaign in Oklahoma owes its beginnings to Karen Silkwood. Silkwood was a twenty-eight-year-old woman who died in a
traffic accident in 1974 while she was en route to a meeting with a *New York
Times* reporter to turn over documents on safety and health violations at a
Kerr-McGee plant in Oklahoma. Fortunately, the Silkwood team of attorneys
and organizers who came to Oklahoma had experience with the national
antinuclear movement. Lynda Jacobs was one of the original Sunbelt Alliance
organizers:

> We formed the Sunbelt Alliance in 1978 as an umbrella organization that
> brought together all the entities working to stop construction at that
> time. The Silkwood folks brought with them the knowledge of how to
> organize a nonviolent civil disobedience action. They were well in-
> formed about the national movement, allowing us the opportunity to
> bring in antinuclear entertainers and raise money as well as awareness
> fast. This made a big impact in Oklahoma. They trained a few of us, and
> then we started training folks across the state. They were very knowl-
> edgeable about organizing and brought critical wisdom that allowed
> Sunbelt Alliance to blossom quickly.[4]

My decision to participate in the action developed slowly. In the beginning,
I did not know if I wanted to be arrested. However, I did know that the current
pace of construction was scary. It is my view that PSO was choosing not to
educate the public about the dangers of nuclear power. The real possibility of
accidents, the lack of knowledge of long-term effects, the problem of how to
dispose of spent fuel rods, the human costs of producing more plutonium,[5]
the risks involved in transportation of radioactive materials, and the cost of
nuclear compared to other forms of energy were not being discussed by PSO.
It seemed to me that the *people* should get to decide about this. I was angry

that a corporation could make a decision about something that would have lasting and devastating effects on Oklahomans for generations. I dearly loved Oklahoma, and I did not like the thought of an accident or of the problems that disposal of spent fuel rods would cause my state.

Evidently there were many who agreed with this position, and fortunately, it was not up to PSO; the burden of proof was on us as citizens. I felt I had a responsibility to do something—fast. The way I saw it, PSO would have the atrocity built before any real action could be taken. Although I believed working within the system to be valuable, I felt that my time would be better spent with nonviolent social change. The Sunbelt Alliance strictly adhered to the theories of nonviolent civil disobedience. This stance was consistent with my ethics, making it easier for me to be involved in this type of movement.

While considering the options, I asked many questions of others—and myself: "Should I trespass or support?" "If arrested, will I have a record?" "Is it worth missing classes and work?" Although my mother and stepfather participated in Sunbelt Alliance activities, and my brother was a member of an affinity group, some members of my family were vehemently opposed to my participation, making the decision more difficult. In the end, my decision to trespass was based on my feelings about children. As I wrote in a journal at the time: "If I cannot come to a decision through other means, I will do it for the children here and to be. They know not what we thrust on them and are innocent victims."[6]

Since nonviolence training was required of anyone who wanted to participate in the occupation, Linda Overbey and Jeff Bagget spent a full day one Saturday training a group of us in nonviolent civil disobedience. The twenty-five or more of us at that first meeting later dubbed ourselves the Foxhounds affinity group. There were already a number of affinity groups in existence and more waiting to be trained.

It was explained that affinity groups were the backbone of the occupation. "Affinity groups have several functions. They are much like tribal communities and therefore serve as a source of support for their members and a family within which one can feel a continual sense of solidarity throughout an action that will be full of tension and possible violence."[7] Our affinity group consisted of students, professors, musicians, carpenters, artists, and various professionals. We grew close quickly, as a lot of planning and readiness is necessary to a successful occupation.

At that time in history, all occupations of proposed nuclear power plants in the United States had terminated within twenty-four hours. We were going over the fence on a Saturday with every reason to believe that we would be arrested immediately; but there was a remote possibility that we would not be arrested until the following Monday, when construction was scheduled to begin. We had to pack everything we felt was necessary as an affinity group for a four-day camping stay. For the next three weeks, we prepared ourselves body and mind for the occupation.

We eventually occupied the Black Fox nuclear power plant construction site together on October 7, 1978. Those of us who ignored the "No Trespassing" sign on the property owned by PSO did so because we felt we had no choice. We backpacked into the site, being careful not to harm the environment—we had even built ladders to go over the fence. As is consistent with nonviolent civil disobedience theory, "If necessary, we will be prepared to move the entire occupying force over the fences without putting one pound of stress on one strand of wire."[8] We followed faithfully over the fences as our affinity groups lined up and were arrested by Sheriff Amos Ward of Rogers County. I was one of 348 people arrested that day.

The Black Fox occupation made a big splash in the national news. The Oklahoma occupation was one of four campaigns scheduled around the nation that day. The others were carried out by the Paddlewheel Alliance at the Marble Hill plant site in Indiana, by the Clamshell Alliance at Seabrook, New Hampshire, and by the Bailey and Chiwarkee Alliance at the Zion Reactor site in Zion, Illinois.

The Foxhounds were jubilant after that first occupation. As consumers, we found the occupation empowering because we were responding to a lack of voice. The utility company was acting exploitatively by disregarding the health and safety of the very consumers who were paying for the product. The consumers had been heard.

My journal entry dated October 9, 1978, reads, "Sunday night/Monday morning after the occupation at Black Fox. I have spoken. There is more to do but I have done much so far. I could never do enough, but for the first time I am satisfied with what I HAVE DONE."

The Foxhounds continued meeting after the occupation. It seemed that affinity group meetings were a necessity for all of us. In those living rooms we formed an everlasting union of minds and hearts. We met tasks with exuberance and enthusiasm because we were committed to the principles of our goal, as well as to each other. I was surprised to find that my nineteen-year-old opinion was as respected as the opinions of those who held doctorates. This experience affected how I perceived the world, and it changed me forever.

During this era in the United States, antinuclear movements were following the precepts of Gandhi's philosophy of nonviolent civil disobedience.
"Gandhians break laws perceived to be unjust (civil disobedience), but adhere
to the principle of non-injury (*ahimsa*), refusing to hurt, humiliate, or hate
another person; they seek to convert, not to conquer, the opponent."[9] This
technique of action is different from traditional methods for strikes and
demonstrations, in that the campaign has to follow certain rules of conduct,
particularly with regard to preparation for civil disobedience and communication with the adversary. The model allows for a prescription to follow,
rather than a description of the problem. For example, hours and hours of
work were spent in communication with PSO, law enforcement, and the
prosecuting attorney.

In her book *Conquest of Violence: The Gandhian Philosophy of Conflict*,
Joan V. Bondurant lists the steps for a successful campaign. Step four is the
"*issuing of an ultimatum:* A final strong appeal to the opponent should be
made explaining what further steps will be taken if no agreement can be
reached. The wording and manner of presentation of the ultimatum should
offer the widest scope for agreement, allowing for face-saving on the part of
the opponent, and should present a constructive solution to the problem."[10]
Consistent with Gandhi's teachings, the Sunbelt Alliance issued the ultimatum in *Stop Black Fox,* a newsletter printed by the Alliance and the *Tulsa Free
Press:* "We of Sunbelt Alliance are giving PSO two options in this action: 1)
Stop construction of Black Fox immediately or 2) arrest us." Continuing on
page 4 under the heading "Why Occupy," the newsletter states,

> For the past three years, Citizen's Action for Safe Energy (spearheaded
> by Carrie Dickerson) has been the people's advocate in the courtrooms
> of Tulsa and Oklahoma City in a tremendous effort to bring the invali-
> dities and inconsistencies of Nuclear Power before the various City,
> County, State and Federal regulatory agencies. The irresponsibility and
> special interest coercion of these agencies was made most apparent
> when they recently issued Public Service Company of Oklahoma a Lim-
> ited Work Authorization. Therefore, Sunbelt Alliance has chosen to
> occupy the Black Fox Site in an effort to stop the construction of a
> random death machine by nonviolently placing our bodies on the line.

Countless hours were spent in planning the occupation and in negotiations
with law enforcement. Rule number seven in Bondurant's book states that
there should be a "*persistent search for avenues of cooperating with the ad-*

versary on honorable terms: Every effort should be made to win over the opponent by helping him . . . thereby demonstrating sincerity to achieve an agreement with, rather than a triumph over, the adversary."[11] Many hours of negotiations were spent with the sheriff and county prosecutor. During a meeting with Sid Wise, chief prosecutor of Rogers County,

> we affirmed our commitment to the principles of nonviolence to all parties and personally assured Sid Wise that the Sunbelt Alliance will cooperate with him in the prosecution of any participant in the October 7 action who does not adhere to the nonviolence guidelines we have set forth. These guidelines are: 1) Everyone must receive preparation in nonviolent direct action before taking part in the action—either in support or as an occupier; 2) Everyone must be a member of a recognized affinity group; 3) No damage or destruction of Public Service Company property; 4) No running at any time; 5) No dogs; 6) No drugs or alcohol; 7) No weapons of any kind; 8) No breaking through police lines; 9) No verbal abuse of police or security guards; 10) In case of confrontation, we will sit down.[12]

Following the archetype of other antinuclear organizations, the Sunbelt Alliance's affinity groups consisted of approximately twenty individuals who were trained together and would stay together during the occupation; each affinity group chose a spokesperson who could vote at a larger Alliance meeting; decisions were reached through a relentless commitment to the process of hearing everyone's opinions, a process that replaced "voting" with the seeking of *consensus:*

> Consensus is a process for making group decisions without voting. Agreement is reached through a process of gathering information and viewpoints, discussion, persuasion, a combination of synthesis of proposals and/or the development of totally new ones. The goal of the consensus process is to reach a decision with which everyone can agree. Consensus at its best relies upon persuasion rather than pressure for reaching group unity.[13]

Information was carried back to individual affinity groups by the spokesperson and others attending Alliance meetings.

Soon after the October 7 occupation, the Sunbelt Alliance started talking about protesting a reactor core that was en route to Wolfe Creek, Kansas. There were reports that it was to be placed on a faulty concrete pad. The reactor was scheduled to come up the Arkansas navigational channel on a barge and would be docked at the port of Catoosa (between Inola and Tulsa). One night at a Foxhound meeting, we amusingly discovered that most of us did not want to stand up on the hillside and chant "No nukes!" to a time bomb. But we wanted to block that oven and could not, in clear conscience, do it any other way. So around October 30, the Foxhounds stood up in an Alliance meeting and said we wanted to block the nuclear core with our bodies. According to my journal, heated discussion ensued between members who wanted to protest without civil disobedience and the Foxhounds and others who felt that being arrested would be more effective. We obtained permission and began to organize the action to block the reactor core.[14]

The details of this action were unique in that we considered using boats to blockade the reactor core in the water. As the time grew closer, the weather turned very cold, and the entire navigational channel in that area froze. We chose instead to descend an icy slope on a rope and block the barge as it docked. "The 17 who were arrested crossed under a fence erected around the dock and slid down the icy slope, clinging to a rope tied to a fence post. Less than an hour after the barge had arrived, 17 Sunbelt members were arrested by Rogers County Sheriff Amos Ward and three deputies."[15] The loud sound of the barge cracking the ice as it approached us was eerie and dramatic.

On March 28, 1979, the Three Mile Island nuclear power plant accident changed the sense of urgency in a way that none of us would have wished. As noted in my journal that day,

> Brian Hunt and Hal Rankin were in a trial concerning civil disobedience in relation to the Reed Report. We were picketing outside the Federal Building where their trial was to be held. Some guy walked up to us and said, "Have you heard about the accident?" A flame went up through my body. Brian just called and said "they are evacuating pregnant women and children within a 50-mile radius." What right have they to make people fall down helplessly in front of a death machine run by them for their private abundance of wealth? A group of us are going down to PSO to demand they respond to the Three Mile Island evacuation announcement.

The accident at Three Mile Island strengthened the Oklahoma movement. Three Mile Island, coupled with the success of the first occupation and lots of subsequent organizing, brought many new members and sympathizers to the Alliance.

Kyle Cline, Kathryn Greene, and I took on the task of becoming staff to prepare for a second occupation. We were single college students with part-time jobs and lots of enthusiasm. Many (if not all) of the other members worked hard as well; there were now more than seven hundred of us, so there was a lot of preparation. Organizing phone lists, training new members, holding press conferences, maintaining a speakers' bureau—all this kept us very busy, and our prized offset copy machine buzzing.

On June 2, 1979, in accordance with the International Days of Protest, the Sunbelt Alliance, in conjunction with other groups in the United States and around the world, planned to participate in a nonviolent occupation of Black Fox Station. A May 16 journal entry reads,

> My body and I are not friends; we are not even speaking. Long days, long nights. Just eating, sleeping, and the occupation. The most important thing is my work right now. First, my own participation in the occupation counts on my work, then everyone else's participation. Consequently, I am obsessed. My brain is continually organizing and reassessing. Even in my sleep: I wake up still in the Sunbelt, I slept with the Sunbelt. But—I'm good.

Finally, the weekend of the occupation arrived. We went out early on Friday to set up registration tables. It started raining hard that evening, and most of us had water in our sleeping bags and tents. Early the next morning, it was still pouring rain and very chilly for June. I ran around handing out trash bags to those who did not have rain gear. We were hit with the one thing we had not covered in our training sessions: cold weather in Oklahoma during June. We trudged, and I do mean trudged, on a lengthy hike through cold rain, mud, and water. Unfortunately, a number of people had to be hospitalized for hypothermia.

As before, we followed Sheriff Amos Ward to the booking trailers. Some of the press was arrested on June 2. According to my journal that day, "We started chanting 'freedom of the press' as they walked up the steps to the trailers, and slowly one by one they turned around with a sudden look of understanding. I will never forget that."

Leading us over the fence during this occupation, as well as the preceding 1978 occupation, was a group of Native Americans. I was proud that the Alliance was inclusive of many types of people, of all ages and economic backgrounds. American Indians were well represented and served in leadership roles, while African Americans were underrepresented, as was consistent with national campaigns.

Influence from the American Indian community was strong from the beginning within the Sunbelt Alliance. When asked how this began, Lynda Jacobs said, "We were going to a sweat lodge where they were openly accepting non-Indians. They became involved in the antinuclear work. This Native American leadership brought the connection of the spiritual component for Sunbelt Alliance. They did a prayer before the occupation and led us over the fence."[16]

There were 339 people arrested that day in 1979. As with all the other arrests, we were charged with misdemeanors. Our hard-working legal team continued to work with the courts on our behalf, volunteering hours and hours' worth of legal expertise, research, and negotiations. They defended us expertly, and they did it with great heart and soul.

According to Joan V. Bondurant, Gandhi's method provides the means through which an individual can come to know what he or she is and what it means to evolve. "Dogma gives way to an open exploration of context,"[17] she states. I believe that this concept "took" with me. The Sunbelt Alliance began a process that still shapes my life. I learned that I could change the world and eradicate problems. I learned that the scope of the political landscape is mine to alter. This made it seem plausible to open a battered women's shelter, to begin a sexual assault program for universities, to live for twenty-five years in an intentional community that has always worked on a consensus model, and to live in a way that is true to my ideals. I am not alone. We found each other in the Sunbelt Alliance, and this experience has fostered many community actions, organizations, and programs.

The Sunbelt Alliance achieved its goals. Many of us wanted this energetic bundle of people to stay together and become active in other issues. There were many heated discussions as we tried to determine a way to keep the Alliance active, perhaps with other political agendas. At the time, I was upset that we could not agree on a new path. But I have come to believe now, some twenty-six years later, that the Alliance did exactly what it set out to do. We have no nuclear power plants in Oklahoma!

One of the good things about living in a conservative, largely rural state is that there is no competition among groups working for radical social change, so when one comes along, sympathizers rush to join. The Sunbelt Alliance brought together people willing to work very hard and make sacrifices for the cause. I believe that working together in such a community brought out the best in all of us. But the concept of the *campaign* is what fueled and nursed the Alliance. "It excludes the use of violence," Gandhi asserted, "because man is not capable of knowing the absolute truth and therefore not competent to punish."[18]

To have had a blueprint for organizing was critical to Oklahoma. The techniques employed by antinuclear activists, and the direction the Silkwood organizers provided, were crucial to our success. I personally believe that the effectiveness of this model made the Oklahoma campaign successful. These nonviolent civil disobedience campaigns were unique in Oklahoma— 704 people were arrested in nine months. To have so many people involved in an organized campaign of resistance to a corporate decision may be unique in Oklahoma history.

NOTES

1. Each group was required to have "support people" who stayed at the campsite. "Offsite support will strategically make a lengthy 'wait out' possible," according to the Sunbelt Alliance and *Tulsa Free Press* newsletter dated September/October 1978. Support people were vital in that they could maintain communication with the media, provide rapid transportation, and communicate with families.

2. There were a great many individuals who contributed to and were an integral part of this story. In the interest of efficiency, I have for the most part not used names unless they help tell my story.

3. Citizen's Action for Safe Energy was critical to the legal intervention against the nuclear power plant. For a personal historical perspective of this organization, see Carrie Dickerson, *Aunt Carrie's War Against Black Fox Nuclear Power Plant* (Tulsa, Okla.: Council Oak Publishing Co., 1995).

4. Interview with Lynda Jacobs, May 1, 2004.

5. Most processing plants are located in impoverished, predominantly nonwhite areas. Some uranium mines are located on American Indian reservations. I have personally seen children playing near radioactive mill tailings on one reservation.

6. Journal entry, September 9, 1978, found in a journal that I and my friend and roommate Kathryn Greene kept together.

7. *Non-violence,* a Sunbelt Alliance handbook explaining the concepts of non-violence as it pertains to the occupation of the proposed Black Fox nuclear power plant. The document is undated, but refers to the October 1978 occupation.

8. *Stop Black Fox* (Tulsa: The Sunbelt Alliance) and the *Tulsa Free Press,* September/October 1978, 2.

9. Virginia Coover et al., *Resource Manual for a Living Revolution* (Philadelphia: New Society Publishers, 1977), 14.

10. Joan V. Bondurant, *Conquest of Violence: The Gandhian Philosophy of Conflict* (Princeton, N.J.: Princeton University Press, 1958), 40.

11. Ibid., 39.

12. *Stop Black Fox*, 1.

13. Coover et al., *Resource Manual for a Living Revolution*, 14.

14. The next night, Halloween, fourteen members stole into the construction site before dusk and chained themselves to bulldozers. Although this action was not approved by the Sunbelt Alliance, the fourteen got good press and became known as the "Halloween 14."

15. Bob Bledsoe, "17 Protesters Are Arrested at Barge Site," *Tulsa Tribune*, January 4, 1979, 1D.

16. Interview with Lynda Jacobs, May 1, 2004.

17. Bondurant, *Conquest of Violence*, 236.

18. Ibid., 40.

CHAPTER 9

Under the Rainbow

THE SEARCH FOR GLBT EQUALITY IN OKLAHOMA

Christine Pappas

Christine Pappas holds both the Ph.D. and J.D. from the University of Nebraska. Since 2001, she has been Assistant Professor of Political Science at East
Central University. In 2004, she was selected for the university's Teaching Excellence Award, and in 2005 she was named the Oklahoma Political Science
Association's Teacher of the Year. Pappas edited Dorothy Thomas's collected
short stories, *The Getaway and Other Stories,* and wrote *More Notable Nebras-
kans.* She was also the founding editor of *Plains Song Review,* an interdisciplin-
ary journal. Her research interests are public law, minority group representation, and political science pedagogy.

  Most of Pappas's research addresses questions of how minority groups—
including women, African Americans, and gay, lesbian, bisexual, and transgendered people—are treated in a democratic society where decisions are based
on majority rule. Most relevant to her contribution here is her biweekly political
column for the *Gayly Oklahoman.*

The rainbow is a symbol of pride adopted by the worldwide GLBT (gay, lesbian, bisexual, and transgender) movement. Rainbow stickers adorn queer people's cars, and rainbow flags can be seen flying at gay community centers and stores. More than symbolic of pride, the rainbow serves as a powerful metaphor for the difficulties inherent in GLBT political success. When they are presented together, the colors form a beautiful and meaningful array, but independently, each color lacks strength and meaning.

Divisiveness and a lack of shared vision among GLBT groups in Oklahoma are one roadblock to achieving political goals as the GLBT community seeks beneficial policy from both the courts and the political branches of government. Interest groups that lack resources and consensus, as well as the general public's support, will have trouble competing against stronger, better endowed groups.[1]

One of the most important issues facing GLBT people is securing funding for HIV/AIDS research and care, and this issue underscores just why it is so important for GLBT groups to be able to pull together for political success. The possibility of success was called into question on November 2, 2004, by the landslide passage of State Question 711, a broadly written bill that bans same-sex marriage, as well as the undefined "benefits of marriage."

The first gay person in Oklahoma lived here long before the Stonewall Inn riots of 1969.[2] There were "two-spirited people" (as homosexuals are called by some Native Americans) as well as both closeted and "out" Boomers, Sooners, and settlers. Oklahoma City was home to a softball team called the "Sooner Queens" in the 1940s and 1950s, and there were many clubs where gays could drink and dance.

Being publicly gay, however, was and is not without its risks. A former proprietor of a popular lesbian bar recalls that in the 1950s, "police would take tag numbers of cars at bars and inform people's work places, and women could be arrested for playing poker and dancing together."[3] Portrayals of homosexuality in the statewide newspaper the *Oklahoman* were uniformly negative, commonly emphasizing the sexual orientation of criminals and reporting on how many gay people were ousted from federal government service in the 1950s.

Lynn Riggs, the gay Cherokee author of the play *Green Grow the Lilacs* (upon which the smash hit and iconic musical and movie *Oklahoma!* are based), lived and created his art in the context of early 1900s Oklahoma. In his essay "Lynn Riggs as Code Talker: Toward a Queer Oklahomo Theory and the

Radicalization of Native American Studies," Craig Womack, a gay Creek/ Cherokee, demonstrates that Riggs could not reveal his homosexuality in his letters because he found Oklahoma (and the country at large) to be "an extremely hostile and oppressive society from which he had to hide most of his life, erasing his gay identity from his public identity in order to survive."[4] He and thousands of other Oklahomans lived out their lives "in the closet."

For a variety of reasons—including homosexuals' closeted status—it is impossible to know the exact size of the GLBT population in Oklahoma. We do know, however, that the 2000 U.S. Census recorded 5,763 same-sex couples in Oklahoma (594,391 nationally), which is probably an undercount.[5] Extrapolations made by Alfred Kinsey in 1956 resulted in his theory that 10 percent of any population is gay; however, the more accepted percentage, even among opponents of gay rights, is somewhere around 2.8 percent for men and 1.4 percent for women.[6] These figures were also cited by Lambda Legal, a gay rights legal defense organization that argued on behalf of Tyron Garner and John Lawrence in the historic 2003 U.S. Supreme Court case *Lawrence v. Texas*.[7]

For most of our history, we, like Lynn Riggs, have been terrified to "come out of the closet" and let our queerness be known. This fear is especially felt in Oklahoma. Fear of what? Rejection by our churches and families, termination from our jobs, entrapment by police, eviction from our houses and apartments, and harassment from strangers are just a few of the more common fears. In Oklahoma, gay bashing is a common and accepted political tactic, most famously attributed to U.S. Senator James Inhofe, who seems to have won his 1994 Senate election on the basis of a strategy of "the three G's: God, gays and guns."[8]

Discrimination based on sexual orientation is perfectly legal in Oklahoma, as are crimes motivated by hatred of GLBT people. Even when police are notified to deal with particularly egregious forms of harassment, such as assault and battery, the same norms that drove the crime seem to drive official indifference. For example, on October 19, 2003, two young gay men in Norman were chased three miles and physically assaulted. When they reported the act to the Norman police as a hate crime against gay men, the officer they spoke with told them, "We're not interested in that." Today, times are changing, and there are rich and powerful gay people who are no longer scared to come out of the closet to defend victims of antigay violence. Once this assault was made public, a group called the Cimarron Alliance Foundation (CAF), just one of several powerful gay or allied groups, stepped forward with legal support to make sure that the two young men were treated equitably.[9]

The political landscape is definitely changing in positive ways for the GLBT community, both in Oklahoma and in the rest of the country. GLBT people are becoming more willing to be seen and heard. The gay novelist Andrew Holleran provides two clues to this transformation: "AIDS changed everything in gay life—and so did the Internet."[10] Much attention has been paid to the HIV/AIDS crisis and how it has shaped GLBT people's connection to politics. It is common knowledge that the AIDS pandemic and the U.S. government's inaction, especially under President Ronald Reagan, forced many gay men out of the closet in the 1980s and early 1990s, to lobby for increased attention to the disease. AIDS served to politicize and mobilize a group of people who had previously not thought of themselves as a group at all.

Groups pushing for attention to AIDS in Oklahoma "started with nothing," according to one activist; they baked cookies in order to raise money.[11] In Oklahoma, local chapters of the group ACT-UP participated in political rallies and passed out information about safe sex and AIDS to local high schools.[12] There was a clear legislative victory in 1987, when the legislature passed a law mandating AIDS education in public schools.[13] As late as 1993, a hostile climate toward AIDS funding still existed in the state. In an unsigned editorial in the *Oklahoman*, it was suggested that AIDS research should not garner so much federal funding, because "AIDS still claims most of its victims in the United States as a result of personal behavior—homosexual activity or intravenous drug use," suggesting that HIV/AIDS patients "deserved it."[14]

More recently, the Internet has been a welcome forum for GLBT individuals seeking community and validation of their identities. As one young Oklahoma woman wrote, "The Internet has affected my queer identity by allowing me to be more open and not have to face retaliation (such as occurred in the Matthew Sheppard case)."[15] Using the Internet, even closeted and fearful GLBT people in Oklahoma can join in the gay community at large through Web pages, chat rooms, and pseudonymous email addresses, perhaps increasing the likelihood that they will one day join the political movement.

The relatively small size of the Oklahoma GLBT community and its status as a disliked group in society work against it when it comes to political action. Studies have shown that the most successful interests in American politics have strong group cohesion, ample political power, and a positive social construction among the polity at large.[16] The importance of how a group is viewed at large is key to political success, because the majority must support minorities in whatever benefits those groups receive.

In Oklahoma, partially because of the substantial socially conservative influence of Baptist (and other) churches that condemn homosexuality as perverse, the social construction of GLBT Oklahomans is patently negative. For example, in 2002, when the School Bullying Prevention Act was introduced in the Oklahoma legislature to address the problem of bullying against schoolchildren, its coverage included gay students. Because the number of gay kids is so small, they were dependent on the goodwill of the majority in order for the bill to pass. Because of GLBT people's negative social construction, however, the language concerning gay children was eventually struck before the rest of the bill passed.[17] A group with a negative social construction, such as the GLBT community, will not win beneficial public policy. Even more troublesome, society as a whole will actually support policy that punishes such groups and takes away their rights and benefits.

There may be hope that the social construction of GLBT people in Oklahoma is changing, and the source of the change may be surprising. For a century, the *Daily Oklahoman* has been the leading newspaper in Oklahoma City and in many parts of the state. Therefore, the statewide news that most Oklahomans receive pertaining to the GLBT community has been filtered through the lens of the *Oklahoman,* and until recently this lens was not a particularly flattering one. Between 1901 and 2000, more than 30 million stories appeared in the *Oklahoman,* 8,196 of which contained the word "homosexual," 2,524 of which contained "lesbian," and 726 of which contained "bisexual," suggesting that GLBT people have not been invisible in Oklahoma.[18] However, the majority of portrayals of GLBT people between 1950 and 1970 were quite negative. Sexual orientation was most frequently included in a news article when it was connected to vice and other sorts of deviant activities. In one early column that discussed homosexuality, titled "Deviation, Sin, or Illness," the author argued that "when homosexuality claims a sufficient percentage of men and women, their culture falls apart." She urged readers to " 'please, please help us to relieve the homo's tragic plight.'"[19] Other early articles mentioning homosexuality dealt with the Red Scare and how Joe McCarthy drummed gays out of the federal government in the 1950s.

In the past few years, perhaps as a result of the change in editorial control, coverage of GLBT issues in the *Oklahoman* has evolved from completely negative to relatively compassionate. There have been articles on GLBT political rallies and issues pertaining to GLBT Oklahomans, as well as decent coverage of big events, such as the Oklahoma City Pride Parade. One article's headline read, "State Bill Reaffirms Stance on Adoptions by Gays," but the text of the lengthy article included quotes from gay parents worried about losing

their children.[20] The most surprising, and perhaps challenging, article pro-
filed a transgendered Oklahoma City police officer as she struggled with her
decision to transition from being a man to being a woman while maintaining
her job on the police force. The article, entitled "Two Lives, Two Struggles,"
was compassionate and long (encompassing almost all of two pages, including
the front page).[21] Although there was a firestorm of letters to the editor
protesting the story, the fact that it appeared suggests that the social construction of the GLBT community may be changing for the better.[22]

THE RISE OF THE GLBT POLITICAL
MOVEMENT IN OKLAHOMA

As democracies, the U.S. and Oklahoma governments are majoritarian in
nature. Constituting just a small portion of the population, and with few
political allies, the GLBT community is finding it difficult to achieve lasting
political success. Interest groups are successful when they can pressure the
policy process for favorable policy, or when politicians look to members of the
group as a bloc for key votes.[23] The Oklahoma legislature has no use for GLBT
people as a voting bloc because we are too small to bother with, and if the
public at large saw legislators trying to curry our favor, there would be negative electoral repercussions. The same argument can be made for the governor
of Oklahoma, although the governorship has symbolic power even without
any sort of concrete support. The judicial branch is not a political branch,
which means that it possesses more independence from electoral forces.[24] The
question remains, then, whether the GLBT community, acting as an interest
group, can affect Oklahoma's government.

In 1994, an essay by Thomas E. Guild, Joan Luxenburg, and Keith Smith was
included in the predecessor to this volume, "An Oklahoma I Had Never Seen
Before": Alternative Views of Oklahoma History. Titled "Oklahoma's Gay Liberation Movement," it analyzed two components of the gay equality movement
in Oklahoma: community and political organizing, and legal action. The
authors concluded that although lawsuits to attain parity for gays had been
quite successful in Oklahoma, gay community organizing seemed to lag about
ten years behind the national average. The Stonewall Inn riots—generally
considered the moment of conception of the national gay rights movement—
occurred in 1969, whereas the first public gay rights group was not formed in
Oklahoma until 1979, when Bill Rogers and others spearheaded the creation of
Oklahomans for Human Rights (OHR).[25]

Since 1979, many other GLBT political groups have formed in Oklahoma, perhaps bringing the level of political organizing up to par with the rest of the nation. Another important early force for women's and lesbian equality is Herland Sister Resources, which was formed in 1983 and celebrated its twentieth year in 2003.[26] The women of Herland "rallied to stop rape and pass the Equal Rights Amendment and they stood up defiantly against oppression in any form—sexism, racism, heterosexism, misogyny, or homophobia."[27] Herland continues to be a community-building presence in Oklahoma City today. In the mid-1990s, a now-disbanded group called Simply Equal participated in rallies and lobbied legislators through postcards and letters. There are many other vital groups. Pride Network Incorporated sponsors the Oklahoma City Pride Parade each summer. The Cimarron Alliance Foundation focuses on spreading information about gay and lesbian issues and takes up legal issues. Cimarron Equality Oklahoma is a political action committee that openly lobbies politicians, and even placed a full-page ad in *USA Today* in 2004 bemoaning the Oklahoma legislature's support for a constitutional amendment banning gay marriage.[28] The Oklahoma Gay and Lesbian Political Caucus (OGLPC) is a pressure group that lobbies various officials, and is also responsible for publishing a voter guide before major elections. OGLPC sends out a lengthy questionnaire regarding support for gay rights, and candidates are ranked according to their answers.[29] Tulsa Oklahomans for Human Rights (TOHR) formed as a branch of OHR in 1980, but was established as a separate group in 1985 when OHR's membership dwindled. TOHR has sponsored a Gay Information Line since 1985 and also sponsors the Tulsa GLBT Community Center, which has existed in various locations since 1996.[30] Central Oklahoma Stonewall Democrats is an Oklahoma City–based club within the national Democratic Party. The Oklahoma Freedom and Equality Coalition is an umbrella group that brings together more than twenty different Oklahoma GLBT groups that seek equal rights through education, advocacy, and grassroots organizing.[31] Many other social groups exist as well, adding to the vitality of the Oklahoma GLBT community. On an Oklahoma City Web site designed for the GLBT community, there are links and contact information for thirty-one organizations, fifteen HIV/AIDS services, and five news sources, including the *Gayly Oklahoman,* which recently celebrated its twentieth anniversary of bringing news to the regional gay community.[32]

Can these various groups work together to achieve political goals? American politics is largely conceived in a "pluralist" way, meaning that each group must fight for and defend its own interests; the allocation of scarce government resources comes down to which groups are the strongest and best-organized. To have its interests represented in government, an interest group needs three things: money, members, and an effective leadership organization that can achieve group cohesion.

MONEY

In his book *The Power Game*, Hedrick Smith wrote, "the big gun of lobbying, the political weapon of choice, is money. It looms over the political landscape like the Matterhorn."[33] With money, an interest group can finance the political campaigns of friendly politicians, or help remove hostile ones. It can mobilize the grassroots with elaborate postcard campaigns, or wine and dine politicians, seeking to directly influence policy makers. Money has the added benefit of hiding other flaws in the group: a lack of members can be remedied with membership drives, or a lack of leadership can be solved by hiring a new superstar to provide the spark the group needs.

Some groups in the GLBT community seem to have a lot of money for expensive projects. For example, it must have cost thousands of dollars for Cimarron Equality Oklahoma (CEOK) to run a national ad in *USA Today*, taking Oklahoma to task for considering the Marriage Protection Amendment, and CEOK regularly sends out polished and professional fundraising appeals, hoping to add to its coffers. Other groups in the GLBT community have raised money in tiny increments through bake sales and the like, cherishing every penny. The *Herland Voice* makes it clear that some pretty extensive scrimping and elbow grease are the only things that saw Herland Sister Resources through its twenty years of existence.[34] One hopes that the disparity in money does not affect how each group and its particular issues are represented within the GLBT movement in Oklahoma.

MEMBERS

In his famous book *The Logic of Collective Action*, Mancur Olson wrote, "It is often taken for granted, at least where economic objectives are involved, that groups of individuals with common interests usually attempt to further those common interests."[35] Olson continues to explain that, in fact, unless the group is very small and the addition of one more member will truly make a difference, or unless there is some coercive force at work, rational self-interested people actually will not act in their own or their group's self interest. What effect does this theory have on the success of the GLBT political movement in Oklahoma? Sadly, it predicts that people are less likely to join groups, even if it is in their own self-interest.

Most people join interest groups because they expect to get some benefit in exchange. The benefit might actually be a material benefit, such as a discount on their health insurance. Less tangible benefits that attract members to interest groups include the good feelings people have when they are working toward a cherished goal. There are numerous reasons why GLBT people are drawn to interest groups. Many join because they want to help lobby the government to create beneficial policy for GLBT people. Groups such as OGLPC and Stonewall Democrats see it as their goal to lobby, especially through organizing Lobby Days at the Capitol and sending out Action Alerts to their members. Consider the comments made by one woman in regard to lobbying the Oklahoma City Council about hate crimes legislation in 1995: "We were a wonderful group of lesbians and gays and transgenders and straight human rights activists. We knew the proposals would fail, but we also knew our cause would prevail."[36] The main benefits this author receives from her political action are not tangible at all; she gains the benefit of working with people like herself, as well as working for a cause in which she believes.

Attracting quality members to an interest group is key to its survival. Ronald J. Hrebenar writes, "Perhaps the most fundamental resource of any organization is the unique composition of its membership."[37] For example, a group of lawyers may have the lobbying skills and ego strength to sell the merits of their group both to the public and to public officials. On the other hand, poor people who lack education and other resources important to effective lobbying will fail to get their message across. A key to the GLBT movement in Oklahoma is people such as Keith Smith, a professional lobbyist, who sends out e-mails stating exactly which politicians to contact, what to say, and how to say it. This type of expertise is very useful to a group trying to marshal its members effectively.

The total population of all GLBT people in Oklahoma may be relatively small; it is a diffuse group, scattered among city, town, and country. However, the success of an interest group lies less in sheer size than in cohesiveness and organization. It is hard for a broad-based group such as women to organize, which is precisely why the National Organization for Women has had such a difficult time becoming an effective political player.

What do women want? It depends on whether you ask Phyllis Schlafly or Betty Friedan. Breaking down GLBT into its component parts may be useful.

Gay men want . . . what? Doesn't the answer still depend on social class, race, and education? A well-heeled gay activist in Oklahoma City may not see the need for protection of employment rights in the way that a gay mechanic in Lawton might. Lesbians are also split, primarily among those who wish to pursue a feminist agenda of women's rights as opposed to gay rights. For example, the feminist women at Herland Sister Resources who were first politicized by the Equal Rights Amendment campaigns of the 1970s hypothetically are torn between their allegiance to gay groups such as OGLPC and women's groups seeking feminist aims. The rift between feminist lesbians and gay men seems to have been present in the GLBT community from the start. Several groups—the OGLPC, for example—elect both a male and a female cochair, simply to keep gender parity, but dominance by men remains a problem in most groups that contain both men and women.

EFFECTIVE LEADERSHIP ORGANIZATION

Much attention has been paid to the interest group "entrepreneur," the person who provides the spark to get the organization off the ground. There are several such "entrepreneurs" working in the Oklahoma GLBT scene, and they are present at nearly every function one could attend. For example, Paul Thompson is involved with OGLPC, and Keith Smith with Central Oklahoma Stonewall Democrats; Edward Kromer and Paul Bashline took Pride Network, Incorporated and the Oklahoma City Pride Parade to a new level; Wahru Cleveland was integral to Herland Sister Resources; and Bill Rogers is credited with creating Oklahomans for Human Rights. Leaders are important for getting groups started, but it is often their officers, boards, and general memberships to which a lot of the work falls. These groups are vibrant, but in a lot of ways they create walls and subtle animosities within the GLBT community. Sometimes leadership roles are not smoothly passed or shared, and whole groups have folded because of interpersonal struggles. These problems seem to be due to lack of shared vision, as discussed below, or perhaps are the result of too many talented leaders fighting over too few rewards. Questions of political strategy seem particularly divisive.

Leaders are important because they can enhance group cohesion. As is the case with the GLBT movement with its many different groups, leaders who can promote a shared vision and compatible goals can be very important to overall success. Groups have problems with cohesion when the "inclusive organization cannot absorb the units."[38] Defining both goals and strategies can be very difficult, especially when radical social activists attempt to work in a political climate designed to accommodate only slow, incremental change.[39]

SUCCESS IN THE LEGISLATURE?

The GLBT movement in Oklahoma seemed to be achieving substantial gains until May 2004. The climate shifted during the summer of 2003, when the U.S. Supreme Court decided *Lawrence v. Texas. Lawrence* holds that under the doctrine of privacy, states cannot ban sodomy—either homosexual or heterosexual—between consenting adults. *Lawrence* obliterated the legal basis for regulating homosexual conduct, and it seemed as though a new era of rights protection was forthcoming.

In Oklahoma, openly gay politicians such as Oklahoma County Commissioner Jim Roth and Norman City Council member David Ray were elected by voters despite their sexual orientation. When GLBT activists staged a counter-rally at the state capitol on February 17, 2004, to protest the proposed Federal Marriage Amendment and its definition of marriage as between one man and one woman, the event was covered respectfully in the *Oklahoman*.[40] Allies in the legislature, including Senator Bernest Cain, chair of the Human Resources Committee, were effective at keeping antigay legislation from getting out of committee.

Then, without warning, House Bill 2259 passed both the Oklahoma House and Senate during the 2004 legislative session, over the strenuous objections of the GLBT community's key lobbyist, Keith Smith. It was enacted by a vote of the people in November 2004, redundantly adding language to the Oklahoma Constitution to ban gay marriage. During that same legislative session, House Bill 1821—relating to adoptions by out-of-state couples—was amended with the following language: "This state, any of its agencies, or any court of this state shall not recognize an adoption by more than one individual of the same sex from any other state or foreign jurisdiction."

Nobody is quite sure how House Bill 2259 turned into State Question 711 (the "Marriage Protection Amendment"), but the reactions to it rippled through Oklahoma's gay and ally community, where it was met with a mixture of indignation and anguish. When HB 2259 was introduced in the House by Republican Mike Wilt, it concerned penalties for child sexual abuse; a similar bill was introduced in the Senate by Republican Glenn Coffee, which is standard procedure. When the House bill was reported out of the Criminal Justice Committee, it still concerned child sexual abuse, and during the markup process, representatives made several thoughtful amendments. When the bill was taken up in the Senate, it included additional coauthors (Republicans Ken Corn, James Williamson, and Daisy Lawler) and added an incredible amendment: *AMENDMENT NO. 1. Page 1, strike the title, enacting clause and entire bill. . . .*

Additional language added to what was henceforth called the "Marriage Protection Amendment" called for an amendment to the Oklahoma Constitution to be placed on the November 2004 ballot. The measure read in part: "Marriage in this state shall consist only of the union of one man and one woman." There was minimal debate, and only seven senators voted against HB 2259. A press release from the Oklahoma Freedom and Equality Coalition summed it up best: "The Oklahoma State Senate today subverted the intent of the Oklahoma Constitution, state law, and its own rules by converting HB 2259 into a proposed amendment to the Oklahoma Constitution."

Keith Smith was in the Senate chamber when the measure passed, and his attempts to "love the bill to death" with unpopular amendments failed. He summarized his feelings about it in an impassioned and widely circulated e-mail bulletin: "It was terribly painful to sit there in the Senate Gallery by myself and see the numbers go up on the board and slowly realize we were going to lose by a handful of votes on the crucial and most important vote for tabling amendments."[41]

The House was even more likely than the Senate to pass this bill, so it was no surprise when only four representatives voted against it. House Speaker Larry Adair, a Democrat, had an opportunity to kill the measure, but he didn't. Nor did Democratic governor Brad Henry veto it, although it would have been pointless, since the House and Senate's majorities far surpassed what would be needed to override. Terry Gatewood, chair of Cimarron Equality Oklahoma, condemned the proposed amendment: "Oklahoma already bans its gay and lesbian citizens from the rights and responsibilities of civil marriage, so the Amendment is simply a statement of intolerance and meanness."[42] On November 2, 2004, State Question 711 passed by a whopping statewide majority, 75.6 percent to 24.4 percent.

The passage of House Bill 1821 has a similar story. The issue of adoption of Oklahoma children by same-sex out-of-state couples arose when Attorney General Drew Edmondson issued an opinion stating that Oklahoma must recognize such adoptions, regardless of whether the parents were eligible to adopt in Oklahoma. HB 1821, introduced by Rep. Susan Winchester, a Republican from Chickasha, initially did not mention same-sex couples, but Rep. James Williamson—the same Republican who had spearheaded the alteration of HB 2259—amended this bill as well. The bill passed both houses easily, and Governor Henry signed it into law on May 3, 2004.[43]

The lessons that HB 2259 and HB 1821 can teach us are twofold. First, the GLBT movement is practically powerless when it comes to influencing the members of the legislature, especially when those members are in the public eye. Second, if a group has a negative social construction and is despised by the public, as seems to be the case here, politicians can curry favor with the public by actually punishing groups by supporting punitive public policy. Passing the Marriage Protection Amendment and restricting the adoption of Oklahoma children by out-of-state same-sex couples were cheap and easy ways for legislators to win public support simply by restricting the rights of GLBT people.

SUCCESS IN THE COURTS?

As the essay by Guild, Luxenburg, and Smith elucidates, GLBT people in Oklahoma have a history of using the state courts to achieve a measure of equality. For example, in 1972 the ACLU sued the University of Oklahoma for refusing to recognize a gay campus organization, and a Cleveland County district judge demanded that the group be recognized.[44] Turning to the courts is a popular strategy for unpopular minority groups because in this forum it is possible that justice can win over popular sentiment. In most other states, research shows that state courts can be significantly more liberal than federal courts; therefore, GLBT legal advocacy groups focus their litigation at this level. This liberalism, however, is not found in Oklahoma (or several other southern states). In fact, in Oklahoma, the federal courts—a conservative force in many other states—are far more hospitable to GLBT legal action than are Oklahoma state courts.[45]

Post v. Oklahoma, a 1986 case decided by the Oklahoma Criminal Court of Appeals, offers a good example of the conservatism of Oklahoma courts.[46] The *Post* case interprets the Oklahoma Constitution's ban on sodomy, which states that sodomy—all sodomy—is a "detestable and abominable crime against nature." In *Post*, the court decided that the ban itself is unconstitutional under a right to privacy as applied to heterosexual sex, but it is not unconstitutional as applied to homosexual sex. In applying *Post* in another case, the Court explained, "This Court, relying on federal constitutional law, held that an individual's constitutional right of privacy encompassed the private, consensual acts of sodomy between heterosexual adults."[47] Although the *Post* distinction was mooted by the U.S. Supreme Court case *Lawrence v. Texas,* which used privacy grounds to bar distinguishing homosexuals from heterosexuals when it comes to banning sodomy, *Post* was important because it preserved the criminal basis for prosecuting (and persecuting) GLBT Oklahomans. Therefore, the Oklahoma Supreme Court demarcated a clear class of deviants in homosexuals, who could be sent to prison for up to ten years for being convicted of sodomy, without wielding the same penalty for straight people. This distinction lasted from 1986 until it was obliterated in 2003. Criminalizing homosexuality is symbolically important because of the "age old equations . . . sodomy = homosexuality and homosexuality = criminality."[48] More than any other law, the homosexual sodomy ban justified unequal treatment of members of the GLBT community.

Almost two decades after *Post* was decided, another pivotal case was adjudicated, but this time at the federal court level. When Oklahoma City, led by Republican mayor Kirk Humphreys, argued that gay pride banners hung for Gay History Month (October) and the Pride Parade would not be permitted because they constituted "social activism," the Cimarron Alliance Foundation sued them in federal court. The U.S. District Court found that Oklahoma City had violated GLBT groups' first amendment rights and supported their right to display gay pride banners.[49] This legal victory was reported widely in the *Oklahoman,* and became known as an important success to GLBT groups throughout the country. One of the original banners was installed in a GLBT history museum in San Francisco.[50]

So how good are the courts at protecting the rights of Oklahoma GLBT people? Even though the Oklahoma Court of Criminal Appeals handed down the odious *Post* decision, lower state courts have done a better job of giving us equal rights than either the legislature or the governor ever could in the current hostile climate. However, even more than state courts, U.S. federal courts have been and probably will continue to be the source of more rights for GLBT people in Oklahoma. It was the U.S. Supreme Court that made the *Post* rule obsolete, and it was the U.S. District Court that forced Oklahoma City to allow gay pride banners to hang. Oklahoma state courts would have given us neither of these decisions. In short, because the state of Oklahoma treats GLBT people so poorly, in both the political and judicial branches, GLBT Oklahomans may have to look exclusively to federal courts for basic civil rights protections.

FRAMES

Amber Hollibaugh, a self-described "lesbian-sex radical ex-hooker incest survivor rural Gypsy working-class poor white trash high-femme dyke," offers a hint in her book of why the GLBT movement in Oklahoma will never be as strong as it could be.[51] There are few people (if any!) who share her experiences and categories, which is precisely the reason the GLBT movement cannot cohere. Hollibaugh writes, "We keep those secrets about sex and desire and the erotic as we have kept other secrets like class and color and addiction —because they seem too dangerous or too explosive, or we are too powerless, to have them acknowledged inside our communities or the larger heterosexual world."[52] Why are secrets kept within (and without) the GLBT movement? The answer is the same for any group of people who come together to solve a problem: individual differences must be subsumed in order to find commonalities. In the GLBT movement in Oklahoma, the bonds holding individuals together within the movement are so fragile that they can barely withstand differences within the group. The movement is in constant danger of bursting apart into its constituent parts. Ironically, diversity, which in so many other contexts fuels creativity and solves problems, here cleaves the movement. Interest groups depend mainly on cohesion for their strength—all individual members must be on the same page as the collectivity, and when they are not, the group's power is lost.

Using another example, Wahru Cleveland, also known as Barbara, writes in the *Herland Voice,* "I am a black woman, womanist, feminist, diverse sexual-orientation person. My life's experiences are deeply connected to culture and struggle, as well as my woman identity."[53] In just considering these two strong women and their diverse and unique experiences, can we be sure that we have the material for a political movement? What if we add bisexuals, transgenders, and gay men to the mix? Will they find common ground? The overall goal is GLBT equality, but this goal is complicated by subsidiary goals such as increased AIDS funding, gay marriage, hate crimes legislation, and employment discrimination protection, as well as new issues that continue to come to the fore.

The intersections between individual and group interests are sometimes called "frames."[54] Issues can be "framed" either narrowly, so that only a very discrete set of people may see it as in their interest to fight for the issue, or more broadly. An appeal calling for "social justice" is broadly framed, encompassing the interests of many, but the concept is so brittle that any more definition would cause the coalition to crumble. Just the concept "GLBT" or "sexual orientation" is problematic, as we have begun to see, with the divergent wishes of gay men, lesbians (both feminist and traditional), bisexuals, and transgendered people.[55]

Frames can be altered: made to bridge between groups, as perhaps the relationships between the constituents of the GLBT community might suggest. Together, they may fight for a more inclusive conception of sexual orientation, but, in fact, each distinct constituency has its own unique issues. Lesbians may be more economically oppressed than gay men, or lesbians with traditional values may be more interested in the right to marry than gay men or feminist lesbians. To be successful, it seems that each group has to subvert its own unique goals in order to reach the collective benefit of more equality for all. If a frame is strong and keeps the groups united, there is a higher possibility for success, yet the underlying lack of cohesion always exerts a destabilizing force. These weakness are summed up by a former GLBT activist: "Everyone wants to be on top. Everyone wants to get all the credit for themselves. What this does is to water down the message. The focus is totally lost. These actions continue to break the community apart and divide our resources and energy."[56] More often than not, members of the Oklahoma GLBT community find themselves fighting each other, and not prejudice, the real enemy.

NOTES

1. David Rayside, *On the Fringe: Gays and Lesbians in Politics* (Ithaca, N.Y.: Cornell University Press, 1998).

2. The Stonewall Inn is a bar in the heart of New York City's gay district. Police raided the bar on June 29, 1969, which touched off two days of rioting. Sometimes referred to as the "big bang" in the GLBT movement, the incident represents the first time that GLBT people and their straight allies fought back against police brutality and homophobia. See Dick Leitsch, "Acting Up at the Stonewall Riots," in Mark Thompson, ed., *The Long Road to Freedom: The Advocate History of the Gay and Lesbian Movement* (New York: St. Martin's Press, 1994), 28–29.

3. DJ, as told to MOC, "Out and About in OKC, before Stonewall," *Herland Voice* 111, no. 6 (June 1999): 1.

4. In Craig Womack, *Red on Red: Native American Literary Separatism* (Minneapolis: University of Minnesota Press, 1999), 277.

5. Census data are available at http://factfinder.census.gov/home/saff/main
.html?_lang=en (accessed August 16, 2004). All GLBT people are undercounted,
because these figures refer only to same-sex couples who cohabit.

6. Peter Spring and Timothy Dailey, eds., *Getting It Straight: What the Research
Shows about Homosexuality* (Washington, D.C.: Family Research Council, 2004), 42.

7. *Lawrence v. Texas,* 000 U.S. 02-102 (2003).

8. "God, Gays and Guns," *Economist* 5, no. 333 (November 11, 1994): 27.

9. Paula Sophia, "Cimarron Foundation Town Hall Meeting," *Gayly Oklahoman*
22, no. 3 (February 1, 2004): 1; Christine Pappas, "The Night the Music Stopped at the
Copa," ibid., 10.

10. Quoted in Christine Pappas, "The Internet and Queer Political Identity," *Gayly
Oklahoman* 20, no. 19 (October 1, 2002): 11.

11. Excerpted from an interview with Margaret Cox, March 6, 2004.

12. Bryan Painter, "AIDS Group to Continue School Anti-AIDS Drives," *Oklahoman,* November 22, 1991, 3. ACT-UP stands for "AIDS Coalition to Unleash Power."

13. Paul English, "AIDS Education Required in Schools," *Oklahoman,* April 25,
1985, 2.

14. "Deadlier Disease Ignored," *Oklahoman,* January 16, 1993, 12.

15. Personal correspondence, n.d.

16. Ann Schneider and Helen Ingram, "The Social Construction of Target Populations: Implications for Politics and Policy," *American Political Science Review* 87, no. 2
(June 1993): 334–47.

17. SB 992 (1992), codified as Title 70, Sec. 24-100.2.

18. Tabulations by the author based on searches conducted online in the *Oklahoman*'s archive at http://newsok.com. Articles are available in full text between 1901
and 2004. Analysis conducted on April 10, 2004. Data was also collected on the words
"gay" and "queer," although the multiple meanings of these words complicated the
content analysis. The word "gay" was used 12,167 times during 1991–2000, and seems
to be the *Oklahoman*'s appellation of choice for homosexuals during this period. The
term "queer" is used to refer to homosexuals to the exclusion of other meanings by
approximately 1970. "Queer" appeared only 143 times from 1971 to 1980 and generally
carried negative connotations until it was reclaimed by the advocacy group "Queer
Nation" between 1991 and 1995, and was listed as part of the title of the popular
television show *Queer as Folk* between 1996 and 2000.

19. Edith Johnson, "Deviation, Sin or Illness," *Oklahoman,* December 31, 1957, 10.

20. Judy Gibbs Robinson, "State Bill Reaffirms Stance on Adoption by Gays,"
Oklahoman, May 1, 2004, 7A.

21. "Two Lives, Two Struggles," *Oklahoman,* February 8, 2004, 1

22. See, e.g., Michael Bratcher, "Gay Students Face Ridicule, Report Says," *Oklahoman,* December 9, 2003, 4; Leonard Pitts, Jr., "Shocker: Gays Live among Us,"
Oklahoman, January 7, 2004, 15A.

23. Graham K. Wilson, "American Interest Groups," in Jeremy J. Richardson, ed.,
Pressure Groups (Oxford: Oxford University Press, 1993), 131–44.

24. In Oklahoma, there are two courts of last resort, the Oklahoma Supreme Court,

which handles civil actions, and the Oklahoma Court of Criminal Appeals, which reviews criminal decisions. Judges on both of these courts are appointed by the governor and are subject to statewide retention votes of the people. Federal judges are appointed by the president to lifetime appointments, therefore further insulating them from political pressures.

25. Thomas E. Guild, Joan Luxenburg, and Keith Smith, "Oklahoma's Gay Liberation Movement," in Davis D. Joyce, ed., *"An Oklahoma I Had Never Seen Before": Alternative Views of Oklahoma History* (Norman: University of Oklahoma Press, 1994), 328–41. OHR has since disbanded.

26. *Herland, 1983–2003: Celebrating 20 Years* (Oklahoma City: Herland Sister Resources, 2003).

27. Ibid., 1.

28. Fundraising literature disseminated by Cimarron Equality Oklahoma, May 2004. The ad features a picture of the state of Oklahoma with a "closed" sign hanging across it. The headline reads, "Oklahoma: Going Out of Business." The ad appeared in *USA Today* on May 10, 2004.

29. See, e.g., "OGLPC Voter Guide Now Available," *Gayly Oklahoman* 20, no. 16 (August 15, 2002): 1, 11.

30. Andrew Hicks, "On the Move with TOHR," *Gayly Oklahoman* 22, no. 7 (April 1, 2004): 1, 4.

31. Paula Sophia, "Freedom and Equality Coalition," *Gayly Oklahoman* 22, no. 4 (February 15, 2004): 1.

32. http://www.gayokc.com, accessed May 1, 2004.

33. Hedrick Smith, *The Power Game: How Washington Works* (New York: Random House, 1988), 218–19.

34. See, e.g., Jo L. Siske, "La Salle De Femmes," *Herland Voice* 22, no. 2 (February 2004): 1, 3.

35. Mancur Olsen, *The Logic of Collective Action* (Cambridge, Mass.: Harvard University Press, 1965), 1.

36. Sybil Ludington, "As Long As I Breathe . . . ," *Herland Voice* 13, no. 2 (February 15, 1995): 4.

37. Ronald J. Hrebenar, *Interest Group Politics in America,* 3rd ed. (Armonk, N.Y.: M.E. Sharpe, 1997), 24.

38. Ibid., 135.

39. Rayside, *On the Fringe,* 3.

40. Carmel Snyder Perez and Ryan McNeill, "At the Capitol: Gay Marriage Debate Reaches Oklahoma," *Oklahoman,* February 18, 2004, 4A. For more information, see, e.g., Paula Sophia, "State Capital [*sic*] Marriage Rally," *Gayly Oklahoman* 22, no. 5 (March 1, 2004): 1.

41. Keith Smith, "We Lost Today," e-mail bulletin, April 15, 2004.

42. http://www.eqok.com/42395.html, accessed May 15, 2004.

43. Carmel Perez Snyder, "Adoption Ban among 17 Bills Signed," *Oklahoman,* May 4, 2004, 3A.

44. Guild, Luxenburg, and Smith, "Oklahoma's Gay Liberation Movement," 332–33.

45. This result is unique among states, largely because of Oklahoma's extreme conservatism. Pinello argues that state courts are more liberal than federal courts when it comes to gay rights protection, but it seems that Oklahoma is the exception that proves the rule. See Daniel R. Pinello, *Gay Rights and American Law* (Cambridge: Cambridge University Press, 2003). Also, there is a probable pitfall because federal courts' support for GLBT people seems to waver. Joyce Murdoch and Deb Price argue in their book *Courting Justice* that just as frequently as the Supreme Court supports GLBT rights, the Court denies them; *Courting Justice: Gay Men and Lesbians v. the Supreme Court* (New York: Basic Books, 2001). For example, yes, GLBT people scored a victory in the Colorado case *Romer v. Evans* (1996) when the Court struck down discriminatory legislation there. However, gays lost in *Boy Scouts v. Dale* (2000) when the Court found that the Boy Scouts could ban gay men from their den meetings and pup tents.

46. *Post v. State,* 715 P.2d 1105 (Okla. Crim. App. 1986).

47. *Hinkle v. State,* 771 P.2d 232 (Okla. Crim. App. 1989), 234.

48. Murdoch and Price, *Courting Justice,* 334.

49. Paula Sophia, "Banner Ordinance Unconstitutional," *Gayly Oklahoman* 20, no. 19 (October 1, 2002): 1.

50. Personal correspondence, September 17, 2003.

51. Amber L. Hollibaugh, *My Dangerous Desires: A Queer Girl Dreaming Her Way Home* (Durham, N.C.: Duke University Press, 2000), 7.

52. Ibid., 267.

53. B. Wahru Cleveland, "From La Salle De Femmes to Herland: Why Not the Same Name or Same Direction," *Herland Voice* 22, no. 3 (March 2004): 1.

54. The term is Irving Goffman's. Frames help organize experiences and guide action, both collective and individual. David A. Snow et al., "Frame Alignment Processes, Micromobilization, and Movement Participation," in Steven M. Buechler and F. Kurt Cylke, Jr., eds., *Social Movements: Perspectives and Issues* (Mountain View, Calif.: Mayfield Publishing Co., 1997), 211–28.

55. Queer groups often have what is known as the "Alphabet Soup" problem: so many different constituencies are included that group members may sense an overall lack of identity. Groups may include "A" for Allies, "I" for Intersex, "Q" for Questioning, or any other queer group to which they wish to try to bridge their frame. A former GLBT activist wrote, "I am consistently amused that almost weekly I see a new group, a new name, a new mission but led by the same people. Something new for the alphabet soups that the GAY community has become. L.B.G.T.T.Q." Personal correspondence, October 17, 2004.

56. Personal correspondence, October 17, 2004.

CHAPTER 10

Oklahoma Poverty, Religion, and Politics

LESSONS FROM ECONOMIC HISTORY

Alvin O. Turner

Alvin O. Turner is a lifelong Oklahoman. His Ph.D. is from Oklahoma State University, and he has taught at four different Oklahoma institutions of higher learning. Currently, he is Professor of History, Dean of the School of Humanities and Social Sciences, and Acting Dean of the Graduate College at East Central University. He has written widely on various subjects in history and popular culture. His latest book, *Letters from the Dust Bowl,* is an edited collection of the important papers of Caroline Henderson.

Turner's essay here is a written version of a presentation he made at the "Religion, Freedom, and Prosperity in Oklahoma" conference at East Central in 2001. His deep insights into the state, based on both personal experience and historical knowledge, are evident.

Varied business and political interests, along with state government agencies, have sponsored a wide range of studies during the past decades focusing on means to improve the state's economic standing. All measures of state economic health place Oklahoma near the bottom of the fifty states, with only Mississippi or Arkansas likely to challenge it for that status. The studies have suggested a variety of solutions, but the vast majority of these are simplistic solutions to complex problems and are characterized by an absence of historical understanding. At best, such studies turn a blind eye toward many of the historic roots of Oklahoma poverty, frequently confusing causes and effects. As a result, there is a near-unanimous conviction that constitutional provisions and popular attitudes reflecting populist influences account for the state's present inability to compete successfully in the regional and national economy.[1]

Oklahoma achieved statehood during the Progressive Era, when the spirit of reform influenced changes in every aspect of American life. William H. "Alfalfa Bill" Murray, the president of the Constitutional Convention, was an advocate of a variety of reforms earlier called for by populists. An overwhelming majority of the convention delegates likewise supported such populist measures as the long ballot and other direct democracy features and restraints on corporate power. Murray was also a primary example of the populist style, noted for its appeals to the lowest common denominator in politics. The resultant combination of constitutional provisions, subsequent legislative actions, and a persistent tradition of political demagoguery clearly have had negative effects on Oklahoma's development. However, some of the measures associated with populism were characteristic of the more respectable progressives as well, who often represented the scientific or academic views of government and society. These groups also supported many of the Oklahoma constitutional provisions now labeled as populist, including the implementation of Jim Crow provisions. In addition, they have been as likely as any other group to participate in political corruption or support other actions detrimental to the state's development.

A better understanding of Oklahoma's economic history establishes that fundamental weaknesses were compounded by the decisions and practices of varied interests and groups. Moreover, the state's history explains both past and present poverty and its populist tendencies. Oklahoma's economy was founded on a nineteenth-century economic model that rested upon expected returns from agricultural production at the beginning of a century-long decline in agricultural prospects in a region where crops are always at risk. Historical failures to protect the interests of Native American populations and other minorities, destruction of the human and physical resources of the state, and the failure to address related problems do more to explain the state's poverty than does the populist heritage.

This chapter is adapted from a paper originally presented at a conference held at East Central University in 2001. The conference followed a year-long seminar that addressed questions arising from the Weber thesis, which suggested a correlation between certain teachings of Protestantism and the rise of capitalism.[2] In contrast, Oklahomans frequently refer to their state as "the buckle of the (Protestant) Bible Belt," yet they remain locked in relative poverty. Part of this apparent discrepancy results from a misapplication of the Weber thesis, which identified specific teachings such as the Puritan dilemma, wherein Calvinists struggled for evidence of their election. Because their theology left them in doubt about their ultimate relationship with God, they struggled to succeed in order to accumulate material evidence of God's favor. That tension and the other qualities of Protestantism defined by Weber are not prominent in the primary Oklahoma religious expressions.

More to the point, other conditions characteristic of the rise of capitalism have been absent in Oklahoma as well. Weber never argued that Protestantism inevitably led to capitalism; he asserted that it did so in particular contexts. One of these was a location in time and place that permitted the emergent capitalists to gain from their efforts. Working hard produced profits, and invested profits produced more wealth, thereby affirming the Protestant work ethic as an underpinning for capitalism and strengthening its hold in the culture at large.

Neither the geography of Oklahoma nor its historical setting permitted the conditions the Puritans encountered in the New World that encouraged capitalism. Simply stated, Oklahoma got off to a bad start and has never recovered from its initial difficulties. Oklahoma developed as an agricultural state, frequently on poor-quality land with settlement largely completed within ten years of an absolute trough for agricultural prices that began with the panic of 1893. That economic disruption marked the beginning of an uninterrupted national shift from an agrarian economy to an industrial one. Farmers and related economic interests, communities, and states have suffered accordingly since that time.[3]

This development meant a weak economic foundation for everything that would be built subsequently. The small family farm no longer offered a means of success in the emerging twentieth-century economy. Even if it had, Oklahoma's agricultural economy would not have produced the kinds of economic gains that had been true on earlier frontiers because of geographic changes the settlers encountered. These required greater expenses in production due to increased costs for such things as obtaining water, fencing, and building shelter. Also characteristic of the Great Plains and adjacent areas, distance factors increased dependence on the railroads and added still more costs to offset the farmer's potential profits. The likelihood of substantial gains was reduced even further by regular weather-related disasters, typical of the plains environment, and relative declines in agricultural prices.[4]

Even before these factors shaped the state's subsequent history, others were destroying much of the economic potential of the tribal peoples who remain a significant component of Oklahoma's population. Evidence for this may be seen by correlating the American Indian populations of Oklahoma counties with their poverty rates. Twenty-three of the thirty-two counties that exceed the state's rural poverty rate of 17.5 percent also exceed the average of 7.9 percent Indian population. Similarly, of the seven poorest counties that exceed the 23 percent rural poverty levels, six have Indian populations near or exceeding two times their state population per capita. Every other social indicator confirms that there are hard cores of Native American population groups located in pockets throughout the state, including relatively prosperous counties, who are not reflected in these dismal statistics. In contrast, only nine of the counties that exceeded rural poverty rates had less than the state average for Indian population. Eight of these were among the westernmost counties, where geographic factors such as those described above have had their sharpest impact. For example, all of these counties experienced significant population drops in the past and prior decades, with most having reached their peak populations before 1920.[5]

The irony in these statistics is that the largest numbers of poor counties outside of western Oklahoma are within the historic tribal domains of the Five Civilized Tribes. These tribes were recognized as being well on the road to assimilation by the time of their forced migrations to Oklahoma in the 1830s and 1840s. That designation reflected their economic status as well as their literacy rates, their acceptance of Christianity, and other measures of their accommodation and assimilation of the prevailing culture. Complex factors account for the present poverty of many of their descendants, but any meaningful discussion of those factors must recognize the impact of the destruction of the economic gains of four generations of successive tribal populations. Those who were forced to Indian Territory along the many trails of tears also left behind improved lands and businesses. Those who were able to find the strength or resources to rebuild had those gains destroyed by the Civil War.[6]

The scope of physical destruction was as severe in Indian Territory as in any region of the South. Resultant tribal economic problems were compounded by more forced relocations, the loss of lands, and other measures that weakened their governments. Subsequent gaps in federal enforcement meant that Indian Territory became an outlaw haven, creating the seedbed for an outlaw-tolerant culture. Bootlegging flourished throughout the territorial period and then shaped Oklahoma politics through the first fifty years of statehood. That tradition and others soon included acceptance of malfeasance in public office. The impact of weak law enforcement also affected tribes' economic develop-ment, notably in the federal failure to enforce restrictions against intruders into the tribal domain. The generation of tribal peoples who rebuilt amid these struggles then lost many of those gains through the allotment process. The allotment of lands in severalty was defended as a means to force tribal assimilation, but its most immediate impact was to expose individuals and families to years of legal chicanery and other devices used to deprive them of the possession of or profits from their lands. Oklahoma's early state history is filled with abundant evidence documenting the role of local and state leaders in the plunder of tribal resources, with the Creek orphan scandal only the most conspicuous. Moreover, no one would seriously argue that federal and state efforts to address the educational needs of the Indian population were successful during this dismal period of time.[7] The tribal people who persisted and gained success despite such pressures then encountered the economic devastation of the Great Depression.

Arguably the most drastic consequence of this chain of destructive forces was its impact on the hopes and aspirations of the people who were affected. That conclusion is illustrated by the story of one anonymous Chickasaw man. When queried by an agent, in about 1840, why he was not more ambitious in building the farm he was operating in Indian Territory, he replied that he had already built one farm, and since the government had taken that one from him, he saw no reason to invest his labor in another.[8]

There are important parallels between these experiences and those of the Plains Indians and other tribal groups in the state, which often produced even worse results. Essentially a Stone Age people when they were defeated mili-tarily in the 1870s, the Plains tribes were expected to adapt to the prevailing cultural practices and economic systems within a generation. That expecta-tion carried with it the virtual assurance that it would fail; neither the time allowed, the commitment of resources, nor tribal assets were adequate. Thus, families were forced into farming at the very time when prospects for farming were in general decline nationwide. Moreover, they were expected to farm in western Oklahoma at a time before anyone really understood how to farm on the Great Plains, with limited help and even less equipment. In 1876, just before the outbreak of the last Southern Plains War, old Cheyenne men were out breaking sod around the Darlington agencies with sharpened sticks so that they could plant the corn that would burn up in that summer's heat.[9]

The tribes of western Oklahoma were also frequently victimized by a culture that permitted the continued robbery of tribal peoples, treating them as a resource to be exploited. The Osage oil murders were the most extreme manifestation of that tendency, but less dramatic examples were common, and community and state leaders were frequent participants. Tragically, recent events have established that the hardships that many tribal people encountered in the past were exacerbated by practices of the Bureau of Indian Affairs. As a result of that agency's accounting practices, many families were cheated of income from their oil-bearing properties. The problem became so severe that Congress called for reconciliation of all affected accounts in 1987. As of this writing, seventeen years later, a final reconciliation has yet to be made; the BIA indicates that it is unable to fulfill the mandate, and the most conservative estimates are that at least $2.7 billion was unaccounted for in a single twenty-year period from 1973 to 1992.[10]

Oklahoma's historic oil development and the number of Native Americans in the state ensure that much of this money would have benefited Oklahoma tribes. Similarly, in the decade of the 1980s alone, Koch Industries was charged with using fraudulent measurements to cheat royalty owners of their profits from oil production. Much of that oil came from Indian lands in Oklahoma. A U.S. Senate investigation of these charges terminated in 1992 after Senator Don Nickles of Oklahoma and other influential senators intervened on behalf of Koch Industries.[11]

Black Oklahomans also share a dismal history. Segregated education ensured that most blacks would receive minimal education, which limited job and other economic opportunities. The threat of violence further impeded black initiative or business expansion. Other individuals and communities suffered direct losses resulting from white violence toward blacks. The race riot that took place in Tulsa in 1921 was the nation's worst to that point in American history; it killed an estimated hundreds of people and destroyed the commercial center known as the "Black Wall Street."[12]

The failure to protect individual and economic rights in these particular areas has been mirrored in widespread toleration for lawlessness in numerous others, each affecting the state's economic potential. These historic factors and the resultant attitudes were shaped by forces that prevailed long before the populist institutions and attitudes deplored by present-day economic thinkers. Descendants of the bootleggers who flourished in the lawless Indian Territory would shape Oklahoma politics well into the twentieth century. Outlaws such as Pretty Boy Floyd moved with impunity through many areas of the state and were often regarded as folk heroes.[13]

Meanwhile, Oklahoma earned a dubious distinction for political corruption. The most conspicuous example of this pattern was seen in the scandals that rocked the state in the 1970s and 1980s. From 1976, when former governor David Hall (1971–75) began serving a federal sentence for bribery, until 1987, 246 Oklahoma officials were convicted of federal crimes, including 165 county commissioners representing sixty of the state's seventy-seven counties. A series of scandals in which state treasurers were implicated, charges of campaign finance irregularities, a related guilty plea from another governor, and the Southwestern Bell rate case dominated news in the next decade. In 2004, the state's legislature impeached the insurance commissioner for crimes in office.[14]

In retrospect, perhaps the most disturbing aspect of these events has been the public response. The state legislature and executives failed to enact substantive reform while local responses reached the level of low comedy, defending the commissioners as good old boys corrupted by the system. Thus, many of the men who had participated in practices that had cost Oklahoma taxpayers in excess of $200 million annually spent their last days of freedom surrounded by well-wishers, some of whom were raising funds for appeals.[15]

A pattern of dramatic economic booms followed by the inevitable busts also continues to influence Oklahoma's economic potential. The fortunes of the state's oil industry offer the most dramatic example of this effect, while the land runs and early town speculation are comparable examples that add to the impact of the long-term cycles that affect agriculture.[16]

Oklahoma's five land runs are more often celebrated than lamented, but they also provide an important example of wasted investments. First, hundreds of thousands of people expended limited capital in a hazardous effort for what was often a fruitless venture. Most either failed to gain a claim or found that they did not have the resources or had not found the quality of land necessary to succeed. Difficulties stemming from their limited resources were compounded by bad planning, particularly with regard to the timing of runs. For instance, the Cherokee Outlet land run took place in September, which meant the settlers would have no chance of a crop until spring, at the earliest. That decision, together with a drought then affecting the Plains, necessitated a nationwide appeal to help save the starving settlers.[17]

Pressure to seize a claim virtually ensured that much marginal land would be taken, especially after the government sought to limit prior access to the available lands. Thus, the months following the runs were inevitably followed by an exodus of those who had succeeded in establishing claims. Such problems were typical of every run and often marked the loss of further investments in barns, housing, or even storefronts.[18]

The hard lessons offered by the land runs, however, did not end government policies promoting agricultural expansion, which often led to more wasted investments. In conjunction with World War I, farmers were encouraged to plow and plant from fence row to fence row. All too often that policy led to the sowing of seeds for a future environmental disaster, as well as the inevitable economic bust once the wartime stimulus ended. Two generations later, federal policies encouraged a different kind of agricultural expansion, which ultimately was no less destructive to its investors when farmers expanded their landholdings in the midst of the state's last oil boom.[19]

Mass exoduses from Oklahoma following land runs often involved as many prospective businessmen as farmers. The population of the town of Perry was more than 10,000 shortly after the 1893 land run but had declined to less than 3,000 within six months. One measure of the failure of these town investors can be seen in the empty buildings that dot the squares of early Oklahoma boomtowns, some of which were only briefly, if ever, fully occupied by aspiring businessmen. A second wave of failed town investments followed the spread of rail lines across the state. Many of these were also doomed to failure, as were the towns that had been promoted as the "next Kansas City." In 1909, for example, dozens of people paid hundreds of dollars for lots in Foraker. That town reached its all-time population high of 415 the following year; only 25 claim the town as home today.[20]

Even the majority of towns that succeeded did so only as long as there was an agricultural population base to support their businesses. Those conditions changed sharply with major population shifts in the 1930s and 1940s, when Oklahoma began to follow national trends toward urbanization. In 1930, at which time the state was seeing some of the worst results of reliance upon an agricultural base, Oklahoma was still 59 percent rural, whereas the average for the rest of the nation was more than 50 percent urban, according to the 1920 Census.[21]

Oklahoma towns and their investors experienced a final blow in conjunction with the great oil bust of 1982–86. That event produced a 50 percent decline in state agricultural land values, which meant that farmers who had invested in or mortgaged their land were at risk. Correspondingly, farm failure rates tripled; slightly more fortunate farmers lost the value of their earnings from oil and gas leases in failed land investments. Towns and investors and property values suffered accordingly.[22]

Undoubtedly, more people have been affected directly by the loss of agricultural and small-town investments than by the boom-and-bust cycles of the oil industry. That industry, however, has unleashed the most dramatic instances of destructive economic forces, which often produce ripple effects that exacerbate the pressures on agriculture and small towns. The oil bust of 1982 was the last dramatic illustration of a long-term historical force that has regularly destroyed the hopes of investors and the people in Oklahoma. The price for oil peaked at $34 per barrel in 1982 and dropped precipitously to $15 by 1986. The state lost 54,000 jobs in oil and gas, 16,000 in manufacturing, and about 10,000 in both construction and transportation and utilities. The proliferation of new motels that had been built to serve the Boomers in western Oklahoma virtually ensured the bankruptcy of many, creating a twenty-year-long distortion in the lodging business along Interstate 40 through Oklahoma. The related collapse of Penn Square Bank triggered a nationwide crisis in banking and the savings and loan industry, virtually destroying the potential for raising capital in Oklahoma for decades.[23]

A personal example may illustrate the range of consequences and impact on potential investors. I purchased a house at El Reno in 1982 and met every payment for ten years. In year six, despite my excellent credit record, I found no source of credit that would allow me to refinance the house. Finally, after eleven years of payments, I sold the much-improved house for $10,000 less than I had paid for it, and about $5,000 less than I owed.

Previously, the decline of the Glenn Pool, Cushing-Healdton, Greater Seminole, and Oklahoma City booms had triggered comparable statewide economic crises. Dozens of smaller regional booms spawned disasters that affected smaller numbers but were equally devastating to individuals and communities. Besides disrupting future invest patterns, such disasters create psychological barriers to investment. The boom-and-bust psychology has often produced humorous but still deleterious effects on individuals. Some of that humor is reflected in the oft-repeated promise that if God will only send another boom, we will promise not to waste it "this time." But waste it they did. Boom psychology encouraged individuals' acquisition of new automo-

biles or oil industry properties, but rarely resulted in long-term, stable investments. The bankers at Penn Square and elsewhere seemed equally convinced
that the boom would never end.[24]

Communities that tried to meet the burgeoning demands of population
during an oil boom were often left with huge debts to be paid by a shrinking
population. A classic case occurred at Earlsboro, a part of the Greater Seminole pool, which flourished in the 1920s. It took that community more than
fifty years to pay off the bonded indebtedness incurred in an effort to provide services to a population that increased sixfold between 1920 and 1930 and
then began a sharp decline. Other area communities had similar experiences,
while the population of Seminole County increased from 23,000 in 1920 to
79,621 in 1930.[25]

That story has been repeated in countless communities across the state,
producing a kind of Catch-22 in which a town's debt prevents improvements
or maintenance to the infrastructure, which reduces the town's attractiveness
to investors or new residents. The impact of these patterns would be serious
even if they were confined to only a few dramatic instances. In fact, however,
they are typical. The varied sources of booms and busts throughout Oklahoma history have meant that sixty-nine of Oklahoma's seventy-seven counties had a decennial population higher at some point than it would be as the
century ended. The empty buildings in a majority of Oklahoma's towns offer
mute evidence of the legacy of booms and busts.[26]

Even more noticeable scars on Oklahoma's landscape serve as vivid indica-
tors of a third historic factor shaping Oklahoma poverty. Those who sneer at
populist concerns about regulating capitalism should be required to drive
through the countryside around Lehigh or Okmulgee and count the number
of abandoned coal mines or slag heaps. For best results, the trip should end in
the Tar Creek area, which has been recognized as the nation's highest-ranking
Superfund site. That dubious distinction is based on the threat from heavy
metal contamination throughout the area stemming from lead and zinc mining. Even without that threat, the existence of the town of Picher and other
area communities is jeopardized by the potential collapse of mines that un-
derlie towns as well as individual properties.[27]

A century of oil development has left its own scars on the landscape.
Abandoned refineries stand as symbolic and real barriers to economic development in many towns while also threatening area water supplies. Less
conspicuous but representative of significant damage and loss of revenue

potential are countless oil storage pits and salt deposits. Likewise, it is still possible to find abandoned wells from the territorial period that were never properly plugged or other remnants of past oil development efforts, successful and otherwise.

At least some of the blame for such historic damage can be distributed among varied groups other than individualists and other capitalists. The state's most extensive oil booms occurred during an era of flush production before the invention of a bottom-hole pressure gauge that could permit effective measurement of production potential. Similarly, local interests, from community leaders to landowners, were rarely concerned with environmental or other long-term issues when the promise of oil money or other major economic gains seemed possible. But one does not have to be anti-business to question why so much has been left for a poor state to clean up. Nor does one have to be a populist to call for reasonable restraints on business to protect the environment and other aspects of the public interest.

These concerns are particularly pertinent to the situation in Oklahoma, where the relative lack of reinvestment in the state by many of the interests who have exploited its resources has mirrored the petty thief's "smash-and-grab" technique. Tulsa's once-deserved reputation as "the Oil Capital of the World," E. W. Marland's investments in Ponca City, H. H. Champlin's enduring contributions to Enid, and the Phillipses' interests legacy to Bartlesville and elsewhere are among the examples that can serve as significant counterpoints to that charge. They are, however, the best examples from almost one hundred years, and their contributions represent only a small percentage of the billions that could have been invested in the state's cultural and other resources. Further, these individuals and families had all made their fortunes and investments by 1930, and they have few rivals among later oilmen or other industrialists. More typical is a pattern of exploitation in which companies are given incentives to locate in Oklahoma, only to move out a few years later for a more attractive offer, leaving communities and the state with little more than a sense of what might have been.[28]

Variations on most of these stories could be told for most southern and western states. Walter Prescott Webb, for example, made many related arguments in 1944 in his controversial book *Divided We Stand*. Elsewhere he lamented the cultural gap between the North and the arid regions of the West. In contrast today, however, many other southern and western states have enjoyed significant economic growth, placing them at or near, if not surpassing, the levels of economic growth enjoyed by the nation's most prosperous regions. Texas has developed its cultural resources in the same period, to the extent that Webb's assertions seem absurd to today's students.[29]

Some of the economic growth outside of Oklahoma can be attributed to geographic factors. Some can be explained by constitutional or other changes such as those advocated by Oklahoma 2000 and comparable interests calling for the reform of populist institutions. Substantive reform that can produce real change in Oklahoma, however, does not appear likely because of the fourth factor shaping the state's deficiencies in poverty leadership and a tendency to deny problems or believe in simple solutions. For example, most groups recognize the need for educational improvements, but many of the same interests have consistently worked against tax increases, including those intended to address educational needs. The state's historic ambivalence about education funding is directly related to deficiencies in leadership at every level, beginning with media influences. E. K. Gaylord and his son E. L. shaped every aspect of their newspaper, the *Daily Oklahoman,* and of the media empire's policies from early statehood to the recent past. That empire has included the state's leading newspaper, the first television station in the capital city, and a major radio station there. Strident conservatives, they occasionally supported city and state economic development initiatives, particularly when family interests might benefit, but they consistently opposed adequate funding for education. Similarly, Gaylord harshly criticized the state's leadership for increasing taxes to offset budget revenue shortfalls during the economic bust of the 1980s.[30]

Arguably even more detrimental has been the newspaper's support of practices and policies that explain the state's inability to solve its problems by blaming external forces, the historic legacy of populism, or some other largely undefined evil. The *Oklahoman* has consistently offered some of the sharpest criticisms of individual political figures or even the actions of the largely Democratic legislature, but it has been very slow to report on endemic problems. The paper led efforts to prosecute Governors Walters and Hall because it had opposed them from the start of their terms in office, but it practically ignored the Supreme Court scandal, the county commissioner scandal, various misdealings surrounding Southwestern Bell's rate cases, and similar examples of corruption until federal prosecutors defined the depth and scope of the problems.[31]

The Gaylord empire also contributed to a pervasive spirit of denial about Oklahoma's problems. The majority of the state's residents initially seemed to recognize the essential accuracy of John Steinbeck's *The Grapes of Wrath* despite some concerns about details and the coarse language therein. The *Oklahoman* and political and educational leaders promoted a different view. Congressman Lyle Boren asserted that "No Oklahoma economic problem has been portrayed in the low and vulgar lines of this publication." Governor Leon Phillips concurred, encouraging the House Un-American Activities Committee, also known as the Dies Committee, to search for evidence of communism in the state as an explanation for its difficulties.[32]

In the meantime, the state's leading university joined in the spirit of the times, abandoning faculty and programs that had gained national recognition. The "Oklahoma movement in poetry," B. A. Botkin's *Folk Say* collections, and similar efforts were either suppressed or allowed to die by the early 1930s, an era that included campus recognition of the D. D. M. C. (Deep Dark Mystery Club), a secret society that used vigilantism against perceived enemies. Similarly, the refusal of the University of Oklahoma Press to publish Angie Debo's *And Still the Waters Run* marked the university's explicit endorsement of the spirit of denial. Debo had done the unpardonable, naming names and documenting the exploitation of the tribes by community and state leaders.[33]

Some of these actions were undoubtedly a response to a climate of fear generated by the rantings from the *Oklahoman*, investigations by the Dies Committee, the raid on progressive bookstores, and similar stresses. But the spirit of denial persisted in Oklahoma long after these threats ended. Even Angie Debo joined the chorus of those who declaimed *The Grapes of Wrath*. In the meantime, the *Oklahoman* finally acknowledged that a problem existed, but it claimed that "Conditions were worse in other states." That attitude has never been seriously challenged in the popular mind of Oklahomans. To this day, when people talk over coffee or even discuss these issues in college classrooms, most will argue that the Okies were not real Oklahomans, that their numbers were inflated by "Arkies." More often, coffee talk centers on the fortunes of the Sooners, the University of Oklahoma's football team, which was deliberately promoted by university and state leaders to offset an unfair negative image of the state in the 1950s.[34]

If willful ignorance had been perpetuated about only one chapter in Oklahoma's history, it would still be damaging, but the state's history is replete with other examples. The corruption that Angie Debo documented in her studies is still not recorded in the mainstream of Oklahoma historical writings. When the bound volumes of the *Tulsa Tribune* were collected for microfilming, the two basic accounts of the 1921 race riot were missing. And there is no mention of that event in Oklahoma history textbooks until 1972. The suppression of our state's history is mirrored in a continuing refusal to deal with present realities. The recent explanation offered by a state Baptist leader for why Oklahoma has one of the highest teen pregnancy rates in the nation illustrates another aspect of the tendency. Arguing that the problem was caused by the absence of prayer in school, he apparently assumed that policy had had only detrimental effects in Oklahoma. A parallel argument of students in my "Introduction to Oklahoma Cultural Studies" class a few years ago also reflected a refusal to deal with reality; they concluded that the data were erroneous. These convictions were at least consistent with their insistence that Oklahoma's standard of living offset the consequences of its poverty, another widespread belief in the state. It was also consistent with what they had been taught, as nearly everyone educated in Oklahoma schools can attest.

Such attitudes and beliefs virtually ensure that Oklahomans will not commit to long-term systematic efforts to address problems. Instead, there will be a continuation of the pattern that historian Danney Goble has called "here we go again," the pursuit of one quick fix after another. Many of the reforms of the past few decades have been needed; the potential for some was dubious from the start. But from HB 1017 (an effort to improve funding for public education) to horse racing and the recent successful campaign for Right to Work, those reforms have often been promoted or understood as a solution to problems much deeper than they could address. Currently, some Oklahomans await the opportunity to establish casino-style gambling, while others bemoan the legislature's failure to enact more stringent restrictions on tort claims, particularly those affecting medicine. Still others are focused on an effort to increase the number of college graduates in the state while tuition has increased by almost 50 percent in the last five years. Fee increases in the same period have added to the burdens faced by students. But one has to search assiduously to establish that the bonded indebtedness of state agencies has risen sharply in the past decade or that Oklahoma's share of national per capita income has declined sharply since 1990. In 2004, the business section of the *Oklahoman* reported that median income in Oklahoma had declined by $500 the previous year. Interestingly, the article then went on to discuss national changes affecting labor.[35]

Some of Oklahoma's economic problems could possibly be resolved by removal of selected populist features from the constitution. But solutions that recognize other historic problems are necessary if we are to address the root causes of the state's malaise. Any long-term solution must address the impact of the past on the hopes of Indians and blacks and must also recognize the long-term effects of boom-and-bust cycles and a tradition of denial. Ultimately, these solutions require a willingness to face the truth about who we have been and who we are. This means the recognition of strengths as well as weaknesses, the refusal to stop at quick fixes, and a commitment to redressing the legacy of generations of despair.

NOTES

1. William Clark, "Constitutional Reform and Economic Development in Oklahoma," in *State Policy and Economic Development in Oklahoma: 1988* (Oklahoma City: Oklahoma 2000, 1998), 18; Alexander Holmes et al., "Social Culture and Economic Development," in *State Policy and Economic Development in Oklahoma: 1998*, 10–14; Barry W. Poulson, "Ensuring Fiscal Discipline in Oklahoma," in *Oklahoma Policy Blueprint* (Oklahoma City: Oklahoma Council of Public Affairs, 2002), 2; Benjamin Powell, "Expanding Economic Freedom in Oklahoma," ibid., 105; Ann-Marie Szymanski, "Oklahoma Constitutional Revision, Revisited," *Oklahoma Policy Studies Review* 2, no. 1 (Spring/Summer 2001): 13–14; Larkin W. Warner, "Economic Foundations: Lessons from Two Decades of Economic Outlook Conferences," unpublished presentation at Economic Outlook Conference, Greater Oklahoma City Chamber of Commerce, September 22, 1998, 10; Larkin W. Warner, "An Overview of Oklahoma's Economic History," pt. 1, *Oklahoma Business Bulletin,* September 1995, 8–10. Extended treatments of populist and other influences in early Oklahoma can be found in Danney Goble, *Progressive Oklahoma: The Making of a New Kind of State* (Norman: University of Oklahoma Press, 1980), and Worth Robert Miller, *Oklahoma Populism: A History of the People's Party in the Oklahoma Territory* (Norman: University of Oklahoma Press, 1987).

2. Robert Lee Maril, *Waltzing with the Ghost of Tom Joad: Poverty, Myth, and Low-Wage Labor in Oklahoma* (Norman: University of Oklahoma Press, 2000), 4, 91–98, 106; Brett S. Sharp, "Great Expectations and Recent Frustrations: Oklahoma Continuing Quest to Partner with Faith-Based Organizations," Roundtable on Religion and Social Welfare Policy, 2003, 1–3; Max Weber, *The Protestant Ethic and the Spirit of Capitalism* (New York: Charles Scribner's Sons, 1958), 47–78.

3. Robert V. Hine, *The American West: An Interpretive History* (Boston: Little, Brown & Co., 1973), 146–76; Warner, "Overview," pt. 1, 6–12.

4. Hine, *The American West,* 146–76; Warner, "Overview," pt. 1, 6–12; Allan G. Bogue, "An Agricultural Empire," in Clyde A. Milner II, Carol A. O'Connor, and Martha A. Sandweiss, eds., *The Oxford History of the American West* (New York: Oxford University Press, 1994), 303–305; Carlos A. Schwantes, "Wage Earners and Wage Makers," ibid., 445–47; Walter Prescott Webb, *The Great Plains* (Boston: Ginn and Co., 1931).

5. Author's compilation, U.S. Census, "State and County Quick Facts," http://quickfacts.census.gov/qfd/states/40000.html, accessed August 2003.

6. Warner, "Overview," pt. 1, 7–8; *State Policy and Economic Development in Oklahoma: 1998,* 13.

7. *State Policy and Economic Development in Oklahoma: 1998,* 13; Annie Heloise Abel, *The American Indian as Participant in the Civil War* (Cleveland: Arthur H. Clark, 1919), 250–51; Abel, *The American Indian under Reconstruction* (Cleveland: Arthur H. Clark, 1925), 331–36; Angie Debo, *And Still the Waters Run* (Princeton, N.J.: Princeton University Press, 1940), esp. 232–38; Howard F. Stein and Robert F. Hill, *The Culture of Oklahoma* (Norman: University of Oklahoma Press, 1993), introduction and p. xxi; *State Policy and Economic Development in Oklahoma: 1998,* 13.

8. Grant Foreman, ed., "Notes of A Missionary among the Choctaws," *Chronicles of Oklahoma* 16, no. 2 (1938): 178.

9. Robert Nespor, "From War Lance to Plow Share," *Chronicles of Oklahoma* 65, no. 1 (Spring 1987): 42–75; Alvin O. Turner, "Journey to Sainthood," *Chronicles of Oklahoma* 70, no. 2 (Summer 1992): 136.

10. General Accounting Office, "Report to Commissioner of Indian Affairs," Appendix I, May 3, 1996; Ercole Grudi, "Indian Trust Fund, the Billion Dollar Heist," 1–3, http://www.geocities.com/Athens/Delphi/1088/natives/case.htm, cited January 27, 2004; Terry Wilson, *The Underground Reservation: Osage Oil* (Lincoln: University of Nebraska Press, 1985), 134, 135, 145–47.

11. CBS News, "Blood and Oil," http://www.cbsnews.com/stories/2000/11/27/60II/main252545.shtml?CMP=ILC-SearchStories, accessed August 15, 2001; "Senator Don Nickles (R-OK)," *National Journal,* May 16, 1992, www.motherjones.com/news/special_reports/coinop_congress/stock_congress/don_nickles.html, accessed May 6, 2006.

12. Wayne H. Morgan and Anne Hodges Morgan, *Oklahoma: A History* (Nashville, Tenn.: American Association for State and Local History, 1984), 106–107; Stein and Hill, *The Culture of Oklahoma,* 49, 58–59.

13. Warner, "Overview," pt. 1, 7–8; Stein and Hill, *The Culture of Oklahoma,* 208; *State Policy and Economic Development in Oklahoma: 1998,* 13.

14. Richard R. Johnson and Alvin O. Turner, "The Smell of Corruption," in Johnson and Turner, *Oklahoma at the Crossroads* (Dubuque, Iowa: Kendall/Hunt Publishing Co., 1998), 75–89; David R. Morgan, Robert E. England, and George G. Humphreys, *Oklahoma Politics and Policies: Governing the Sooner State* (Lincoln: University of Nebraska Press, 1991), 196–99, 211.

15. Ibid.

16. Stein and Hill, *The Culture of Oklahoma,* 43, 129, 132, 139, 206; Morgan, England, and Humphreys, *Oklahoma Politics and Policies,* 59.

17. Alvin O. Turner, "Order and Disorder," *Chronicles of Oklahoma* 71, no. 2 (Summer 1993): esp. 154–56, 170.

18. Ibid.

19. Schwantes, "Wage Earners and Wage Makers," 440–47; Paul B. Sears, *Deserts on the March* (Norman: University of Oklahoma Press, 1980), 126–27; Oklahoma Academy for State Goals, *Strategy for Economic Expansion in Oklahoma* (Stillwater: Oklahoma Academy for State Goals, 1986), 1–3; Larkin W. Warner, "An Overview of Oklahoma's Economic History," pt. 2, *Oklahoma Business Bulletin,* December 1995, 5–14.

20. James P. Gutelius, *High Lights on Auctioneering* (Kansas City, Mo.: Nazarene Publishing Co., 1922), 140–46; Turner, "Order and Disorder," 170.

21. Warner, "Overview," pt. 1, 10–14.

22. Ibid., 13–18; Warner, "Overview," pt. 2, 5–14; Oklahoma Academy for State Goals, *Strategy for Economic Expansion in Oklahoma,* 1–3.

23. Warner, "Overview," pt. 2, 5–14; Morgan, England, and Humphreys, *Oklahoma Politics and Policies,* 209; Mark Singer, *Funny Money* (Boston: Houghton Mifflin, 2004).

24. Singer, *Funny Money.*

25. John Wesley Morris, *The Agglomerated Settlements of the Greater Seminole Area* (Nashville, Tenn.: George Peabody College, 1941), 3–5; Oklahoma Employment Security Commission, *Special Studies, June 1, 1890–April 1, 1930 Census Enumeration* (Oklahoma City: Oklahoma Employment Security Commission, 1981).

26. Author's compilation, U.S. Census, "State and County Quick Facts"; Warner, "Overview," pt. 1, 11.

27. *Governor Frank Keating's Tar Creek Superfund Task Force: Final Report* (Oklahoma City: Office of the Secretary of Environment, 2000), 1–3.

28. Henry B. Bass, "Hubert Hiram Champlin," *Chronicles of Oklahoma* 32 (Spring 1955): 124–33; John Joseph Matthews, *Life and Death of an Oilman: The Career of E. W. Marland* (Norman: University of Oklahoma Press, 1974), esp. 177–87.

29. Necah Stewart Furman, *Walter Prescott Webb: His Life and Impact* (Albuquerque: University of New Mexico Press, 1976), 3, 77, 101–10, 118–19, 120–24, 142, 172–77; Walter Prescott Webb, *Divided We Stand: The Crisis of a Frontierless Democracy* (Austin, Tex.: Acorn Press, 1944), esp. 19–23, 28, 49–52, 102–103.

30. Morgan, England, and Humphreys, *Oklahoma Politics and Policies,* 4–6.

31. Ibid.; Johnson and Turner, "The Smell of Corruption," 75–89.

32. Maril, *Waltzing with the Ghost of Tom Joad,* 4–5, 107–29; Martin Staples Shockley, "The Reception of the Grapes of Wrath in Oklahoma," *American Literature* 15 (January 1944): 351–61; Marsha L. Weisiger, "The Grapes of Wrath Reappraised," *Chronicles of Oklahoma* 70, no. 4 (Winter 1992–93): 391–414.

33. George Lynn Cross, *Professors, Politicians, and Presidents: Civil Rights and the University of Oklahoma, 1890–1968* (Norman: University of Oklahoma Press, 1981), 87–88, 90, 92–93, 109, 113–19; Richard Lowitt, "Regionalism at the University of Oklahoma," *Chronicles of Oklahoma* 73 (Spring 1998): 157–58, 162–67.

34. Cross, *Professors, Politicians, and Presidents,* 87–88, 90, 92–93, 109, 113–19; Lowitt, "Regionalism at the University of Oklahoma," 157–58, 162–67; George Lynn Cross, *Presidents Can't Punt: The OU Football Tradition* (Norman: University of Oklahoma Press, 1977), 7–10; Weisiger, "The Grapes of Wrath Reappraised," 395, 401–402, 409–10.

35. Paul Monies, "Mixed Signals Blur Job Picture," *Sunday Oklahoman,* September 5, 2004, D1; Oklahoma State Regents for Higher Education, *Brain Gain 2010: Building Oklahoma through Intellectual Power* ([Oklahoma City]: Oklahoma State Regents for Higher Education, 1999).

CHAPTER 11

Unraveling the Mystery of Freedom-Prosperity Inconsistency in Oklahoma

Brian Bentel

Brian Bentel is Assistant Professor of Sociology at East Central University in Ada, Oklahoma. He holds the B.S. in Sociology/Psychology from the University of Wyoming and the M.A. in Sociology from the same institution (his thesis was entitled "The Deceptively Rational Use of Ideology"). Texas A & M University awarded him the Ph.D. degree in 1999 (his dissertation was titled "Societal Fragmentation and the Postmodern Crisis of Identity").

This essay was originally presented at the 2001 conference "Religion, Freedom, and Prosperity in Oklahoma" at East Central University. A version was also published in the *ECU Research Journal,* no. 1 (Spring 2002). Alvin O. Turner, the editor of that journal, graciously granted permission to reprint the essay here, but this version is actually considerably revised.

Thomas Frank, in his book *What's the Matter with Kansas? How Conservatives Won the Heart of America* (New York: Metropolitan Books, 2004), makes the basic point that Kansas, like much of the nation, votes self-destructively—meaning conservatively—because social issues such as abortion, gun control, flag burning, and gay marriage distract it from economic self-interest. Is it indeed too much to suggest that many Americans vote for the Republican Party because of its conservative stand on such issues and get in return economic policies that hurt them, that help to keep them in poverty?

Bentel's essay provides food for thought on that issue with Oklahoma as its focus. He flows freely from sociology into economics and history to help us understand the relationship between religion and poverty/prosperity. His essay follows logically after Alvin O. Turner's, for together they provide a complex and sophisticated examination of poverty and prosperity in Oklahoma.

Clearly, religion is an important factor in Oklahoma life, and in Oklahoma history. But as with any important subject, there are different ways to look at Oklahoma religion. Turner and Bentel, and, to follow, Samuel P. Riccobene and Marlin Lavanhar, all look at the subject in non-mainstream, "alternative" ways.

I n April 2001, East Central University in Ada, Oklahoma, held a conference entitled "Religion, Freedom, and Prosperity in Oklahoma." As the "call for papers" that was sent out for this conference showed, examples of the apparent positive relationship among economic, civil, and religious liberties and economic prosperity abound in the international context. Of the top twenty-nine countries in the 1999 Heritage Foundation's Index of Economic Freedom, nineteen have a Judeo-Christian heritage, twenty-two are listed by the Freedom House as "free," and nineteen have per capita Gross Domestic Products in excess of 10,000.

These findings raise an interesting question regarding our state. As part of the "Bible Belt," Oklahoma is one of the most religious states in the nation. Its people enjoy the same basic liberties as those in other states, and it is rich in resources. So why, then, is it one of the poorest states in the nation, ranking among the lowest with respect to the quality of living? Oklahoma ranks forty-sixth in per capita personal income, with an average income equivalent to 80 percent of the national average; it has the fourth-highest divorce rate in the nation; it ranks forty-fourth in overall health status; and it was one of only two states (with Arkansas) in which the mortality rate increased between 1990 and 1997. The Progressive Policy Institute's New Economy Project ranks Oklahoma fortieth in readiness for the new high-tech jobs and business of the twenty-first century.

The conference challenged participants to explain the peculiar case of Oklahoma—a state in which the assumed relationship among religion, freedom, and prosperity did not exist. However, it was apparent to me and many of my colleagues that the call for papers had answered its own question: there is no mystery here, because Oklahoma-style religion is conducive to neither freedom nor prosperity. Rather than explain how the religion-freedom-prosperity inconsistency in Oklahoma constitutes an "exceptional" case, I will attempt to unravel the very premise of the conference itself.

Most disturbing is that such a critique must be undertaken in the first place. "Of course there's a strong positive relationship between religiosity and prosperity," quipped a particularly sarcastic colleague. "I mean, look at Afghanistan—I've never seen such a booming economy! And that Japan! Those atheists are living in cardboard boxes!" While the joke is obvious to some, others—apparently even in academia—continue to see religion as a panacea. It is not uncommon for this Oklahoma professor to hear our citizens, including college students, rue the loss of prayer in school, blaming this tragedy for everything from the Columbine massacre to teen pregnancy (indeed, in Oklahoma, prayer may be a major form of birth control).

It is perhaps a talent of our species to ignore mountains of evidence if those mountains support conclusions that threaten cherished beliefs. Must the trouble be taken to spell out the obvious—that superstition and economic development are not particularly compatible? That extremes of religiosity and extremes of poverty typically go hand in hand? That those who prefer not to question the dogma of ancient religious texts are not likely to question their own exploitation in today's economic climate?

Consider the levels of economic development for the twenty nations with the highest levels of atheism. Those nations and the estimated percentages of their populations who classify themselves as atheists, agnostics, or nonbelievers are as follows:

Sweden, 46–85 percent
Vietnam, 81 percent
Denmark, 43–80 percent
Norway, 31–72 percent
Japan, 64–65 percent
Czech Republic, 54–61 percent
Finland, 28–60 percent
France, 43–54 percent
South Korea, 30–52 percent
Estonia, 49 percent
Germany, 41–49 percent
Russia, 24–48 percent
Hungary, 32–46 percent
Netherlands, 39–44 percent

Britain, 31–44 percent
Belgium 42–43 percent
Bulgaria, 34–40 percent
Slovenia, 35–38 percent
Israel, 15–37 percent
Canada, 19–30 percent[1]

Two groups are represented here. The first, constituting about two-thirds (13) of the list, are nations that clearly fall into the category of "developed." In other words, they are democratic "First World" nations with high levels of economic development, democracy, and civil rights. The remaining seven are mainly former Soviet bloc nations. Although they are not fully "developed," neither should they be placed in a "Third World" category. Because atheism was promoted by the state under communist rule, we should not be surprised to find countries such as Slovenia and Russia here. But if religiosity is so crucial to freedom and prosperity, why do so many in developed nations shy away from religious belief?

So begin the mountains of evidence. Yet despite these mountains, the voice of reason often rings unheard, for to hear it is to call into question something much more powerful than reason. It is to question what by definition must not be questioned: the sacred.

The purpose of this essay is to analyze the theoretical relationship between two variables in Oklahoma: "liberty" (including economic, religious, and civil liberty) and "prosperity" (by which we mean the standard of living of Oklahomans). One perspective, which for the purpose of this discussion will be called the "liberty breeds prosperity" thesis, asserts that a society's economic prosperity depends upon its level of liberty or "freedom." According to this perspective, "liberty" is a general force that is reflected in signs of liberty such as religious expression, unfettered economic activity, and civil liberties. A society in which these signs are apparent should also be a prosperous one.

This assertion (or we might use the term *ideology*) reflects particular political interests that will be discussed later. At the same time, we must recognize that the "liberty breeds prosperity" principle, in the most general sense (and if we do not bother to examine it critically), is well accepted in the United States. Americans are fond of pointing out that our great prosperity is due to the fact that we live in a "free country," where economic opportunity is limited only by one's aspirations, and where religious and other sorts of expression are not limited at all. The best policy decisions, therefore, will be those that favor liberty rather than regulation (be this government regulation of business, religion, or people's personal lives).

If a society shows a low degree of economic prosperity—as does Oklahoma, as is reflected in a variety of census statistics, including average income, health status, and mortality rates[2]—there are a few conclusions that might be drawn. One is that liberty is lacking in the society in question, in which case the "liberty breeds prosperity" thesis is supported as it stands. Another is that liberty is apparent in the society but not actually present, in which case, again, the thesis is supported. If, however, liberty truly exists and prosperity is absent, we must conclude that the "liberty breeds prosperity" thesis is somehow flawed or invalid, or that some special circumstance has affected the impact of liberty on economic prosperity for the case in question. All the above conclusions apply to the liberty-prosperity inconsistency in Oklahoma. That is, the liberty-prosperity thesis can be criticized on all counts.

This is not to say that the thesis is worthy only of criticism. As is true of many flawed theories, the liberty-prosperity idea is not totally without merit. This being the case, a modified theoretical framework can clarify the relationships between the variables in question, with new variables added as required.

INEQUALITY IN THE BIBLE BELT

If one flaw in the "liberty breeds prosperity" thesis presents itself particularly strongly, it is the idea that religious expression causes—or at least coincides with—economic prosperity. While the idea can be countered logically, it may be helpful to start by considering certain facts that stand in opposition to this notion. The opposite assertion—that the association between religious expression and prosperity does not exist—is suggested by data on levels of inequality in Bible Belt states and on income levels of different religious groups.

What qualifies as the Bible Belt is subjective, but it is typically taken to mean the strip of states running "from Texas north to Kansas, east to Virginia, and south to Florida."[3] A state is popularly called a Bible Belt state when it is known for particular patterns of religious activity. Although frequency of church membership and attendance may be a factor, at least as important is the type of religious practice and belief: Conservative Protestantism. Because there are many strains of Conservative Protestants in the South and elsewhere, it is not accurate to make sweeping statements about the character of these groups.

Data collected by George Barna may be of help here. Barna, a conservative Christian, uses social science methods to gather information about religious practices, trends, beliefs, and associations between religious variables and others (such as income). Although Barna does not define the fundamentalist aspect of Conservative Protestantism, he does provide definitions for "born again" and "evangelical," traits associated with Bible Belt Christianity. To be born again, a Christian must make "a personal commitment to Jesus Christ that is still important in [his or her] life today," and agree that "when I die, I will go to Heaven because I have confessed my sins and have accepted Jesus Christ as my savior." To be classified as "evangelical" by Barna's standard, a Christian must be born again and "say their faith is very important in their life today; believe they have a personal responsibility to share their religious beliefs about Christ with non-Christians; believe that Satan exists; believe that the eternal salvation is possible only through grace, not works; believe that Jesus Christ lived a sinless life on Earth; and describe God as the all-knowing, all-powerful, perfect deity who created the universe and still rules it today."[4]

Although there seems to be a clear association between being "born again" and the Bible Belt, it is not correct to say that Conservative Protestants as a whole can be described as both evangelical and fundamentalist. It may be important to distinguish evangelism, which is characterized by a doctrine of sharing one's faith with others, from fundamentalism, which is characterized by a doctrine of (claimed) strict adherence to literal interpretations of the Bible.

Whether or not Conservative Protestant sects and denominations qualify as evangelical or fundamentalist, Bible Belt Christianity is overtly religious—in other words, it is expressive, spilling into the everyday lives of its adherents. We can compare this way of life to that of more moderate Christian denominations (for instance, Catholics and liberal Protestants such as Lutherans and Episcopalians), who might be more likely to hold the idea that religion "has its place," and that place is church.[5] Such groups define the very goal of religion in a different way. For example, for an Episcopalian, church may not be "about" evangelism but about connecting with the community, while for a Unitarian, "good works" may be given primacy. More moderate forms of Christianity are also more likely to recognize alternative sources of truth and authority. Other data from Barna help us to understand these different approaches, and to place beliefs associated with Conservative Protestantism in the South.[6] Consider:

- While 50 percent of southerners describe themselves as born again, 40 percent of westerners, 39 percent of midwesterners, and 28 percent of those living in the Northeast are classified as born again.
- Southerners are more likely than others to believe that the Bible is totally accurate in all of its teachings. This belief is held by 52 percent of those living in the South, 45 percent of those in the West, 40 percent of those in the Midwest, and 37 percent of those in the Northeast.
- Those living in the South feel more of a responsibility than the average American to tell others about their faith. Approximately 45 percent feel a responsibility to share their faith with others, compared to 34 percent of westerners, 31 percent of midwesterners, and 22 percent of northeasterners.
- More than 76 percent of those living in the South state that their faith is very important in their life, compared to 67 percent of those living in the Midwest, and 61 percent of those living in the West or Northeast.

With our admittedly imperfect definition of the Bible Belt, let us now look to some evidence regarding associations between economic prosperity and Bible Belt status. The list below includes all definitive and possible Bible Belt states, in order of income inequality ranking. Lower numbers indicate higher levels of inequality. Data are from the U.S. Census and represent the average degree of income inequality over a period of approximately ten years (1990–1999). Alongside this ranking, I have added the official percentage of the population living below the poverty level for each state. (The average poverty rate for the United States as a whole is listed by the census bureau as 12.3 percent.)[7]

Louisiana (4), 19.6 percent
Texas (7), 15.4 percent
Kentucky (9), 15.8 percent
Virginia (10), 9.6 percent
Alabama (11), 16.1 percent
Georgia (12), 13 percent
Florida (13), 12.5 percent
West Virginia (14), 17.9 percent
Mississippi (15), 19.9 percent
North Carolina (17), 12.3 percent
Oklahoma (18), 14.7 percent
Kansas (21), 9.9 percent

Tennessee (27), 13.5 percent
Arkansas (28), 15.8 percent
Missouri (33), 11.7 percent
South Carolina (36), 14.1 percent

By "inequality," I mean the degree to which (in this case) income is received disproportionately by a small proportion of the population (the richest). To the extent that inequality exists, the standard of living for the average person tends to fall. Note that all but five states from the Bible Belt list fall into the top twenty most unequal states, and the average ranking for the list is about 17. (If this list were "average" in inequality, the figure would be close to 25.) Among the top fifteen most stratified states are such clearly Bible Belt states as Texas, Louisiana, Alabama, Georgia, and Mississippi—with Oklahoma close behind at number 18.

It is important to note that while inequality is related to poverty, it is not the same thing. Hypothetically, a society could be very equal and very poor (e.g., everyone is equally starving) or very stratified and very rich (e.g., although there are great differences between classes, even the lowest classes have plenty of money). The latter possibility is not supported by the evidence when it comes to the Bible Belt, as the poverty rates listed above indicate. Out of the sixteen states listed, only four—Virginia, North Carolina, Kansas, and Missouri—show poverty rates lower than the national average (and we might note that these states tend to hit "above the belt" geographically).

Thus, while inequality does not necessarily indicate squalor for the poorest, it seems to be associated with it. Median household incomes by region further demonstrate the relationship between inequality and poverty in the South. The median household income for the United States as a whole is $42,100; for the Northeast it is $45,100; for the Midwest it is $44,600; for the West it is $44,700; and for the South it is $38,400.[8] Data from Barna tends to complement what the census reveals: "Income appears to be inversely related to identifying oneself as a 'born again Christian.' We found that only 26 percent of those who earn at least $60K a year call themselves born again, while 44 percent of those who earn under $60K a year identify themselves as born again Christians."[9]

What we should conclude from this rough look at the Bible Belt is not that Conservative Protestantism necessarily causes inequality and lower income, but that, at the very least, it seems to be associated with inequality and low income rather than with economic prosperity. Thus, the observation that

Oklahoma is an enigma because of the simultaneous presence of high religious expression and low prosperity makes little sense. Instead, given the pattern as it stands, the assertion should be that this lack of prosperity is predictable. Indeed, both the census data and Barna's findings conform to associations between class and denomination revealed by other sociological research.[10]

On a more intuitive level, it may be hard to imagine a member of the "old money" New England elite speaking in tongues, handling snakes, or testifying to whoever will listen. We may find the occasional Mercedes in the parking lot of the Pentecostal church, but in sociology we deal in aggregates. The cold statistics listed so far corroborate what can be observed casually: Episcopalians tend to be more economically affluent than, say, Southern Baptists (i.e., the so-called "Liberal Protestants" do better economically than the conservative denominations). While these associations can be demonstrated empirically, our purpose here is to explain them, and thus to shed light on the lack of prosperity that can be found in a Bible Belt state such as Oklahoma.

RELIGIOUS LIBERTY IN THE BIBLE BELT

Although it is not central to the critique undertaken here, it may be worth our time to call into question an assumption revealed in the previously cited "call for papers"—that the abstract concept "religious liberty" is indicated by signs of religious *expression* in a society. Logically, expression could indicate either that individuals are free to express religious beliefs (as suggested by the thesis) or that they have been pressured to do so by state or informal agents of social control. In societies such as Iran and Saudi Arabia, it is against the law *not* to engage in certain behaviors that express religion. Likewise, although religious non-expression is formally protected in the United States, in my experience it is informally expected, at least in my area of Oklahoma, at private (and occasionally state-sponsored) activities such as rodeos, sporting events, public schools, and civic clubs, where the assembly or group normally includes a Christian prayer (even though there are bound to be non-Christians present) alongside other collective rituals such as the Pledge of Allegiance.

This being the case, we might say that a high level of religious expression is rather a sign not of liberty but of religious conformity. Because individuals in such societies are likely to feel pressure to conform to religious practices that they do not normally observe, those societies may be accurately judged to be *lacking* in religious liberty. If religious liberty is part and parcel of liberty generally, a high degree of religious expression may even be a sign that the society in question lacks liberty. If this is so, why not define religious liberty to mean religious non-expression? To do so makes the same mistake as the original, but in the opposite direction; it may be that some force is keeping people from religious expression, as was the case in the former USSR.

Defining societies with a great variety of religious expression as "religiously free" might make more sense. By such a definition, a social and geographic region where one category of religious practice predominates does not seem comparatively "free." Living in rural Oklahoma has placed me in countless situations where Christians have led those present in prayer—but never Muslims or Hindus or Wiccans, even though I knew such faiths to be represented in the audience. Indeed, I have witnessed Catholics express hesitation about revealing themselves! If we can agree that religious liberty, and thus perhaps liberty generally, is not especially great in the Bible Belt, then the inequality rankings, poverty rates, and median income data mentioned above make more sense, and in fact will jibe well with the "liberty breeds prosperity" thesis; in other words, we are talking about a society in which people are in some sense repressed or limited in their behavior—and it shows in prosperity measures.

LIBERTY FOR WHOM?

If the claimed positive relationship between "religious liberty" and "prosperity" does not hold when religious liberty is measured by a society's level of religious expression, it is a result of the way "religious liberty" is measured rather than a basic logical flaw in the "liberty breeds prosperity" thesis. A second flaw, similarly, does not concern the connection between liberty and economic prosperity—it has to do with a lack of specification of the concepts "liberty" and "prosperity."

The implication of the thesis under criticism is that liberty is a general social force that is reflected in such examples as economic, civil, and religious liberty. In other words, we are told that there is a characteristic of society called "freedom" or "liberty"—a characteristic that a society can have more or less of. How will we know the extent to which this characteristic exists in a given society? We see it when people are allowed to trade freely, speak freely, worship freely. In accordance with the "liberty breeds prosperity" thesis, there is no point in distinguishing one type of freedom from another, because they are all part and parcel of the same social force. Breaking the variable "freedom" down further serves as much purpose as breaking a crayon in half: the two halves can be used for different purposes, but they are the same thing in essence.

My position, on the other hand, is that while we may be able to collapse civil and religious liberty into the general category of "civil liberties," economic liberty means something very different and must be treated in its own right. Economic liberty refers to a lack of state regulation of business, while civil liberty is commonly taken to mean a list of individual rights guaranteed by the state, such as the right to free speech, political action, security from state invasion into the home, and religious practice. The American Civil Liberties Union focuses on civil liberties, and is not particularly interested in the details of, say, the laws regulating the banking industry. Likewise, the concern of the American Enterprise Institute is not whether Muslim girls are allowed to wear veils in the public school system—the AEI persistently calls for reduced government regulation of business. If both civil and economic liberties are nothing more than "reflections" of the general social force "liberty," we should expect them to coexist peacefully in a free society. If such can be shown not to be the case, then there is some reason to doubt the wisdom of conceptually combining the two as one force. Before an argument is presented against the peaceful coexistence of civil and economic liberty, we should note that the two *are* often conceptually combined. The "liberty breeds prosperity" thesis has taken economic liberty and "thrown it in" with civil liberty in an attempt to associate the two for ideological purposes (i.e., the idea is to convince the many of this equivalence so that the few may benefit). To understand exactly how and why this ideological synthesis of concepts exists, we must look back to social changes that occurred in the West at the beginning of the modern era.

The change from medieval to modern was fueled in part by ideologies of civil liberty—ideologies that helped motivate and organize the lower classes and bring about social change, and in some cases violent revolution. Enlightenment ideology, a reflection of resurrected ideas from the golden ages of ancient Rome and Greece, concerned civil more than economic liberty. Reason —not capitalism—was touted as the ultimate means of, and precondition for, freedom.[11] The point is that the civil liberties sought by these thinkers, though they are little different from the liberties sought by Americans today, were not deliberately associated with economic freedom in the sense of free-market capitalism. Particular Enlightenment thinkers varied in their advocacy of industrial revolution and the accompanying social revolution that ultimately increased the sociopolitical power of middle-class factory owners and merchants,[12] but whatever the motivation for this Enlightenment reasoning, it was used by a burgeoning economic elite in Europe. "Liberty for all!" was the cry of the revolutionary, but "Liberty for us!" (i.e., the budding capitalists), remained the underlying motivation.[13]

Freed from interference by the aristocracy, a new capitalist elite could pursue its own interests. Some of the freedom acquired by this group could not help but benefit the rest of society: absent a formal caste system, it was possible, theoretically, for certain talented or lucky people to rise through the social hierarchy. Other benefits of the new order might include some degree of participation in government, access to mass-produced, free-market consumer goods, and increased education. Still, it can be argued that, especially at the early stages of capitalism, a tendency existed for the exploited serf to become an exploited industrial worker.[14]

History shows a slight drop in living standards for any given society entering its industrial phase, followed by a slow increase. For a while it appears that freedom has triumphed for all—civil *and* economic liberties have led us to greater prosperity. This increase reaches a maximum, however, when benefits to citizens begin to exceed the usefulness of such benefits to business, and business fights back with repression of the worker: increased hours, a reduction in pay, layoffs, child labor, and at times brutal discipline of workers. It is at this point that a popular movement must create additional benefits, such as we saw with the labor movement in early-twentieth-century U.S. history, and earlier in Western Europe.

Although U.S. workers and their First World counterparts fought risky and often bloody battles to gain labor rights (another sort of civil liberty), in the United States many of the results turned out to be short-term. Efforts by business—anti-labor PR campaigns, legal changes such as "Right to Work," and the like—have been so successful in weakening unions that today union membership is strikingly low compared to other First World societies.[15] The proportion of workers who belong to unions is approximately 13 percent in the United States, while in Germany it is 34 percent, in England 42 percent, and in Japan 27 percent.[16] Related to this are lower average wages for American workers compared to their First World contemporaries. In 1998, Germany, Belgium, France, Austria, Denmark, the Netherlands, Japan, and Finland boasted higher average wages than the U.S.[17]

More disturbing is that the average U.S. hourly wage that year was around

$22, an amount that would have thrilled a great majority of Oklahoma la-
borers (whose rate of union membership, by the way, was only 8.9 percent in
2002). This seemingly generous average wage may be more indicative of the
dual labor market—a situation in which one sector of the economy (typically
large corporations in specific low-competition industries) pays good salaries
and benefits, while another (e.g., retail, restaurants) keeps wages and benefits
as low as possible.[18] In general, we must be careful when comparing averages
between the United States and other First World nations. Often our average is
"average" not so much in the sense of "typical" as in the sense of representing
a deceptive midpoint between the very rich and the very poor.

The conceptual collapsing of economic and civil liberties facilitates the
battles that elites have waged against labor and other reasonable attempts to
curtail the relentless pursuit of profit. Today, the old Enlightenment ideal of
freedom is used by U.S. conservatives to justify economic exploitation of
underdeveloped regions such as Oklahoma, the rural South generally, and the
Third World.[19] The concepts of civil and economic liberty have been melded
in an effort to convince the general population that a reduction in economic
freedom for the corporate elite precedes a total loss of individual freedom.
Americans are reminded about the Soviet Union, a society that purportedly
lost its civil liberties because it lost free-market capitalism: democracy (civil
liberty) and capitalism (economic liberty), it is contended, must necessarily
go together. Warren Burger, in his preface to the copy of the U.S. Constitution that I keep in my office, plainly states that immigrants flock to the
United States because the liberties granted by our constitution give people
opportunities.[20]

Profit margins increase when corporations operate in places that do not
regulate things such as wages, workers' rights, and pollution; this is why
businesses have been shifting to such havens for several decades. While this
sort of economic liberty is well and good for corporations, we must understand that such regulations are ideally designed to protect common people
from the abuses of powerful business interests. Such abuses amount to increased private profit subsidized by the public (in environmental damage,
unsafe working conditions, etc.). For instance, a polluting industry profits
more when the costs of cleanup are borne by the public. These may be costs to
the state if it does the cleanup, or health costs to those poisoned if no one does.

Ironically, the free-market champion Adam Smith warned against socializ-
ing the costs of doing business, arguing that businesses will be unmotivated to
increase efficiency if the public picks up any of those costs. In fact, Smith did

not call for a laissez-faire (unregulated) market, but rather for one regulated by fair rules in which monopolies, which he viewed pejoratively, could be prevented.[21] In a democratic society, the most rational way for the general public to protect its interests, when such interests clash with those of the powerful elites, is through the government. This statement requires qualification—even in ostensibly democratic societies, the government can be controlled by powerful groups (typically business, or the government workers themselves), and to the extent that this is the case, the people will not exert power through it.

However, as the case of Western European socialism demonstrates today, business *can* be kept in check by the people's will. Although some may define this as a lack of liberty, and point accusingly at the slowness of such economies, they mysteriously overlook certain crucial facts: these societies lead the world in measures of the prosperity of the average individual (as compared to that of the business elite). Measures of health in democratic socialist nations rival those of the United States (which ranks thirty-ninth worldwide in a measure of the population's general health, despite being first in health-care expenditures), their poverty rates are a fraction of ours, and we have not even mentioned crime.[22]

The point, relevant to the conceptualization problems of the "liberty breeds prosperity" thesis, is "Liberty *for whom* breeds prosperity *for whom*?" As the thesis stands, "prosperity," like "liberty," is treated in too simplistic a manner—the question of "prosperity for whom?" is ignored. Instead it is taken for granted that prosperity for a society (as measured, for instance, by an expanding economy) means prosperity for all, or at least most, individuals. For the major part of the 1990s, the term was used to describe the United States—the logic being that a booming economy is the best indicator of prosperity. Thus, there is an assumed relationship between economic prosperity for business and prosperity for others. The most interesting point is that this is usually the case: when the richest get richer, other classes may gain as well. But for the first time in U.S. history, economic developments in the 1990s did not produce that result. During this period of economic expansion, a time when businesses could not find adjectives powerful enough to describe the profits they were making, the average citizen did not see an increase in prosperity (toward the end of the decade, there were improvements to the tune of a few percentage points, but not for all; for instance, the very poor got even poorer).[23]

This is not to say that Americans weren't working. Another common assumption is that a drop in unemployment means a rise in the standard of living, and yet the 1990s brought high employment alongside low wages, reduced benefits, and little job security. It can be argued that these conditions are in part what allowed the record expansion of the economy in the 1990s,[24] although, as has been made clear in recent years, the artificial boosting of corporate earnings via questionable accounting practices also played an important role. It is crucial to note that both the permissive tax law and the relaxation of traditional labor protections represent, in a sense, "freedoms" for business. Unfortunately, as is clear with this example, one party's freedom is often paid for with another's suffering. (Just ask a former Enron employee.)

The "liberty breeds prosperity" thesis thus holds—but only if it is recognized that in a society with competing groups, a gain in freedom, and thus prosperity, for one group often comes at the cost of a loss in freedom, and thus prosperity, for another. In a nation such as the United States, and especially in a state such as Oklahoma, where it is well accepted that "what's good for business is good for everyone" (i.e., where civil and economic liberty are conflated), we can expect only that prosperity will land in the laps of those who have the freedom to exploit those whose freedoms have increasingly been taken away.

RETURNING REASON TO THE MODEL OF LIBERTY AND PROSPERITY

To understand the essential flaw of the "liberty breeds prosperity" thesis requires that we return to its source: the Enlightenment thinkers. While these thinkers espoused freedom as we do today, they emphasized reason as a precondition of freedom.[25] It was reason that allowed people to see the flaws of the outdated and exploitative monarchies and change them to more democratic forms of governance. Reason had this power because it made no assumptions, recognized no authorities, religious or secular: reason's power lay only in logic and facts. The force of reason lies behind decisions, made long ago in Western societies, to replace traditional doctrine with scientific theory, and to replace traditional tyrannies with government of and for the people. While such outcomes of reason have hardly been perfect, it can be argued that they are an improvement over a society in which the sun revolves around the earth "because the church says so."

The current American ideology of "liberty breeds prosperity" (embodied in such political philosophies as "trickle-down" economics) has retained the idea of "freedom" without its necessary precursor, "reason." In the absence of reason, said the Enlightenment thinkers, *there can be no freedom*.[26] It is only when citizens are aware of the true relationships between social policies and outcomes that they can effectively support policies that are in their interest, and resist those that are not. Without reason, the serf accepts the idea that the king deserves to live in luxury while he and his family starve, because he has been assured by the church that the king's authority is "divinely ordained." Likewise, without reason, the American worker accepts that he or she is not entitled to affordable health care, fair wages, or a safe working environment, because in our value system it is justifiable for bosses to make as much money as they can—but not for workers to "rock the boat" (i.e., make a living wage) by, say, joining a union.

The problem with the implicit corrective is that reason is not easy. It requires hard intellectual work, and a willingness to question current understandings of reality. Thinking about, and being critical of, the dominant perspectives of one's society is difficult. Believing in, and conforming to, the dominant perspectives of one's society is *not* difficult. As human beings, we are feelers and believers before we are rational analyzers. We want to belong to groups, to be accepted by them—to feel secure. Religious organizations—in particular, organizations that espouse abandonment of critical thought in favor of faith in doctrine—give us all the good feelings and security we could want without challenging prevailing economic thought.

A colleague of mine in political science once made the comment that to get elected in the state of Oklahoma, one must remember the three Gs: guns, God, and gays. Of course, the key is to be *pro*-guns, *pro*-God, and *anti*-gay. Howard Dean made the same point in defense of his controversial statement that he wanted to "reach out to the guys with Confederate flags on their pickup trucks." Dean noted that until the people of the South learn to ignore such conservative rhetoric, they will see no improvement in what actually matters: education, health care, and jobs.

Conservative Protestantism is also associated with an uncritical commitment to conservative values generally, including nationalism, obedience to authority, self-reliance, hard work, and the sanctity of free-market capitalism. This assertion is supported by data from Barna that link dogmatic religious beliefs to conservative political behavior (e.g., those who see the Bible as literally true are more likely to support right-wing policies).[27] In some ways, such conservative values overlap greatly with general American values, but in other ways they can be described as "extreme" (this is not to say that all conservative values are negative, or anti-freedom). In particular, and most relevant for our purposes, conservatives tend to believe that we should obey authorities, work hard, and blame individuals, including ourselves, for their lack of economic success, as opposed to criticizing an imperfect social system, which they seek to "conserve." When we combine the political conservatism of Oklahoma with the regional Protestant tendency to be uncritical, and the dominant American belief that economic liberty—allowing businesses free rein—is good for all of us, we have a recipe for exploitation in the Bible Belt. In this climate, Oklahoma continues to lag economically, at least with regard to living standards for the average person (witness the state's abysmal rankings in income and health).

In my small Oklahoma town, the local economic development committee finds that one of our biggest assets when it comes to attracting industry is a standard of low wages alongside a strong work ethic. On an old Oklahoma road map I have, Governor Frank Keating mentions this work ethic in a message that seems to have been directed to industry more than to tourists. Oklahoma, like every other state in the union, is willing to put itself out for business, offering a variety of "corporate welfare" incentives at the state and local levels that, along with out-and-out bribes, exempt companies from certain regulations (i.e., restrictions of their "freedom").[28] And what better way for a state to compete with the Third World—where business has traditionally gone to reap the benefits of willing, powerless labor and lackluster regulation of industry—than to become more like it? Judging by the measures of prosperity already mentioned, our state is well on its way to this status.

This critical look at such cherished values as religious expression and the free-market system should not be taken as a denouncement of them. The freest and most prosperous societies today (in the sense of civil liberties and average standard of living) have abandoned neither. Rather, they have treated each in a reasonable manner. In the case of religious expression, democratic socialist states such as Germany, the Netherlands, France, and Denmark have not sought to repress particular religious groups with state intervention— even though some of these nations (e.g., Denmark) have declared an official national religion.[29] What we must pay special attention to is that the First World, with the exception of the United States, is a secularizing world nonetheless (as reflected in the rates of atheism cited earlier). The explanation for this secularization process is debatable, but it can be argued that religion is needed less in a society with less squalor and fewer social problems. In other words, individuals may have less reason to pray for good fortune, or to turn to the comfort of religion when things are going badly, in a society where the state provides protection for workers, quality education, and welfare for the poor.

This decline in religion may also have something to do with the high quality of public education and the lower cost of higher education. In Denmark, for instance, a person can quit work and go to college, and the state will pick up the tab for both tuition and living expenses.[30] The result of such policies is the development of an intellectualized population that stands in polar opposition to the dogmatic ideals, such as an uncritical submission to authority, characteristic of Conservative Protestantism. Although religion remains— even fundamentalist slants—it does not have the impact on reason that we find in the Bible Belt. Uncritical dogma does not make sense to intellectuals, but it is a seductive path for those seeking answers they can find nowhere else.

The same logic can be used to understand why regulation of business and industry is seen as positive in many other First World nations, while Americans continue to view such practices as disastrous for economies. Democratic socialist societies have abandoned the idea of "the invisible hand," the idea, touted by some economists, that by letting all people compete in their own interests and without regulation, an equilibrium in which all people benefit will be achieved—in other words, an "invisible hand" will reach in to make sure that no one gets too much or too little. The abandonment of this idea, an idea that is exactly the same as the belief that economic liberty necessarily leads to prosperity for all, can be reached through reason—through an educated population who can see the true relationship between social policies and outcomes for them, rather than accepting, on authority, that the hand actually exists and functions. (We should note that my use of the concept "invisible hand" here represents an interpretation of Adam Smith's term by the American right, not the idea as he actually used it.)[31]

European corporations that once turned to the Third World for cheap labor and few restrictions on industry now come to the United States.[32] In their own societies, prosperity for the common man may be high, but business is not booming—because its explosion has been limited by reason. In other words, in these societies it may be that prosperity is up for the average person precisely because dogmatic religion and unfettered capitalism are on the way out. Ironically, in those parts of the world that are becoming less and less Christian nominally, we see more and more Christian behavior in the sense of ensuring the welfare of one's fellow man. In the United States, "welfare" is a dirty word because it is seen as "unfair" to give people money they didn't earn (even though about half of those "lazy people" are children). In democratic socialist states, the general population sees the poor as a more appropriate recipient of state funds than fabulously wealthy multinational corporations.[33] For some reason, this idea is unfathomable to American sensibilities.

IDEOLOGY IS NOT GOOD THEORY

Reason is the key, but our society, when compared to others in the First World, is lacking in reason. The American public education system is ranked at or near the bottom for First World nations and below those of some developing nations.[34] Our college freshmen are puzzled by basic algebra, challenged by the need to write complete sentences. We prefer to watch television rather than read, to judge politicians by their "character" rather than their policy decisions. More than 130 years after Darwin's revelation (and the subsequent scientific revolution), we are still holding debates over whether the Book of Genesis might be a better explanation of the origins of life on earth.[35] In the Terri Schiavo case, overlapping conclusions held by medical experts were worthless in the face of those who simply "believed" the brain-dead woman to be sentient.

We are not all unreasonable, but as a nation we exhibit a marked lack of intellectualism that is astounding to many foreigners, who are puzzled at how the United States remains an economic and military superpower. Although not all of us may know it, much of the rest of the world sees us as something of a joke—an insensitive and dim-witted bully. This was the case long before the George W. Bush administration began its drive for world domination (and the establishment of a de facto police state in America). In the Bible Belt, matters are worse. Just a few years ago, the ACLU had to defend an Oklahoma teen who was expelled from school because she was thought to have "put a hex on one of the teachers." That was the official reason given for expelling the Wiccan, who was also prohibited from wearing the symbols of her religion (so much for religious freedom).[36] This example is singular but not isolated; that such a case would even require resolution in court tells us something about the state of our cultural consciousness.

In the absence of reason, we must settle for uncritical acceptance of ideology. Ideologies are beliefs about "the way things ought to be," which may or may not be based on facts or logic. While ideologues call on facts, even scientific research, to support their views, those views are not held up to scrutiny. Ideologues want to believe—and want *us* to believe—their version of reality whether or not it resembles reality as judged by reasoning persons. They want this because these ideologies must be believed if they, or those who employ them, are to remain in a position of hegemony.

The "liberty breeds prosperity" thesis, while not completely false, is largely ideological: it is something that has been sold to the public to allow large businesses to remain profitable for those who own and run them. It is not difficult to find this sort of sales pitch in the popular media. For instance, in 2001, President Bush shot down a bill that would have let carpal tunnel sufferers qualify for unemployment compensation.[37] Carpal tunnel syndrome is a painful condition that results from compression of a nerve in the forearm; it is common among typists, waitresses, beauticians, and others who work intensely with their hands. Opponents of the bill noted that we must think carefully before passing a law that would cost us "billions of dollars." Of course, the bill would have cost corporations, not "us," all that money. Again we see the collapsing of categories: "economic regulation is not good for *us*." Another bill, passed in 2005, called for the revamping of bankruptcy laws, so that people who owed huge debts to credit card companies could no longer escape through Chapter 7 bankruptcy (by filing under Chapter 7 instead of 13, they could, theoretically, keep their home). Politicians who supported the bill, which was lobbied for by (surprise) credit card companies for many years, assured us that it would affect only those who could "afford to pay." They failed to mention that it would also affect credit card companies' already enormous profits—to the tune of about $1 billion per year.[38] Such a bill makes "good sense" to Americans because it doesn't seem fair to allow people to squirm out of debt they legitimately owe to creditors. Again we seem to have forgotten who it is that we are taking freedom away from (the poor and middle class) and giving it to (the rich), and thus who ultimately prospers. But after all, don't the elite deserve their hard-earned profits?

Judging by America's response to repeated tax cuts in the face of overwhelming deficit spending, the answer is in: "Absolutely!" The current administration's tax cuts, which have now expanded to the so-called "death tax" and capital gains, are disturbingly similar to Reaganomics of the 1980s. The 2001 cut was based on the promise of a surplus that, opponents recognized, might very well not materialize. Now, of course, we can say that it definitely didn't, as every economist worth his or her salt made clear years ago.[39] About half of the Bush tax cut went to the top 1 percent of the richest Americans, and although it was designed to take effect over a period of years, much of it was taken "up front" (perhaps just in case what happened to the economy happened). Reagan multiplied the national debt by cutting taxes, then borrowing to cover some of the costs of the cuts (and reducing social programs for the rest). Bush has done, and continues to do, exactly the same thing, although he has especially favored borrowing. Tax cuts are justified in a variety of ways, the most notable of which is "to stimulate the economy and produce jobs." For cuts in spending for the non-rich, such as schoolchildren or federal workers, the more baldly mendacious rhetoric "To save money for the war on terror!" has been repeatedly invoked.

We might recall other rhetoric employed in the 2001 controversy over tax relief, which went something like "It's your money; you should decide how to spend it." This statement reflects the ideal of economic freedom—that the government should not control your money. The arguments of the Bush administration are nothing new (as we noted, Bush is essentially Reagan II), and have been employed by conservatives for years in Oklahoma and elsewhere. For instance, shortly after 9/11 (the timing couldn't have been better), Oklahoma became a Right to Work state by popular vote, thanks in part to massive advertising campaigns, financed by business, with slogans such as "Vote Freedom." Alongside this slogan was additional propaganda about how Right to Work would increase wages—again we see the conflating of deregulation for business and economic prosperity for all.[40] These examples are a true consequence of American acceptance of the pro-business ideology that economic freedom is essential for overall prosperity. What we must ask is why this ideology must be promoted if its accuracy is obvious. As the old saying goes, "The proof of the pudding is in the eating." If low regulation of business bred prosperity for all, the average standard of living (as measured by poverty rates, health, crime, etc.) in the United States would be superior to that of the rest of the Western world, and no one would need convincing. Europeans would envy us, and perhaps emulate our methods to increase their own prosperity. As it stands, European (and Japanese) corporations have looked to their American counterparts for ideas because this nation's elites retain the lion's share of liberty and prosperity. The European Union Constitution was rejected by the French and Dutch partially because European elites had done their best to make it more friendly to business.[41]

A FINAL NOTE: RELIGION IS NOT A CAUSE

Although this essay is primarily a response to the thesis that liberty breeds prosperity, a word should be said about the insinuation that free religious expression is more than a reflection of freedom generally—namely, that religious expression itself, and Christian religious expression in particular, may have a direct causal effect on prosperity. This suggestion (we might call it the "*religion* breeds prosperity" thesis), while less insidious than pro-business ideology, is ideological nonetheless, and has been supported by misleading arguments.

For instance, the call for papers points out that societies with a Judeo-Christian heritage, such as the United States and the nations of Europe, have done well economically and have relatively high standards of living. However, to say that particular nations have a "Judeo-Christian" heritage is not the same as saying that they currently have a high incidence of Judeo-Christian belief and expression. For instance, although many nations in Western Europe are "officially" Christian, we have seen that actual belief and practice have declined. In addition, the true relationship between a Judeo-Christian heritage and economic prosperity in Europe may be different from what we expect. That these societies have First World status may be due in large part to their dominance during the colonial and postcolonial periods. The explanation for this dominance is complicated, and may indeed have something to do with a mission to "spread the faith." Still, Christianity affected the colonizers much differently than it did the colonized. Nations under colonization are hardly good examples of "free" and "prosperous" societies, even if they can be defined as highly free in the economic sense. Former colonies of European empires—including the United States—staged revolutions precisely because the economic development of the colony was impeded by the economic development of the empire.

Thus we may note that while many European and North American societies with a Judeo-Christian heritage are doing well, the same cannot be said for societies in Central and South America, Africa, and other places that took up Christianity during the colonial period. Japan should also be invoked as an example here, because it is an opposite example—a society with virtually no Christians (and little religion of any kind) that has bloomed economically. The criticism may be raised at this point that Japan is a special case, possibly because it is Eastern, possibly because it was spared by its conquerors after World War II and given an economic shot in the arm. This criticism, that some cases are unique, is a good one—and it can also be applied to the "religion breeds prosperity" thesis. The irony is that Max Weber, the sociological thinker who often made this criticism, has been repeatedly invoked to support the "religion breeds prosperity" thesis.[42]

A relationship between religion and economic prosperity was suggested by Weber, whom sociologists consider to be one of several important classical theorists. The basic thesis of Weber's *The Protestant Ethic and the Spirit of Capitalism*[43] is that Calvinist doctrines of asceticism and predestination, and Luther's doctrine of "the calling," may have "sparked" capitalism in the West. Weber thus challenges the ideas of thinkers such as Karl Marx, who see religious ideas as a reflection of economic forces. For Marx, the economic system is the base upon which all other aspects of society are built. Religious ideologies support the economic system—they do not create it.[44]

Weber warned against such absolute statements, noting that we should be careful in applying all-encompassing "grand theory" to something as complex as social phenomena. Instead, each phenomenon must be understood in relation to its particular place in history—its relation to a complex set of forces, many of which are particular to a time and place. Weber did not believe that broader explanations were *impossible,* just that they should be approached carefully, not employed in a knee-jerk fashion. Thus, although he argued that a certain brand of religiosity sparked capitalism in the West, he did not, and would not, say that Calvinism, or any religion, for that matter, would necessarily have the same effect across history and cultures.

• • •

Although it may seem otherwise, this essay was not written to denounce the practice of religion or business. Both institutions are part of a free society. Instead, it has been my purpose to enter reason into the equation—to point out that reason is required to ensure that a balance of liberty, and thus prosperity, is achieved. This must always be necessary in a world where people do not always share common interests—where one group's freedom is another's slavery. In a truly free society, civil and economic liberties will be in balance, so that when prosperity comes, it is directed at most citizens instead of a small elite.

This balance has not been achieved in the state of Oklahoma because we, more than other states, lack reason. Our workforce is undereducated, poor, and superstitious. In this sense we resemble the labor pool available in the Third World, and so we can only expect to be treated similarly (as we are).

The solution is not to suppress Conservative Protestantism, but to promote intellectualism, letting regional religious values run their course. An added perk of an educated, enriched, and empowered population, capable of making political decisions in its own interests, is that this population will be more prepared for the technical and cognitive demands of twenty-first-century work. This achieved, we should be completely satisfied if, after making intelligent political decisions and occupying a well-paid professional job, the quintessential Oklahoman makes his or her way to church.

NOTES

1. Phil Zuckerman, "Atheism: Contemporary Rates and Patterns," in Michael Martin, ed., *The Cambridge Companion to Atheism* (Cambridge: Cambridge University Press, 2005).

2. U.S. Census, 2000.

3. http://www.explanation-guide.info/meaning/Bible-belt.html.

4. Barna 2001 (http://www.barna.org).

5. Wade Roof and William McKinney, *American Mainline Religion: Its Changing Shape and Future* (Piscataway, N.J.: Rutgers University Press, 1987).

6. Ibid.

7. U.S. Census, 2000.

8. Ibid.

9. Barna 2001.

10. Roof and McKinney, *American Mainline Religion*.

11. E.g., John Locke, *On Civil Government* (1690), and Jean-Jacques Rousseau, *The Social Contract* (1762).

12. Alan Swingewood, *A Short History of Sociological Thought* (New York: St. Martin's Press, 2000).

13. William Doyle, *Origins of the French Revolution* (Oxford: Oxford University Press, 1999).

14. Phyllis Deane, *The First Industrial Revolution* (Cambridge: Cambridge University Press, 1980).

15. Patricia Sexton, *The War on Labor and the Left: Understanding America's Unique Conservatism* (Boulder, Colo.: Westview Press, 1992).

16. *United Nations Human Development Report* (Oxford: Oxford University Press, 1994), 194.

17. Harold Kerbo, *Social Stratification and Inequality* (Boston: McGraw Hill, 2000).

18. Ibid.

19. Michael Lind, *Made in Texas: George Bush and the Southern Takeover of American Politics* (New York: Basic Books, 2002).

20. Warren Burger, preface to the Constitution of the United States (U.S. Constitution Bicentennial Commission, 1991).

21. Adam Smith, *An Inquiry into the Nature and Causes of the Wealth of Nations* (1776).

22. Kerbo, *Social Stratification and Inequality*.

23. Ibid.

24. Ibid.

25. Irving Zeitlin, *Ideology and the Development of Sociological Theory* (Englewood Cliffs, N.J.: Prentice Hall, 1994).

26. C. Wright Mills, *The Sociological Imagination* (Oxford: Oxford University Press, 1959).

27. Barna 2001.

28. Donald Barlett and James Steele, "Corporate Welfare, a System Exposed," *Time*, November 9, 1998.

29. http://www.nationmaster.com.

30. http://www.copcap.com.

31. David Korten, *When Corporations Rule the World* (San Francisco: Berrett-Koehler Publishers, 2001).

32. Barlett and Steele, "Corporate Welfare."

33. Kerbo, *Social Stratification and Inequality*.

34. Alexander Higgins, "Poor Marks for U.S. Education System," Associated Press, November 26, 2002.

35. "Kansas Educators Debate Evolution," Associated Press, May 6, 2005.

36. http://www.aclu.org/religion/schools.

37. http://www.laborresearch.org.

38. Jeanne Sahadi, "House Passes Bankruptcy Bill," April 14, 2005, http://money .cnn.com/2005/04/13/pf/bankruptcy_bill/index.htm.

39. "10 Nobel Economists Endorse Kerry: Experts Criticize Bush's 'Reckless and Extreme Course,' " Reuters, August 25, 2004.

40. The word "freedom" has for some time been co-opted by the right, but in current times we have perhaps seen its most Orwellian, "doublespeak" application. The Patriot Act is meant to "protect our freedoms," apparently by keeping them locked up in a secure place. In seeking a flag-burning amendment to the Constitution, conservatives placed the protection of a symbol of freedom above the actual freedom it supposedly represents. Our brutal bombing campaign against Afghanistan, which killed most of the soldiers and at least 5,000 civilians, was dubbed "Operation Enduring Freedom." Our illegal invasion of Iraq—which by some estimates has killed more than 100,000 Iraqis (a substantial proportion of which were civilians)—was given the code name "Operation Iraqi Freedom." We must ask the question: With that much freedom going on, why are such overt declarations necessary? We didn't have to call D-Day "Operation Free Europe."

41. "Dutch Say No to EU Constitution," June 2, 2005, http://news.bbc.co.uk/2/ hi/europe/4601439.stm.

42. For just one example, see Robert Barro, "Is Prosperity Next to Godliness?" *Business Week*, December 10, 2001.

43. Max Weber, *The Protestant Ethic and the Spirit of Capitalism* (New York: Charles Scribner's Sons, 1930; original German ed. 1904–1905).

44. Karl Marx and Friedrich Engels, *Marx and Engels on Religion* (Amsterdam: Fredonia Books, 2002).

CHAPTER 12

A Liberal Presbyterian in
the Oklahoma Bible Belt

Samuel P. Riccobene

Samuel P. Riccobene is an ordained Presbyterian minister who holds the B.A. degree from Austin College in Sherman, Texas, and the M.Div. from Austin Presbyterian Theological Seminary in Austin, Texas. He is currently Minister at Large in South-Central Texas.

If Brian Bentel's essay began to suggest that there is another way, an alternative way, to view Oklahoma's religious culture, Riccobene documents that fact with experience.

A s a Presbyterian pastor, I came with high hopes to pastor a church in Oklahoma. I reckoned that once the community where I lived and the members of the church where I pastored got to know me, they would count my liberal positions on social issues as one voice among others. We would be conversation partners holding our views separate but our faith in common. I would visit folks in the hospital, marry their children, attend football games, conduct funerals, baptize, and go about carrying out the functions of my ordination. We would live together, happily ever after.

Sadly, that did not prove to be true. Being both liberal and Presbyterian means that I hold democratic principles and Christian values as important

195

and sacred. I could not, in good faith to the New Testament Gospel message, keep my liberal values out of my sermons.[1] Church members and friends who accepted me, along with my opinions, were in the minority. The years I spent as a pastor in Oklahoma challenged me and gave me the opportunity to rethink my values and to further solidify them. But in the end I chose to heed the words of Scripture found in Matthew 10:14, to "shake off the dust from my feet" and move on.

Dictionaries define *liberal* in terms such as "generous in giving"; "not narrow or bigoted"; "broad-minded"; "favoring reform or progress, as in religion, education, etc."; "specifically favoring political reforms tending toward democracy and personal freedom for the individual"; "in education, an academic college course including such fields as literature, philosophy, languages, and history, as distinguished from professional or technical subjects." A liberal, therefore, is one who advocates greater freedom of thought or action. And *liberality* is defined as "munificence; the quality of being liberal"; "a particular act of generosity"; "absence of narrowness or prejudice in thinking; impartiality; broad-mindedness."

"The Heartland" is a label that was imposed on Oklahoma by newspapers and television reporters during the media frenzy following the 1995 bombing of the Alfred P. Murrah Federal Building. However, people in the Heartland of Oklahoma turn out to be suspiciously heartless toward people and ideas perceived as a threat, something counter to the norm, or new. For clergypersons, relocation to small towns (even to cities) in Oklahoma can be difficult. Presbyterians and other "mainline" clergy tend to be more highly educated than the general public and bring to their parishes the gifts of their various educations. My pastoral colleagues agreed with this assessment when I posed the question about their experience of Oklahoma hospitality: our presence seemed challenging to locals' hopes and dreams, an artificial kind of placement into a strange land. Kathleen Norris, talking about a similar reality in the Dakotas, says that clergypersons are mistrusted, seen as short-time intruders who are too educated to be able to relate to life in small farming or ranching communities.[2] Therefore the opportunity to make change or to be changed is often missed. Liberal generosity gives way to suspicion and isolation.

This American Heartland of ours goes along beating out rhythms of displaced Indians and politically conservative politicians; of greedy, greasy booms and busts in the "black gold" oil patches (patches now over-pumped and dependent on elaborate systems of water separation, storage, and shipment to refineries). Subtly, methodically, the invasion of U.S.-style capitalist development and big-box merchandisers puts family businesses to death in the name of bargains for shoppers. Equality and equal opportunity give way to economic *in*equality. If this is the heart of U.S. democracy, we need radical heart surgery.

Who will save the Heartland? For that matter, what will save the country from its current cultural departures from the traditions of freedom that made our nation strong? Will the people who live in Oklahoma be able to make attitudinal changes that will ensure true democracy, religious freedom, and equality of life for their and others' children and grandchildren?

Religious freedom, for example, has spawned a plethora of churches in which Oklahomans can choose to worship. But to be a faithful Muslim, Jew, or Hindu is to be self-isolated. How can a culture be so accepting of subtle changes that have created radical economic and sociopolitical division and yet be resistant to change and the presence of unique new cultures at the same time?

The Sooner State has a relatively small populace, a hodgepodge of humanity centrally self-isolated and hidden in small cities and small towns, enjoying the opportunity to shop at Wal-Mart Super Stores and eat Sunday dinner at Church's Fried Chicken and other fast-food franchises. It appears to be a place where in just three generations, the Oklahomans depicted in John Steinbeck's *The Grapes of Wrath*, the Joad family, grow physically fat and yet remain essentially uneducated, impoverished, and hungry for education and an illusive better life.

Government statistics show Oklahoma to be economically poor, with low funding for education and high incidences of domestic abuse. Voter turnout is consistently low. Instead of practicing the democratic traditions of government by and for all the people, upholding the principles of equality of rights, opportunity, and treatment that have shown promise in decades past, the Joads appear to be insensitive to their own condition. High school football, the prom, buying things advertised on television, the family routine, and a paycheck seem to take precedence over political action, voting, and promoting the common good. The Okie State—the Heartland—has cultural angina. This illness of the heart seems to stop the heart's compassion and understanding—traits particularly necessary in order for an isolated people to welcome others or to accept their differences and face inevitable changes.

Ironically, the center of the grand land to which Oklahoma belongs mimics much of the rest of the nation—the nation that some have called the greatest experiment in democracy in recorded history, and which is now more a culture of haves and have-nots. In a place of broadmindedness there seems to be a fear that has given rise to conservatism of the worst kind. Instead of a land open to new ideas such as equality, one finds in rural and much of urban Oklahoma "the core of political conservatism"—"a resistance to change and a tolerance for inequality."[3] Instead of places of welcome, churches are the most segregated communities in the United States, particularly in rural places such as Oklahoma. Ethnic groups are systematically isolated in sections of cities and towns rather than being invited into all neighborhoods. Speaking about one's religion or party politics is something that mothers warn their children not to do, with the result being a lack of social discourse and of progress toward equality and new opportunity.

Some highlights and signs of better health exist, of course; as in all of life, generalizations and judgments such as have been penned here often promote more anger and resistance than the intended change for a better life for all. The eastern third of Oklahoma is indeed geographically a grand and beautiful land, and Tulsa, a gleaming jewel, is perhaps the nation's best-kept secret as a wonderful place to grow up, watching the mighty Arkansas River roll along. Many people do understand hospitality and offer it. Others are quite open to a diversity of opinion and race. And I admit that I have found healing solace in the quiet isolation of Oklahoma's western plains.

Perhaps the largest positive memory I have of Oklahoma comes from people who should not be there at all. If one listens, really listens, to the feelings and words of individuals from the thirty-eight displaced tribes of American Indians living in Oklahoma, one will receive respect, hospitality, and lasting friendships. To learn that the receiving of a blanket or beads or an invitation into the religious circle of fellowship is more a reflection on the goodness of the giver than on the merit of the receiver is to be open to a whole other way of living, of valuing relationships. Native American Presbyterian congregations welcomed me and included me in their circle of fellowship services, and I felt more welcomed there than in white Presbyterian churches. Oklahoma is the home of Wilma Mankiller, an excellent speaker and the former chief of the Cherokee Nation; of the annual Red Earth Celebration of dancing and drumming in traditional Native American tribal costumes and more. These tribes and their culture offer a way of linking life itself to the joy that comes from nurturing Mother Earth. Dominant white churches, busi-nesses, and the government of the state of Oklahoma capitalize on American Indian ethnicity. Ironically, Indian Nations Presbytery is the name of the home office of fifty or more Presbyterian churches in the Oklahoma City area. While a Native American presence is strong in Oklahoma, respect for tradition and the American Indian people themselves remains low.

And so it is against this background that I wish to present liberal Presbyterian opinions on homosexuality and racism—issues that represent for me some cultural coronary blockages in the Heartland. If these blockages are not ultimately unclogged, they could lead to further division, inflexibility, and perhaps even civil strife akin to that which our nation suffered in the middle of the nineteenth century during the Civil War. If the reader gains more knowledge about these issues, perhaps some solutions to social division and less human frustration will result.

When I returned to my boyhood home state after forty years, I was excited, seeking to minister and be ministered to. Instead I experienced isolation, suspicion, and, finally, eviction. The messages I offered created conflict with the majority of folks—open tolerance of cultural diversity and behavioral changes, issues of racial unity and harmony, integration of gay and lesbian persons, separation of church/state issues such as prayer in schools and at football games, open political debates, exposing violent militia groups, resisting manipulative religious fundamentalism, and strengthened gun control are a few examples of systems that need to be addressed.

I have had the opportunity to live in a variety of places and to study at a liberal arts college. Those opportunities made me more liberal because they exposed me to more people, places, and ideas. Therefore my arguments come not only from my education and personal experience as a pastor and student of Scripture, but from a variety of life experiences.

Although I make no claim to scholarship, I do honor the method of Scriptural interpretation generally known as *contextual translation*. This kind of translation is done in partnership with a variety of Bible scholars, interpreters, and translators who have written down their ideas over time, beginning with first-century historians. The King James Version (or translation) of the Bible was a highly scholarly undertaking for its time and produced what are still some of the most beautiful English interpretations of the original manuscripts. Psalm 23, "The Lord is my shepherd, I shall not want . . . ," is among them. Understanding the context in which the books in today's Bible were written is also achieved through conversation with contemporary scholars, scholars who have access to archaeological and anthropological discoveries from the Holy Land that predate the manuscripts used by those who translated them for the King James Version of the Bible.[4] Questions demand serious study: Who wrote the books in our Bible? When did they write them? To whom or for whom were they written? Why were they written? This kind of study, one hopes, culminates in a more helpful interpretation of what those ancient texts mean about God, and the direction they give for our lives today.

As an example of this kind of interpretation, because I am an ordained clergyperson in the Presbyterian Church USA, everything I say and do is always (I hope) a correct interpretation of the will of God for my behavior toward God, humankind, and all creation entrusted to our care. This is my context for ethical living. For me to be Christian is to live my life according to God's will. I am bound by my faith to point out injustices when I see them. And the Bible is my ethical law book.

Similarly, a judge must take into consideration all the pertinent information in law books and previous court decisions that are available when she makes a final decision about a case before her in court. As an example, society at large may argue for and against legalizing gay marriage in order to extend or block the availability of government-sponsored health care or day care to children of same-sex partners and would do so through the courts—not based on what God might mandate through the Scriptures, but on constitutional, economic, or legal grounds. In church circles, however, debate always includes God's plan, what the Bible says, or whether or not the behavior in question is, in the eyes of God and the church, a sin. And for Presbyterian Christians, such decisions and judgments are not made by individuals for individual reasons; rather, they are reached through a legal church process that takes into consideration all the facts of the issue before a conclusion is drawn about God's will and the morality of the matter.

Current public debates over issues such as gay unions, abortion, and prayer in schools point us to the radical differences between liberal Christian thinking on the matter, as I have tried to explain, and the literal translation of the so-called "religious right." To be Presbyterian in the Bible Belt is to be different from many other Christian Oklahomans.[5]

THE MATTER OF RACISM

The Reverend Dr. Peter Gomes, Plummer Professor of Christian Morals at Harvard College, opines that the Bible as we know it stays the same, but people's minds and attitudes change as the world changes. To make his point, he quotes a contemporary North American religious icon, the Reverend Dr. Billy Graham: "Our consciences should be stirred to repentance by how far we have fallen short of what God asks us to be as agents of reconciliation. . . . Of all people, Christians should be the most active in reaching out to those of other races, instead of accepting the status quo of division and animosity."[6]

Yet a Christian man who befriended me in Oklahoma had this to say about mixed marriage: "I'm not a racist, but just watch out if one of 'them' tries to marry one of my children." Over the centuries, the Bible has been used to justify all manner of evil and oppression against persons who were ethnically different from those in power. One oft-heard quote during the period of slavery in the United States was, "The Bible says that servants should obey their masters" (Ephesians 6:5). We can accept such a statement as true and behave accordingly—accepting slavery, apartheid, segregated schools, and the like. Or we can do what I've been taught to do, and look at the moral values and principles that the Bible presents *between the lines.*

Peter Gomes says that this is the difference between the Bible's "letter and its spirit."[7] While today it is typically only the radically fundamental elements in our church culture who would claim this biblical authority and intentionally bring harm to a group of people, much of the stigma from the past still manifests itself in racial division.

The reality of racism is quickly denied by white people, who will often say something like, "I'm not a racist. I know a number of Indians very well." The following are direct quotes from Native American people with whom I spoke while conducting research for this essay. They point out well the current climate of racism in Oklahoma.

SPR: Tell me about your experience of racial prejudice. Have you experienced anything lately that you feel was racist?

First Woman: Not anything current, but it is an ongoing, subtle thing. We are the ones that are the "minority minority." Because a woman first and then to be Native American. It is out there and I feel it all the time. This is denied by the culture in power, but if you are a person of color you feel it. All ethnic people have a lot in common in this way. You know, each one of us face it from time to time within our own little communities. Because in Oklahoma, as a Native American woman, I do know that we have our difficulties. But when we hear it, we do not respond to it. For example, after college in my very first job, I recall facing a statement from a coworker: "Well, I just say give it back to the Indians." And it just burned me up. I wanted to say, "What do you mean, 'give it back to the Indians'?'" I wanted to respond, but I couldn't, because it made me feel lesser. I couldn't say anything. I was the only Indian in the office at the time. Then they will apologize and say, "Oh, but you are different than the others." But that doesn't help. I then know full well that I have to be very careful around the person who said such a thing and brought my feelings out.

SPR: Have you talked with others about your feelings?

Second Woman: At a multicultural event and at a previous women's conference sponsored by the Presbyterian Church (USA), I began to hear more about this culture of oppression. One's own personal awareness becomes more clear that I'm not the only one experiencing this feeling. Once this feeling of racism comes to me, I hold back, not thinking I can do something about it. My feeling is one of helplessness, to do something about racism. To make people understand that God created us all equal. I know I am this color, but I am human.

SPR: I know there has been a movement in the Presbyterian Church (USA) for the past few years to try and change the names of sports teams, to show more sensitivity to Native Americans. How do you feel about this effort?

First Man: Yes, I think this is good. You don't realize how it makes us feel. It is a reminder of another time that was not good.

SPR: Is there anything specific you want to say about being Native American in Oklahoma?

Second Man: Native Americans in Oklahoma have been trying to be in the mainstream. I think reservation Indians are facing things in another way. But, okay, people find it very difficult to survive in the current culture, whether it is in the job market, fitting into the community, or whatever. And that's how we know about racism existing. Beginning in the Kennedy years, I think, a law came from the Equal Opportunity Commission; it was a federal law trying to make equal opportunity for different tribes/ethnic people. This law and the work of the US EOC, groundwork, was done in the seventies. But I haven't heard anything about the results of that since. You know, when I first moved to [this small rural town], I was working in the main office in Oklahoma City of what is now known as the Bureau of Indian Affairs. Before I left to move, the governor of my Nation at that time said, "I will tell you, though, that [town] is a little, typical country farm town. They are very prejudiced, and I don't want you to be hurt." So whenever I came to town for the job, I was prepared. I had taken extra training to help me do well at my job and to assimilate at the grassroots level, etcetera. But what I had not prepared myself for was that when I am part of that community, I had to be a member of a church. So my wife and I visited the Presbyterian church. There were only two people who got my attention accepting me. They were so gracious and made me want to come back. So I did. And as time went by, we both wanted to participate in different things but did not feel comfortable. When new people would ask me where I go to church, I told them, but as time went along, local people would ask me, "Well, did they let you in the front door or the back door?" But the pastor reached out to us, encouraging us to take part in the church. For the longest time, we were the only persons with a skin color different from anybody else. It took a long time to begin to feel welcome.

A Native American woman speaking at a gathering of Presbyterians in Oklahoma said this about a more subtle form of racial disharmony: "We don't put words in your mouth, so don't put words in our mouth. We speak so slowly that white folks finish our statements. And all of us understand that. They do it to us all the time. At a work setting, at church, anywhere in America."

It seems that although the average citizen of Oklahoma will not take the initiative to make the kind of cultural changes necessary to create a pure democracy, where liberty and justice for all really exists, there are possibilities. Prophetic voices such as the Reverend Billy Graham's, federal legislation, and even churches and their leadership can—I think must—be proactive with their words, money, and programs. These more liberal approaches to those whose ethnicity is different from the white majority will produce better communication, a more clearly Christian response, and therefore more stable social interaction.

THE MATTER OF HOMOPHOBIA

There is a clear cultural stigma against gay, lesbian, bisexual, and transgendered people. As public awareness increases, so does public rage. People in the United States (including Oklahomans) too often are not kind and gentle toward those whose sexual orientation is different from their own. I often wonder if this is a result of our deep Puritan roots, of the dominant media attention to sex as a marketing tool, or of some ancient cellular fear about ensuring that we propagate the human race. Leonard Pitts, syndicated columnist of the *Miami Herald*, writes,

So what is it you have against gay marriage? You, who are fervently opposed—the number of folks who agree with you is up sharply since . . .
the U.S. Supreme Court struck down anti-sodomy laws in Texas. As
recently as May [2003], 49 percent of us supported some form of gay
marriage, according to The Gallup Organization. The figure has since
dropped to 40 percent. That's a precipitous decline. Don't read me that
part in Leviticus where homosexuality is condemned. I mean, that same
book mandates the death penalty for sassy kids and fortune tellers, by
which standard the Osbourne children and Miss Cleo should have been
iced a long time ago.[8]

By interpreting the Scripture from Leviticus in a more contextual way, Pitts is
thus is able to retain his respect for the Bible while at the same time criticizing
those who translate it literally, verse by verse. He goes on to say,

It just feels wrong to you, doesn't it? At some visceral level, it just
seems to offend something fundamental. Hey, I understand. Once upon
a time, the same gut-level sense of wrong—and for that matter, the
same Bible—were used to keep Jews from swimming in the community
pool, women from voting and black people from riding at the front of
the bus.[9]

Pitts ought to be a preacher. He goes on to argue that even as we hold up
marriage as fundamental to our society, we are actually marrying less, marrying later, and divorcing more than ever before.

As pastor of a church in Oklahoma, it became very difficult for me to speak
about homosexual people, or to use illustrations in sermons that included
them. In one sermon I used the following story.

Shortly after the man with AIDS started coming [to our church], his
partner died of the disease. Ken has a totally lopsided face, ravaged and
emaciated, but when he smiles, he is radiant. He looks like God's crazy
nephew Phil. He says that he would gladly pay any price for what he has
now, which is Jesus, and us.

There's a woman in the choir named Ranola who is large and beautiful and jovial and black and as devout as can be, who has been a little
standoffish toward Ken. She was raised in the South by Baptists who
taught her that his way of life—that he—is an abomination. I think she
and a few other women at church are, on the most visceral level, a little
afraid of catching the disease. But Kenny has come to church almost
every week for the last year and won almost everyone over.

He finally missed a couple of Sundays when he got too weak, and then a month ago he was back, weighing almost no pounds, his face even more lopsided, as if he'd had a stroke. So on this one particular Sunday, for the first hymn, the so-called Morning Hymn, we sang "Jacob's Ladder," which goes, "Every rung goes higher, higher," while ironically Kenny couldn't even stand up. And then when it came time for the second hymn, the Fellowship Hymn, we were to sing "His Eye Is on the Sparrow." The pianist was playing, and the whole congregation had risen—only Ken remained seated—and we began to sing, "Why should I feel discouraged? Why do the shadows fall?" And Ranola watched Ken rather skeptically for a moment, and then her face began to melt and contort like his, and she went to his side and bent down to lift him up—lifted up this white rag doll, this scarecrow. She held him next to her, draped over and against her like a child while they sang. And it pierced me.[10]

After this sermon, a group of powerful laypeople in my congregation invited me into one of their homes and asked me not to refer to homosexuality in my preaching. I agreed not to do so. But as the weeks and months passed, this arrangement took away my sense of justice and forced me to abandon or at least ignore the truths that have become apparent based on my interpretation of the Scriptures. Nearly every Sunday after I made that concession to my parishioners, it seemed as though almost every Scripture passage I preached begged for contemporary illustrations of one social concern or another. In the end I was unable to keep my word to that group of church members. I was compelled to speak the truth of Scripture as I interpreted it through the lenses of my Reformed Presbyterian education. Finally, because I did not want to further divide the church, I left.

"Traditional family values are being threatened by these homosexuals," some say. But are family values really threatened by homosexuals, or—to paraphrase President Franklin D. Roosevelt—is the only thing we have to fear (our own) fear itself? Some are quick to insist, "The Bible says homosexuality is a sin," and then proceed as if this is sufficient evidence to condemn others. But does the Bible really say that? Or is that our culturally influenced interpretation of the Scriptures?

The Reverend Dr. Mel White has been a Christian minister, author, and filmmaker all his adult life. Raised as an evangelical Christian, taught that homosexuality was a sin, he fought to overcome his own homosexual orientation for decades in all ways available to him: prayer, psychotherapy, exorcism, electric shock, marriage, and family. That struggle, and his halting, poignant steps to understand and accept his homosexuality, reconcile it with his Christian faith, and express his sexuality respectfully and responsibly, are described in his book *Stranger at the Gate: To Be Gay and Christian in America.*

White was a ghostwriter for Billy Graham, Jerry Falwell, Jim Bakker, and Pat Robertson until the early 1990s, when the religious right began to step up its antigay rhetoric.[11] "The followers of John Calvin might not know for certain whom God has chosen for salvation," White writes, "but at least salvation is out of their hands; [for we who grew up] in the Armenian or 'holiness' denominations, salvation was up to us."[12]

We Presbyterian pastors know about John Calvin, one of the fathers of the Protestant Reformation. We believe, with Calvin and others, not only that personal salvation is out of our hands, but, above all else, that God is making the rules, and God is the judge—not us. However, many people who are now members of Presbyterian and other Reformed congregations were, like White, raised in the more unstructured religious traditions in which confusion, guilt, and fear were more dominant in Sunday school than the Reformed thought that God is in charge and God is a God of love, not of judgment. Rather than ignore such problems, churches have the opportunity to model appropriate ways to dialogue in Sunday schools, at special events, and in face-to-face conversations with people who are openly gay.

Countering a commonly held opinion in Oklahoma that homosexuals will come in and convert our children to their own sexuality, White says, "from the beginning [childhood through adolescence until today], I had only same sex desires and fantasies. I didn't plan it. I didn't choose it. I didn't desire it. And no one forced it on me. I wasn't recruited, raped, or abused."[13]

Anyone who was old enough to understand the news and who read the papers back in October of 1998 will likely remember the name Matthew Shepard. In "The Gospel According to Matthew Shepard," Paul E. Capetz of the United Theological Seminary of the Twin Cities reconstructs the crime and its apparent biblical theme.

[Shepard was] a young gay man who was kidnapped, tied to a fence, brutally beaten, and left to freeze in the cold night air of Wyoming. Five days later he died a victim of anti-gay hatred. Some commentators have spoken of Matthew's death as a "lynching," likening his treatment at the hands of two straight men to the lynchings of black people by white racists. Matthew's death was not an isolated incident which can be understood apart from the context of historic Christian teaching about homosexuality. From biblical times forward the person engaging in homosexual activity was considered an abomination to God and merited the penalty of death. See this in Leviticus 20: 13.[14]

In this same essay, Capetz condemns the concept of biblicism, "a belief in the authority of Scripture such that what it says about homosexuality overrides every other consideration that might be brought to bear on the issue." He and Leonard Pitts both seem to say—and I agree—that if we took everything the Bible says literally and acted on it, we would all be subject to death or imprisonment.

The question for me is, what does it mean to be faithful to the Bible? And how does a liberal Presbyterian relate this understanding of biblical interpretation to a world that keeps repeating immoral behavior such as genocide at worst and racial prejudice in its more subtle form? Fear, misinformation, and preconceived notions about people of color and people of non-heterosexual identity continue to test the foundations of individual freedom and state and national tolerance. Is it possible to offer ways for people of good conscience to dialogue without violence toward or rejection of the one who is different? How might this begin to happen in public discourse?

Ultimately, of course, this will be up to each individual to decide. But I wish to leave readers with one possible idea. It comes from Professor Paul Woodruff, Hayden W. Head Regents Chair in the Plan II Honors Program and Darrell K. Royal Regents Professor in Ethics and American Society at the University of Texas at Austin. On Wednesday, May 12, 2004, Dr. Woodruff presented this idea in a paper, "Renewing Reverence," at the 2004 George S. Heyer Jr. Lecture at Austin Presbyterian Theological Seminary, which I was able to attend. He reminds us that the ethical concept of reverence is a virtue; how people behave in situations in which they have power over others is the crucial idea here. Confucius says, "Virtue has neighbors"; by this he means that an ethical concept or virtue such as reverence, in order to exist at all, must exist in community. The majority of people in Oklahoma who hold power over Native Americans and homosexual people are Anglo people; to them belongs the opportunity to freely exercise the virtue of reverence toward the others. Woodruff says that those who choose to exercise this virtue freely, and when there is no requirement to show it, are those who are to be most highly respected. So the question for you and for me and for the white power brokers in Oklahoma is this: Do we know and understand this high ethical responsibility, and do we work to put it into practice in our daily living? In other words, do we do the following three things?

1. Do we pay attention to this idea of showing reverence for others, for the land, and for our own families? And do we recognize the value of others?

2. Do we speak the language of reverence with feeling? Do we preach it? Are we prophetic? Is poetry valued? Do we want to shake hands with all people showing courtesy and concern?

3. Do we put our money and time into acts of generosity and respect?

Elected officials, pastors, teachers, and other professionals have the responsibility to behave with reverence toward those who have less power. If we do this as part of our daily routine, it will be noticed, and others are then free to act in similar ways.

If you have read this far, you likely understand that I believe the Heartland needs a new heart. You also understand by now that although I had the opportunity to foster such change in values and behaviors, my activities were frustrated, and I eventually left the state of Oklahoma. Still, my liberal Presbyterian roots and leanings remain strong: favoring reform or progress, as in religion and education, and specifically favoring political reforms tending toward democracy and personal freedom for the individual. I clearly want to be one who advocates greater freedom of thought or action, particularly in places where racial prejudice and oppression of gay, lesbian, bisexual, and transgendered people are condoned. I believe that particular acts of generosity and an absence of narrowness or prejudice in thinking break out in our living every day.

When gays were granted the right to legally marry in Massachusetts, it gave hope that a more open and welcoming culture will evolve in the Heartland. In 2004, the fiftieth-anniversary celebration of *Brown v. Board of Education of Topeka, Kansas,* the suit that ended segregation in public schools, turned the spotlight on us, and we saw the good news of integration, but we also saw how little progress our country has made toward racial harmony since 1954. Even the big-box Wal-Mart company is being challenged to reconsider its strategy: the National Trust believes that an increase in the number of Wal-Mart stores will destroy the unique character of the whole state of Vermont, and political action is under way to block further expansion there. In this instance, the conservative idea of resistance to change is actually supporting the liberal agenda of maintaining diversity in our nation.

Several activities that result in bigger hearts must be encouraged. Individuals in power must be vigilant in reverence toward the land and its people. States must continue to pass laws that promote the common good and uphold the freedoms we have come to enjoy. All people must be educated so that they understand our basic freedoms: to worship as we choose, to speak out on issues without fear of retribution, to receive a good-quality public education, and to be able to pursue our own personal happiness while at the same time defending the rights of others to believe differently. Churches must offer opportunities for their members to learn how to disagree with each other and still respect and value different opinions.

When Jesus was ending his ministry, while speaking to a lawyer, a Pharisee, who asked him which commandment was the greatest, he said, "You shall love the lord your God with all your heart, and with all your soul, and with all your mind. This is the greatest and first commandment. And a second is like it: You shall love your neighbor as yourself. On these two commandments hang all the law and the prophets" (Matthew 22:34ff.). If Oklahomans all behave accordingly, they, and the nation along with them, will be truly open-hearted. If Confucius is right, and virtues such as the ones above do have neighbors, perhaps our liberalism will extend to the rest of the world as our circle of neighbors grows wide.

NOTES

1. I define the term "liberal" here as it applies to a style of thinking and living, not as it is often used politically.

2. Kathleen Norris, *Dakota: A Spiritual Geography* (Boston: Houghton Mifflin, 1993), 55.

3. "Anatomy of Conservatism," editorial, *Christian Century Magazine,* September 6, 2003, 7. See also "UC Berkeley News," July 22, 2003, http://www.berkeley.edu/news/media/releases/2003/07/22_politics.shtml.

4. See the various texts on the Dead Sea Scrolls discovered in 1947 in Qumran caves, the *Nag Hammadi* writings found in 1946, etc.

5. For a clear, practical discussion of many of these differences, see Ted Foote, Jr., and Alex Thornburg, *Being Presbyterian in the Bible Belt: A Theological Survival Guide for Youth, Parents, and Other Confused Presbyterians* (Louisville, Ky.: Geneva Press, 2000).

6. Peter Gomes, *The Good Book: Reading the Bible with Mind and Heart* (New York: William Morrow and Co., 1996), 100.

7. Ibid., 92.

8. Leonard Pitts, "Gays May Be Hope for Marriage," *Miami Herald,* August 4, 2003, 1B.

9. Ibid.

10. Anne Lamott, *Traveling Mercies: Some Thoughts on Faith* (New York: Pantheon, 1999), 64–66.

11. Mel White, *Stranger at the Gate: To Be Gay and Christian in America* (New York: Simon & Schuster, 1994); see http://www.soulforce.org for additional data.

12. White, *Stranger at the Gate,* 23, 24.

13. Ibid., 29.

14. Paul E. Capetz, "The Gospel According to Matthew Shepard: The Theme of Reconciliation in 'The Confession of 1967' from the Perspective of the Unreconciled," *Church & Society,* May/June 2002, 92–93.

CHAPTER 13

Tulsa

A DIVINELY INSPIRED CITY

Marlin Lavanhar

The Reverend Marlin Lavanhar was called to serve as senior minister at All Souls Unitarian Church in Tulsa at age thirty-two, from his position as assistant minister at First and Second Church in Boston, Massachusetts. A Harvard Divinity School graduate, he received his undergraduate degree in sociology from Tulane. He is well-known throughout the Unitarian Universalist Association for his three-year bicycle trip around the world, during which he discerned his call to the ministry. He has made a name for himself in Tulsa as a champion for race riot reparations and as a leader in the battle against a creationism exhibit at the Tulsa Zoo.

Upon seeing the title of his essay, many readers might think first of Tulsa's reputation as a center for fundamentalist Christianity, revivalism, Oral Roberts, and the like. Lavanhar disabuses the reader of that notion in his clever and insightful opening. In attempting to explain the success of Unitarian Universalism, sometimes referred to as "liberal religion," in "the buckle of the Bible Belt," some might be tempted to attribute it to the obvious need in such an environment for an alternative approach to religion. Lavanhar makes clear that the situation is far more complicated than that: Tulsa is in many ways a progressive religious environment.

Tulsans like to claim that they live in "the buckle of the Bible Belt." If Tulsa is indeed the "buckle," then whoever is wearing the belt may need to find another way to keep his pants up. A belt buckle holds everything together and keeps it in place. But at the beginning of the twenty-first century, religion in Tulsa is much more multifaceted and progressive than the title "buckle of the Bible Belt" implies.

In some ways, Tulsa has been a religiously progressive city for decades. For example, many Tulsans do not realize that the city's Council of Churches was the first in the nation to admit Catholics, in 1965. Then, in 1971, they broadened the circle to welcome Jews and Unitarians. As of 2004, Jews and Unitarians were still not accepted in most Councils of Churches in the United States; nor had they been accepted into the World Council of Churches. Tulsa's Council of Churches, which eventually changed its name to Tulsa Metropolitan Ministries (TMM), took the lead again in 1983, becoming the first in the nation to admit Muslims.

Historically, Tulsa's religious communities have come together across denominations and traditions, and by doing so they have achieved some outstanding accomplishments. Working together, they have started Tulsa Senior Services, the Day Center for the Homeless, the Retired Seniors' Volunteer Program, Friends of Early Childhood, Meals on Wheels, and Youth Services of Tulsa, just to name a few. And many of these agencies, such as Youth Services of Tulsa, have come to set the standard for other such agencies nationwide.

In 2003, the University of Tulsa became the first university in the nation to allow the construction of a Muslim mosque on its campus. With this decision, Tulsa once again demonstrated its legacy of religious tolerance and cooperation, and it did so at a time when the country's mood toward Islam was predominantly characterized as apprehensive and fearful. The history of Tulsa, for many decades, has been one not of excluding other faiths, but of embracing them and working together. Such a legacy can hardly justify the title "buckle of the Bible Belt."

Tulsa's Oklahoma Conference for Community and Justice (OCCJ) brings together people of all faiths, and is one of the strongest in the country, having separated itself from the National Conference on May 1, 2005. In contrast, the OCCJ in Oklahoma City had to close its doors in 2002 because it did not have enough community support, and the Dallas and Houston offices have also closed their doors.[1]

According to Nancy Day, the executive director of Tulsa's OCCJ, our city's history of interfaith leadership is carried forward by strong clergy leaders, philanthropists, educators, and volunteers, and by the amazing spirit of cooperation between all the interfaith agencies: Tulsa Metropolitan Ministries, the Jewish Federation, the Islamic Society, the Interfaith Alliance, and the Unitarians.[2]

If all this is not sufficiently atypical for a Bible Belt city when it comes to religion, keep in mind that Tulsa is home to what has become the largest Unitarian Universalist church in the world. There is, in fact, a significant connection between the presence of All Souls in Tulsa and the development of a liberal religious spirit of tolerance and cooperation in the city.

All Souls Unitarian Church was founded in 1921 by newspaperman Richard Lloyd Jones, publisher of the *Tulsa Tribune,* and William R. Holway, the engineer responsible for bringing much-needed Spavinaw Creek water to Tulsa, and for later building the massive Pensacola Dam of Grand Lake o' the Cherokees, generating power and flood control for much of northeastern Oklahoma. Many cities in Oklahoma have a clean water supply and adequate sewage treatment facilities thanks to Holway and Associates. These two men, each of whom had Unitarian family connections, decided to try and start a "liberal church" in Tulsa. Richard Lloyd Jones's father, the Reverend Jenkin Lloyd Jones, was the founder of All Souls Church in Chicago, and is credited with helping spread Unitarianism throughout the western United States. Holway's father-in-law, the Reverend Milton Kerr, was a Unitarian minister in Sandwich, Massachusetts, and later Greeley, Colorado.

The group in Tulsa began when Jones ran an ad in his newspaper inviting people who were interested in starting a liberal church to meet in what is now Tulsa's Old City Hall. The group later came together in Richard and Georgia Lloyd Jones's living room. The Reverend Thomas Byrnes, a Unitarian minister from Oklahoma City, began making trips to Tulsa on Sunday evenings to meet with this nascent group. They met for a time at City Hall, then at Temple Israel. A move to the Majestic movie theater afforded the use of an organ, and also room for the church school to begin in the stairwell and in the loges. Eventually the church bought property at 14th and Boulder, where they built a white New England–style church, which was dedicated on December 7, 1930. The architectural style was chosen to highlight the Unitarian roots in New England and to differentiate the building from the many ornate churches in the city. A good portion of the money for constructing the church was given by the American Unitarian Association in Boston, but Jones also appealed to prominent Tulsa citizens who were not members of the church, and received contributions from several, including C. C. Cole, head of the Boston Avenue Methodist building committee; Frank Buttram; A. L. Farmer; Johnson D. Hill; J. A. Hull; John H. Markham, Jr.; H. O. McClure; Herbert Mason; and Waite Phillips. Twenty-five years later, the church was bursting at the seams with children and adults, and the decision was made to erect a larger building at the present location, 2952 S. Peoria.

The fact that a Unitarian church flourished in Tulsa explains both why the city has been labeled "the buckle of the Bible Belt" and why it does not deserve this title. Tulsa has always been a churchgoing community in which most of the population attends religious services on a regular basis. It is as common for Tulsans to ask one another, "What church do you attend?" at the beginning of the twenty-first century as it was at the beginning of the twentieth. The Bible was, and continues to be, referred to frequently in public conversations in Tulsa, as well as in letters to the editor in the local newspapers and on the political stump. In keeping with Tulsa's strongly religious nature and the role of religion in shaping the city's culture and public discourse, many religious liberals and skeptics have sought out a religious community in which they can explore religious ideas and texts from an intellectual, critical, and historical perspective. Such people have also wanted their children to be biblically literate without being biblical literalists. They sought a church that would spark their children's and their own religious curiosity and moral nature without indoctrinating them into a rigid set of beliefs. Such people found what they were looking for at All Souls.

The oil industry also contributed much to creating the cultural milieu that provided fertile ground for liberal religion in Tulsa. The oil boom brought transplants from the eastern United States and abroad. Among those relocating to Tulsa were a large number of geologists and geophysicists—scientists who knew too much about the earth's history to accept a literal biblical account of its having been created only six thousand years ago. All Souls offered these scientifically minded individuals a religious tradition that accepted scientific truth, and at the same time presented intelligent and compelling interpretations of biblical stories.

Many who arrived from cities in the eastern United States were acquainted with the arts, and they looked for ways to continue to enjoy and experience the music, dance, and performances that they knew. All Souls and its members were seminal in the establishment of such artistic and intellectual efforts as Hyechka, a musical organization; the International Folk Dancers; and Tulsa Town Hall. These groups participated in the growth of All Souls, and members of the church have played significant roles over the years in the establishment of the arts in Tulsa. While the dominant churches in Tulsa were forbidding their members to dance, All Souls was opening its doors for dancing.

Beyond religion and the arts, All Souls became a force in the city when it came to responding to social ills. One of the well-known expressions at All Souls is "Deeds not Creeds." The church has long taught that it is not what you *say* you believe, but rather how you act in the world that makes for a moral and religious life. The church and its members have played active roles in the movements for women's rights, civil liberties and civil rights, and women's right to choose regarding reproductive services. Tulsa's chapter of Planned Parenthood was founded at All Souls, and over the years the church's ministers and members have been strong allies in the establishment and maintenance of legal reproductive rights for women. During the days when abortions were illegal in Oklahoma, women and families seeking assistance often contacted the ministers of All Souls for referrals or donations to get the help they needed. The Unitarian ministers in Oklahoma were part of an underground movement for providing safe abortions administered by medical professionals during the era of legal restrictions on women's reproductive rights. It was through the efforts of All Souls' ministers and members that the (Oklahoma) Religious Coalition for Abortion Rights was founded.

In 1960, All Souls called to its pulpit a man who would go on to be named one of Tulsa's 100 Most Influential Citizens at the time of the city's centennial. Dr. John Wolf was only thirty-two years old when he came to All Souls. Under his leadership, All Souls grew to be the largest Unitarian church in the world, and he quickly became a significant part of the conscience of Tulsa. Not long after arriving in town, he led the charge to reform the corrupt funeral industry. In the process he infuriated every florist and funeral director in the city, but he ultimately helped reform the industry and established Oklahoma's first Memorial Society.

In 1965, Dr. Wolf played a pivotal role in bringing together Tulsa's religious community during the civil rights movement. It was this era and the outstanding clergy community of Tulsa during that time that created the context for the thriving interfaith and ecumenical spirit that exists in the city to this day. When Dr. Martin Luther King, Jr., asked clergy to come march with him in Selma, Dr. Wolf called together the clergy of Tulsa, and they decided to hold a march right here in Tulsa. They began the march with an ecumenical worship service at All Souls. It was the first ecumenical worship service in the history of Tulsa, and it was also racially integrated. There wasn't another church in Tulsa at that time that could have hosted such a service without great controversy. In those days, it was as radical for Southern Baptist and Catholic clergy to worship together as it was for blacks and whites. Dr. Wolf had the wholehearted support of All Souls president Arthur McElroy, as well as the vast majority of the congregation.

The service included Rabbi Norbert Rosenthal from Temple Israel, Dr. Warren Hultgren from First Baptist Church, Rev. William D. Bowles from Memorial Drive Methodist Church, Rev. James McNamee from Church of the Madalene (Roman Catholic), Rev. Finis Crutchfield from Boston Avenue Methodist Church, Rev. Ben Hill from Vernon AME Church, Rev. LeRoy Jordan from First Baptist Church of North Tulsa, Rev. Ben Cauthon from Immaculate Conception Roman Catholic Church, and Rev. Charles E. Wilcox from St. Luke's Episcopal Church.

This integrated interfaith worship service and march galvanized the city and ultimately helped shape its religious life. Suddenly the Baptists and Catholics, Jews and Unitarians and others saw themselves as partners in ministering to the welfare of this young and prosperous city. It was out of this legacy that the Tulsa Council of Churches went on to welcome Catholics and then Jews and Unitarians and eventually Muslims.

It is no exaggeration to say that Tulsa would be a very different city if it were not for All Souls Unitarian Church. However, much credit must be given to the large number of Tulsa's clergy who were courageous at a crucial juncture in the history of their country and their city. Their progressive spirits and actions paved the way for the religious understanding and cooperation that Tulsa has today.

A factor adding to this rare clerical brotherhood and unity may have been a psychiatric experiment conducted in the early 1960s by the Tulsa Psychiatric Foundation, in which groups of ten clergymen met with a psychoanalyst monthly over the course of a year, sharing obstacles and insights. The ministers and priests discovered that human joy and misery knew no denominational boundaries. The bonds established during that time were life-long, and the benefits included an interfaith ministers' Bible study group, which included one of the psychoanalysts, because he could read and translate the Greek dialect of the original texts.

By the late 1960s, Dr. Wolf had established himself as a leader in Tulsa among his clergy colleagues and the public. He counted among his congregants local and state politicians on both sides of the aisle, local and federal judges, and school board members. He was presiding over a fast-growing congregation.

In 1968, when Tulsa's public school system was being mismanaged, Dr. Wolf preached a sermon called "The Last Days of Dr. Mason." Excerpts from the sermon were printed in the *Tulsa World* the next day,[3] leading to the largest attendance ever at a meeting of the Tulsa School Board. That meeting, at which Dr. Wolf was an official spokesperson for the public, indeed led to the last day of Dr. Mason as superintendent of Tulsa Public Schools—he resigned before the night was over.

During his thirty-five years as the senior minister of All Souls, Dr. Wolf was interviewed regularly by the press, and his sermons were occasionally printed in the local newspaper. This was the custom of the *Tulsa World* at the time, under Religion Editor Beth Macklin, who had come to know Wolf in her previous position as executive director of the Tulsa Council of Churches—an organization he was not eligible to join, as he did not "profess Jesus Christ to be his Lord and Savior." Nonetheless, Macklin recruited Wolf to head the council's Social Action Committee.

Another talk of John Wolf's that made the paper—and radio commentary —was titled "Tulsa Is a Hick Town."[4] This lecture, which was delivered to the Day Alliance, may have led to the construction of our Performing Arts Center.

Wolf's fearless tirades against Oral Roberts and his fund-raising tactics also appeared in the paper more than once. In fact, they became an element in the televangelist's own efforts, when Roberts portrayed Wolf as one "who might take over ORU if the fund-raising goals were not reached."[5]

Dr. Wolf's legacy lent credibility to the All Souls pulpit. Tulsa's news media continue to request comments from the senior minister of All Souls about religious and moral issues facing the city and the nation. For example, after the attacks of September 11, 2001, I, the newly called senior minister, age thirty-two, was among only a handful of Tulsa's clergy who were interviewed on television, and in a front-page article in the Sunday *Tulsa World,* regarding what we believed the people of America needed to hear from their religious leaders in the aftermath of the attack. Additional interviews in print and on television since that time have included such issues as the federal government's faith-based initiatives, gay marriage, reparations for the survivors of the 1921 Tulsa Race Riot, and Tulsa's black police officers' lawsuit. The Tulsa media seem to have assessed that the people of Tulsa want to know what is being talked about at All Souls. One reason may be that, at least from a legal and historical standpoint, All Souls and its ministers have been on the moral and ethical high ground on just about every issue for which they have publicly advocated. The record of success is not due to their having chosen issues that were popular. On the contrary, many of the issues for which All Souls has advocated over the years have been unpopular and have stirred scornful labels such as "agitators," "radicals," and "heretics," to the point that the church has twice been picketed by a fundamentalist group.

All Souls has always been at the forefront in Tulsa with issues related to sexual orientation in society and religion. The organization Tulsa Oklahomans for Human Rights (TOHR) began meeting in the Activities Room of All Souls in 1980. The group was, and remains, dedicated to the protection and rights of gay, lesbian, bisexual, and transgender (GLBT) people. That was more than twenty-five years ago, and if All Souls had not housed them, certainly no other church would have. Later that decade, gay and lesbian high school seniors who could not attend their school proms with their dates of choice wanted a place to hold Tulsa's first-ever gay prom, and All Souls invited them to use its Emerson Hall. In 1994, at its annual meeting, the congregation voted overwhelmingly in support of a resolution to add sexual orientation to the city's nondiscrimination ordinance as well as to the city's personnel policies. Furthermore, the ministers of All Souls have been performing religious Ceremonies of Union for gay and lesbian couples in Oklahoma since the 1980s. In 2000, All Souls' music director, Rick Fortner, founded Tulsa's gay men's chorus, the Council Oak Men's Chorale, who rehearsed and performed at All Souls. Then, in 2004, All Souls (and thus Tulsa) hosted the southwestern United States' first conference on transgender issues. This is a time when the civil rights of GLBT persons are increasingly being won around the world and around the nation, and All Souls stands proudly behind its long legacy of support for them and for these important and often unpopular issues.

There are certain circumstances, within as well as outside the church, that have allowed for such a public ministry to take place. The theological position of rejecting creeds and encouraging good works as the foundation for salvation and a religious life is only one reason. Unitarians stand so firm for their causes because most of those causes are more than political and social issues; these are deeply felt moral positions regarding the worth and dignity of every human being. As some religious institutions in the community use theological language and scriptures to advocate for certain social and political positions, All Souls ministers and members feel called to witness for *our* understanding of these issues based on *our* theological and scriptural understanding.

All Souls is part of what is known as the Free Church tradition, which sees God's work in the world in the unfolding of freedom. Such freedom is recounted in the Jews' exodus from Egypt, the American Revolution, the abolition of slavery in America, and the ending of apartheid in South Africa. God is seen working in the world, in the light of scientific pursuits and discoveries and the freedom of people to have self-determination regarding their national and religious leaders. In such a tradition, freedom of thought and unhindered exploration of religious ideas and truths are the norm. Such a culture allows for powerful and potent discussions to take place and for new ideas to take root. Ministers are given the freedom to preach without the restraints of established doctrine and dogma. Laypersons are not expected to agree with everything the minister says; they are encouraged to think for themselves and to let their conscience be their guide.

Such a tradition must be distinguished from one that advocates "believing anything you want." The responsible adherence to one's conscience, within a community bound together by a covenant, is very different from unbounded freedom to think and act however one pleases. It has been said, "It is not that Unitarians have no beliefs; it is that they will not be restrained in their beliefs."

A confluence of people, events, and natural resources has made Tulsa fertile soil for such a church to grow. At the same time, the growth of the church has played a pivotal role in the development of the city and its religious outlook. This symbiotic relationship has led to a city planted in the heart of America, which combines the best of the Bible Belt with some of the diversity, culture, and ethos of a major cosmopolitan city. In Tulsa, one finds the strong commitment to values, civic engagement, and support of community that exemplify the Bible Belt. One also finds a wide range of arts and cultures and a growing willingness to accept and appreciate differences. There are indeed strong forces and trends in the religious life of the city that would lead it away from its tolerant heritage if they could, but the momentum is on the side of freedom and diversity and cooperation. As a minister, I would say that such momentum is divinely inspired.

NOTES

1. "A New Day for OCCJ," http://www.occjok.org/newday.asp.

2. Taken from personal conversations with Nancy Day, Executive Director, OCCJ, Tulsa, dates uncertain.

3. *Tulsa World*, February 19, 1968.

4. Ibid., May 18, 1968.

5. Ibid., April 11, 1989.

CHAPTER 14

Growing Up Okie—and Radical

Roxanne Dunbar-Ortiz

Roxanne Dunbar-Ortiz is a historian retired from California State University at Hayward. But she has deep roots in Oklahoma, and has written about them eloquently, especially in *Red Dirt: Growing Up Okie* (Norman: University of Oklahoma Press, 2006). Her essay here is adapted from that book.

Dunbar-Ortiz is especially useful in helping us see that Oklahoma has a long and proud progressive tradition—even though that does not match up with most people's image of the state.

The working class and the employing class have nothing in common. There can be no peace so long as hunger and want are found among millions of working people and the few who make up the employing class have all the good things in life. Between these two classes a struggle must go on, until all the toilers come together on the political as well as on the industrial field, and take and hold that which they produce by their labor.

—FROM THE CONSTITUTION OF THE INDUSTRIAL WORKERS
OF THE WORLD, 1905

My father's name was Moyer Haywood Pettibone Scarberry Dunbar. When I was growing up in Piedmont, Oklahoma, he would read to me from the framed 1905 IWW Constitution and tell me, "I was born two years after the IWW, and Papa named me after the founders: William Moyer, Big Bill Haywood, and George Pettibone. They were on trial, framed up for murder in Boise, Idaho, during that summer of 1907 when I was born, same year Oklahoma got statehood. Clarence Darrow got them off. One Big Union, that's what your grandfather fought for."

Then Daddy would rail against the current trade unions. Hanging on the bedroom wall beside the IWW Constitution was a framed photograph from 1912 of my father's entire family, my grandfather and grandmother sitting on the wide front porch of their spacious two-story house. All ten children were dressed in their Sunday best. Daddy was five years old in that picture.

Next to the photograph was Grandpa Dunbar's diploma in veterinary medicine from St. Joseph, Missouri, dated 1910. He had moved his family from Missouri to Piedmont, Oklahoma, in 1907, just after Daddy was born, and returned alone to Kansas and then Missouri for three years to study medicine. During those years, Grandma was practically a single mother, caring for five little children in Piedmont, where her entire extended family had settled.

Grandpa Dunbar had joined the Socialist Party when it was founded in 1901—eastern Kansas and western Missouri formed the southwest center of the Socialist Party—but he was attracted to the more radical IWW once it came into being. Already a committed Wobbly when Daddy was born, Grandpa continued his involvement while in veterinary school and returned to Piedmont an organizer, as well as a highly respected professional. Daddy said that Grandpa rotated three teams of horses to make his doctoring calls around a fifty-mile area—cattle and horses were his specialty.

Beside the veterinary diploma and the picture, a worn, thin red book—my grandfather's IWW union book—hung from a string, with "Emmett Victor Dunbar" scrawled inside.

"Why did Grandpa take you all to Texas?" I would ask.

"Danged Klan ran us off, some of them same folks you see in church on Sunday. They're pretty brave when they got sheets over their heads. Nothing but cowards. Papa had to sell out lock, stock, and barrel."

Daddy was fourteen when the family moved to the border town of McAllen in the Texas Rio Grande Valley. Grandfather Emmett died in 1934, kicked by a horse he was doctoring. But my father held the KKK responsible, because a dozen years before, they had beat my grandfather half to death.

Daddy told me over and over about those years before World War I when the Wobblies controlled the town and county where I grew up, and many parts of Oklahoma as well as practically all of the mines and fields and woods of western North America: the glory days. My father liked to tell stories about them while he cleaned his hunting rifle; the smell of gun oil went with the story.

"Your Grandpa organized all the sharecroppers and tenants and cotton pickers and wheat thrashers, all of them migrants from here to yon. Papa got himself elected to the school board, that same school you go to. One time a bunch of landlords tried to take the school with guns, waving their red, white, and blue flags. Papa and all us brothers held up there five days shooting it out with them, and we whipped them good."

"How old were you then, Daddy?"

"About your age—ten, eleven—but I was a good shot. Papa always chose me to ride shotgun on his wagon when he made his rounds doctoring."

"What did the Wobblies want?" I asked. No matter how many times he told me, I loved to hear his agenda of Wobbly dreams: abolition of interest and profits, public ownership of everything, no military draft, no military, no police, the equality of women and all races. "The O-B-U, One Big Union," he would say, and then he would smile to himself, lost in memory.

The Wobblies were mostly anarchists and suspicious of the electoral system, but many of them, like my grandfather, voted for Eugene Debs and the Socialist Party all five times he ran. Daddy explained, "It was different here in Oklahoma than some places. Why, by nineteen and fourteen, Oklahoma had more dues-paying members of the Socialist Party than any other state in the Union—twelve thousand. That year they elected over a hundred Socialists to office."

"So what happened that the Klan drove you all out?" I asked.

"That son-of-a-gun Woodrow Wilson, him and that gangster Palmer and his goon J. Edgar Hoover wiped out the IWW, put them all in jail, or kicked them out of the country. The dadgummed rich wheat farmers bankrolled the Klan. They swelled up like a tick—night riding, killing stock, burning barns and crops, lynching, burning crosses. Good Christians they were."

Daddy, like his father, was a freethinker. I would lower my head whenever he talked about Christians, because I was a devout Baptist. Mama was a hard-shell Baptist convert, and I never missed a church service once we moved to town: Sunday morning and night, Wednesday night prayer meeting, and summer Bible school, camp, and tent revivals. My parents tried not to fight about it, and Daddy would even give me a dime to put in the collection plate. But he would break out singing "Pie in the sky bye and bye," from Wobbly troubadour Joe Hill's "Preacher and the Slave," to the tune of the hymn "The Sweet Bye and Bye," and Mama would steam.

Next to the Klan and Christian hypocrites, Daddy scorned any kind of law enforcement authorities. The Wobbly Constitution said that any worker who joined the army, a militia, or even a police force would be denied membership forever.

Despite my grandfather's former affluence, when my parents married in 1927, they returned to Piedmont as sharecroppers.

"Why are we so poor if Grandpa was rich?" I asked.

My father would shift his eyes away from the IWW Constitution and stare at his gnarled hands. He did not like being reminded that we were poor. Down the street lived two of his mother's sisters, among the wealthiest families in town, meaning they had two-story houses with running water and bathrooms. The big family house where my father grew up still stood, one of the seven big houses in town, but it no longer belonged to our family.

"I did all right until the Dust Bowl and the danged Depression. Why, even rich bankers were jumping out of windows back then. Danged Roosevelt dumped our crops in the ocean and got the bankers back on their feet, then tried to drive us all off the land. I wasn't about to be run off to no California."

Oscar Ameringer became the Socialist Party organizer in Oklahoma in 1907. He was doubtful about organizing farmers. In his 1940 autobiography, *If You Don't Weaken,* Ameringer wrote that he had once regarded farmers as capitalists, not exploited wage laborers, as the owners of the means of production with a great deal to lose from socialism. But after a meeting in Harrah— the town where my mother grew up—he was astonished to discover an America he did not know existed, starving farmers poorer than the white and black workers he had been organizing in New Orleans.

Between 1906 and 1917, the Wobblies and the Socialist Party won converts on a mass scale in Oklahoma. My grandfather was one of the first. They adopted the religious evangelists' technique of holding huge weeklong encampments with charismatic speakers, male and female, usually near small towns (indeed, many evangelists were themselves converts to socialism). Socialists were elected as local officials, and the lampposts of many towns were hung with red flags. In 1915 alone, 205 mass encampments were held. The

Socialists never won a statewide race in Oklahoma, but their percentage of the vote increased from 6 percent in 1907 to 16 percent in 1916 voting for Socialist Party candidate Eugene Debs. In 1914, the Socialist candidate for governor won 21 percent of the vote, and the party won six seats in the Oklahoma legislature, along with a majority of local offices in many counties. But it was not a peaceful process.

"There was a lot of shooting?" I asked Daddy.

"You can say that again, and not just shooting. Wobblies cut telephone wires and dynamited pipelines, water mains, and sewers. It was all around here, but mainly over in the eastern part of the state. Them Seminole Indians were in it, Negroes too. Down in San Antone and the Valley, them Magon brothers from Old Mexico. Boy, the Wobblies sure put up a fight."

In speaking of blacks and poor whites and Seminole Indians rising up together in eastern Oklahoma, I know now that Daddy was referring to a spontaneous event, separate from IWW or Socialist Party organizing, the "Green Corn Rebellion" during the summer of 1917.

In December 1994, when I was poking around in southeastern Oklahoma trying to understand that rebellion, I met an elderly Seminole Muscogee Indian woman who said that she had been only nine years old at the time, but she remembered it, and that her uncle, who she said had been a leader of the rebellion and was imprisoned afterward, had told the heroic story over and over.

"The full moon of late July, early August it was, the Moon of the Green Corn. It was not easy to persuade our poor white and black brothers and sisters to rise up. We told them that rising up, standing up, whatever the consequences, would inspire future generations. Our courage, our bravery would be remembered and copied. That has been the Indian way for centuries, since the invasions. Fight and tell the story so that those who come after or their descendants will rise up once again. It may take a thousand years, but that is how we continue and eventually prevail."

I asked her to explain the significance of the Green Corn ceremony to the Muscogees. "That is our most sacred ceremony, and you could call it our new year, the time of new beginnings. It occurs whenever the green corn comes, sometimes as early as late June, or as late as early August. During that year, 1917, the green corn came late, during the last week of July and early August. It was on August 3, 1917, at the end of our four-day Green Corn ceremony, that we rose up."

My father portrayed the Green Corn Rebellion as a great moment of heroism, a moment of unity, betrayed by the "electric-light city" Socialists, who scorned it. Of course, nothing about Wobblies and Socialists appeared in my U.S. or Oklahoma history textbooks (and very little appears in Oklahoma textbooks even now), so I began to doubt my father's stories, especially about the Green Corn Rebellion.

When I moved to California and was swept up in the sixties as a student, I gained a new pride in my Wobbly/Socialist heritage, but I nearly forgot the Green Corn Rebellion until it reappeared in my field of vision in the mid-1970s while I was working on the book *The Great Sioux Nation,* which grew out of the 1973 Lakota uprising at Wounded Knee. A Muscogee medicine man from Oklahoma, the late Philip Deere, told me a story in 1974 that sounded familiar. At first, he did not name the event but described his memory of it and what he had been told growing up. He would have been about the same age as my father in 1917, ten or eleven years old. Philip recalled the rebellion as conceived and led by Indians.

I searched for published information, trying to verify Philip's version, but found very little indeed that even mentioned the Green Corn Rebellion. Finally, I found the typescript of a 1959 Harvard University undergraduate history thesis by John Womack, Jr., himself from Oklahoma, the biographer of Mexican revolutionary leader Emiliano Zapata, and now a senior professor of history at Harvard.

By 1890, before the Native American republics of Indian Territory were dissolved by the 1898 Curtis Act, which violated treaties with the Native nations and forced their communal holdings into individual allotments, white tenants had already come to outnumber the Indians two to one in Indian Territory. Breaking the law, violence, and corruption were thus the rule, not the exception, in that region, setting the stage for an agrarian rebellion.

And times were hard. More than 60 percent of mortgaged farms were lost to foreclosure during the two years before the Green Corn Rebellion. More than half the farms were worked by tenants. The rates were even higher in the southeastern counties (Pottawatomie, Seminole, Hughes, and Pontotoc) where the rebellion took place. Only a fifth of the farms in that region were worked by their owners, and half of those were under heavy mortgages that carried usurious interest rates of 20 to 200 percent.

Farming in Oklahoma was commercial, with tenants as wage laborers and cotton the king; cotton production doubled between 1909 and 1919, making Oklahoma the fourth-largest cotton producer among the states and firmly establishing a cash-and-credit economy. The other major industries were oil production and coal mining, which spawned boomtowns and attracted large populations of transient workers.

When the government began to draft soldiers for World War I, the white, black, and red farmers in southeastern Oklahoma decided to resist conscription. Their strategy was to come together and seal off an area from outside interference, persuade their neighbors to join, and then march all the way to Washington, D.C., picking up recruits along the way. There they would overthrow President Wilson, stop the war, and reform the domestic economy to "restore to the working classes the full product of their labor." In preparation for the great march, they burned bridges across the Canadian River to keep their liberated area isolated. They cut telephone and telegraph wires so that the besieged could not call for help. They planned to confiscate property in the towns and on the surrounding farms. Anyone who opposed them was to be conscripted in the same way that the federal government conscripted its troops. They agreed that any local authorities who tried to stop them would be met with gunfire, and that they would poison food and well water. They believed they would be joined by the working people's armies of other states and that the IWW and the four railroad brotherhoods would support them for a victorious march on Washington, where they would then take control (since most of the U.S. military would already be in Europe or fighting Pancho Villa in Mexico).

I learned from Professor Womack's account that a group of African Americans set off the rebellion. In early August 1917, a sheriff and his deputy were fired on by some thirty black rebels. Hundreds of African Americans, poor whites, and Muscogee Indians were involved. The rebels were well organized. They divided themselves into details—some to recruit all who had not yet joined the rebellion, others to burn barns, another to blow up the Texaco pipeline, several groups to destroy railroad bridges and cut telephone and telegraph wires, and others to tear down fences and free farm animals to trample cotton fields. After a long summer day of destruction, the five hundred or so rebels congregated in their new liberated zone to feast, celebrate, and rest.

However, the reaction of local townspeople against the rebels was fierce. They organized huge posses to hunt them down. When faced with angry, armed citizens, the rebels dispersed, guerilla-style. During the following days, more wires were cut and bridges hit, while more and more rebels were captured. Pitched battles took place, and hundreds were arrested.

The entry of the United States into the European war in 1917 produced a wave of patriotism and a brutal backlash against the anti-war Wobblies and Socialists in Oklahoma. The Socialists blamed the repression in Oklahoma on the Green Corn rebels. Fiery crosses burned all over the state, and the ranks and resources of the Ku Klux Klan burgeoned. The Klan seized political power in Texas and Arkansas and came close in Oklahoma. My grandfather was one of their victims.

When a core group of native white Americans, the very foot soldiers of empire, began turning socialist and anti-imperialist, even inching away from white supremacy, the government and other centers of power acted swiftly, viciously, and relentlessly to crush the movement. A wave of propaganda accompanied the repression. The D. W. Griffith film extolling the KKK, *The Birth of a Nation,* had appeared in 1915. After the victories of the Russian and Mexican revolutions, Red Scare propaganda flooded newspapers and magazines, and formed the main text of sermons. The landless agrarians of Oklahoma were left with a recollection of hard times and hatred for big government and for the rich and powerful, but also with the memory of a failed movement.

And repression: Oklahoma was kept under careful surveillance long before the McCarthy era. As reported by George Milburn in 1946, "It is a criminal offense, for example, in Oklahoma, to have a copy of Karl Marx's *Das Kapital* in one's library, and anyone suspected of possessing seditious literature is liable to search, seizure, and arrest. Indeed, certain scholarly citizens have been prosecuted criminally and faced with penitentiary sentences, because sober political treatises, regarded as classics elsewhere, in Oklahoma are even more illicit than a bottle of bootleg booze."

So talk about my grandfather and the Wobblies and the Green Corn Rebellion thinned as a new Red Scare escalated after World War II: a Red in the family tree was no longer something to be proud of. The rage about our poverty was covered over with pride for just being white and "real" Americans.

I myself grew fiercely patriotic. Tears brimmed in my eyes when I heard "The Star-Spangled Banner" or pledged allegiance to the flag. I won first prize in a county speech contest for my original oration "America Is Great Because America Is Good." I spent the summer of 1954 avidly watching the Army-McCarthy hearings on television, rooting for McCarthy, adoring the young Ray Cohn. I doubted my father's stories. And my father no longer told the stories.

During the Korean War, I sold Veterans of Foreign Wars crepe paper roses.

Several young men in town were drafted and came home wounded. One of the boys who returned sat with my brother and me and our cousins and told us about Korea. "Why, we're rich here in Oklahoma by comparison. They're lucky to eat a spoonful of rice once a day. We went through this one little village and seen an old man, looked to be a hundred, all dried up and wrinkled, just died in front of us. I stopped to pay my respects, and as I was looking at him wondering what his life had been like, out comes this giant white thing from his mouth, a damned tapeworm five foot long." And we felt lucky to be free Americans fighting communism, proud of our country for helping others.

My father came to believe that his father had regretted being a Wobbly and Socialist, and that he had been hoodwinked by communists. He believed the same about me. I do not believe it for a minute; rather, I think he wanted to forget his father's, and my, idealism, which he was afraid could get me into trouble.

Daddy shocked me a few years before he died (in 2001, at ninety-three) when he told me how brutally his father had beaten him as a teenager. I had never before heard him utter a single negative word about his father. "Boy, it hurt and sometimes put me in bed. He used a horsewhip. After I was about twelve, seems like he had it in for me, and that's why I run off when I turned sixteen. I couldn't take it no more," he said, tears filling his fading blue eyes. That would have been between 1919 and 1923, when the Wobbly and Socialist movements were being crushed and the Klan was on the rise, and my grandfather and his family were targets of KKK violence. Grandpa Dunbar had taken out his frustration on his most devoted disciple.

Yet when I was a student during the sixties in California, Daddy's stories of my Wobbly grandfather were my guiding light, and for that I am forever grateful. As I learned theory and a larger perspective from reading and organizing for civil rights and women's liberation and against the war in Vietnam, I remained aware of the real history and possibilities of grassroots radicalism and believe that I contributed that insight. At the same time, I was, and am, acutely aware of the limitations of narrow provincialism and, particularly for white people, the racism that runs so deep.

• • •

Since the 2004 presidential election, the media have been preoccupied by a "red state–blue state" dichotomy—red states being Republican, and blue states, mostly clinging to the two coasts, being Democratic. Of course, nothing is that simple. Some states have razor-thin majorities of one or the other, while other states have significant regions or cities whose color is different from that of the state as a whole. Yet one thing is clear: Oklahoma fits comfortably into the "red state" category, and has for some time.

The "red" designation is part of the symbolism, and irony, of the title of my memoir, *Red Dirt*. Although the "red state" label had not yet been invented when I created the title, it can be added to the reasons I chose it. First, there's the red soil in rural Canadian County, where I grew up, which my father tried to farm as a sharecropper and tenant. Second, Oklahoma originally was territory that the federal government established for the Indians who were forcibly removed from the Southeast region during the 1830s. My mother was in part descended from the "Redman." Third, my paternal grandfather was a Socialist and a Wobbly, active in the Socialist Party and the Industrial Workers of the World, and was driven out of Oklahoma in the "Red Scare" of the Wilson administration. Not only my grandfather, but at least 20 percent of Oklahomans during that time were "Reds." That is where the irony comes in: Oklahoma has gone from "Red" to "red."

More than ever, that history of "red" Oklahoma is essential in the midst of politicized Protestant fundamentalism, laissez-faire capitalism, and superpatriotism linked with war.

Index

Halloween 14 (antia-nuclear group), 133n14
Han, Ben, 104
Harper, Maurine, 24–28, 35
Harrah, Oklahoma, 223
Harris, Fred R., 120
Harrison, George, 94
Haskell, Charles, 67
Hate crimes, 136, 142, 148
Hauptman, Laurence, 64
Hayes, John, 75
Hayes, Lorraine, 115
Haywood, Big Bill, 221
Health status, 171, 174, 186; in demo-
    cratic socialist nations, 183
Heartland, the, 196, 197
Heavy metal contamination, 162
Henderson, Caroline, 153
Henry, Alice, 57
Henry, Brad, 145, 146
Heritage Foundation, 171
Herland Sister Resources, 140, 141, 143
Herland Voice, 141, 148
Hertzberg, Hazel, 68
Hill, Ben, 216
Hill, Joe, 223
Hill, Johnson D., 214
Hillbilly music, 105–106
"History of the Cattle Industry in Okla-
    homa, 1866–1893" (Lewis), 6
HIV/AIDS research and care, 135, 137,
    140, 148, 204–205
Hoffman, Oklahoma, 47
Holleran, Andrew, 137
Hollibaugh, Amber, 148
Hollins, Jess, 45
Holway, William R., 213
"Home Sweet Oklahoma" (song), 95
Homosexuality, 199, 200, 203–208, 218.
    See also GLBT movement
Hoover, J. Edgar, 222
House Bill 1017, 166
House Bill 1821, 145–46
House Bill 2259, 144–45, 146

House Committee on Indian Affairs, 76
House of Representatives, U.S., 70, 71, 72
House Un-American Activities Com-
    mittee (HUAC; Dies Committee), 75,
    77, 165
Hoxie, Frederick, 66, 68
Hrebenar, Ronald J., 142
HUAC (House Un-American Activities
    Committee; Dies Committee), 75, 77,
    165
Hull, J. A., 214
Hultgren, Warren, 216
Human rights: black civil rights, 53–61;
    GLBT equality, 134–49
Humphreys, Kirk, 147
Hungary, 172
Hunt, Brian, 129
Hyechka (music organization), Tulsa,
    214

I Ain't No Jukebox (music album), 95
Ickes, Harold L., 75, 76, 78, 79
"Idabel Blues" (song), 111
Ideologies, 188–90
If You Don't Weaken (Ameringer), 223
"I Live in the Country" (song), 104
Illegal aliens, 27–28
Income, 166, 171, 174, 186; inequality in
    Bible Belt, 176–77
Index of Economic Freedom, Heritage
    Foundation, 171
Indian Citizenship Act, 68
"Indian Demands Justice, The"
    (Bruner), 73
Indian National Confederacy, 69–70, 71
Indian Nation Presbytery, 198–99
Indian-Pioneer Papers, 11
Indian Reorganization Act (IRA;
    Wheeler-Howard Act), 63, 64, 69–74,
    79, 80
Indians. See Native Americans
Indians, Outlaws and Angie Debo
    (video), 21n24
Indians Abroad (Foreman), 9, 10

Satherley, Art, 105–106
Saturday Evening Post, 105
Savings and loan industry, 161
Sawyer, Sophia, 10
Schiavo, Terri, 188
School Bullying Prevention Act, 138
School prayer issue, 166, 172
Scientific theory, 184
Secularization, of First World, 186–87
Seeger, Pete, 109
Segregation, 37, 39, 44; in churches, 198; in education, 46–47, 53; of public accommodations, 54–57. *See also* Civil rights movement
Self-reliance, 185
Seminole County, Oklahoma, 162
Seminole Indians, 65; Green Corn Rebellion, 224
Senate, U.S., investigation of Koch Industries by, 158
Senate Indian Affairs Committee, 71, 77
Sense of place, 51n18
"Separate but equal" doctrine: and black towns, 40; in education, 53; in the military, 53
September 11, 2001, attacks, 217
Sequoyah, proposed state of, 67
Settlement Bill, 77–80
Sexual orientation issues. *See* GLBT movement; Homosexuality
Sharecroppers, 222, 223, 229
Shepard, Matthew, 206
Shevky, Esherf, 74
Shot of Love (music album), 93
Showman, Paul, 29
Silkwood, Karen, 124
Simply Equal, 140
Sipuel, Ada Lois, 46, 50n16
Sit-in demonstrations, 48, 52–62
Skinner, Tom, 88, 99, 104, 111
Slavery, 201
Slovenia, 173
Smith, Adam, 182–83, 187
Smith, Hedrick, 141

Smith, Keith, 139, 142–46
SNCC (Student Non-Violent Coordinating Committee), 115
Social history: Foreman's work in, 11; Lewis's work in, 6; by women historians, 3–5, 18–19
Socialism, 183, 186, 188
Socialist Party, 25, 221–25, 227, 228, 229
Social services, in Tulsa, 212, 215
Society of American Indians (SAI), 68, 80
Society of Oklahoma Indians (SOI), 68–69
Sodomy, 144, 146, 147, 204
SOI (Society of Oklahoma Indians), 68–69
Sooner Queens softball team, 135
South Carolina, 177
Southern Baptists, 178
South Korea, 172
South of Muskogee Town (music album), 89
Southwestern Bell case, 159
Southwest Youth Conference, NAACP, 60
Soviet Union, 179, 182
Spiro Mounds, 7
Sports teams, names of, 202
Spot Music Awards, 91
Springsteen, Bruce, 109
St. Louis, Missouri, 58
Standard of living, 177; and business regulation, 190; and Judeo-Christian heritage, 191
State Question 711, 135, 144, 145
Steinbeck, John, x, 165, 197
Stillwater, Oklahoma, Red Dirt music in, 93, 94, 95, 97–101
Stonewall Inn riots, New York, 139, 149n2
Stookey, Paul, 111
Stop Black Fox newsletter, 127
Story of Oklahoma, The (Wright), 12, 13
Stragglers (music group), 96